Criminology and Social Policy

Southampton
SOLENT
University

LIBRARY

for reference only

Criminology and Social Policy

Paul Knepper

SAGE Publications
Los Angeles · London · New Delhi · Singapore

© Paul Knepper 2007

First published 2007

 SAGE Publications Ltd
1 Oliver's Yard
55 City Road
London EC1Y 1SP

SAGE Publications Inc
2455 Teller Road
Thousand Oaks, California 91320

SAGE Publications India Pvt Ltd
B 1/I 1 Mohan Cooperative Industrial Area
Mathura Road, New Delhi 110 044
India

SAGE Publications Asia-Pacific Pte Ltd
33 Pekin Street #02-01
Far East Square
Singapore 048763

British Library Cataloguing in Publication data

A catalogue record for this book is available from
the British Library

ISBN 978 14129 2338 5
ISBN 978 14129 2339 2

Library of Congress control number available

Typeset by C&M Digitals (P) Ltd., Chennai, India
Printed on paper from sustainable resources
Printed in Great Britain by The Cromwell Press, Trowbridge, Wiltshire

Contents

Preface

Criminology and Social Policy begins with the premise that what appear to be problems for crime policy are actually problems for social policy and aims to think through the challenges, dilemmas, and obstacles that arise in pursuit of this premise. The title refers to social policy, meaning an area of government intervention directed at improving social welfare. In nearly all occurrences, the term social policy is used in this sense. This book is not about what specialists in social policy have to say about crime and criminal justice. Except for one chapter, it does not offer a critique of crime policies from social policy perspectives. Instead, the focus is on social policy as a response to crime. Why do criminologists believe that social policy presents a better response to crime than criminal justice policy? What do criminologists have to say about major social policy areas – housing, health, education, and so on? Are criminologists right to make crime reduction a goal of social policy?

These questions suggest the three major parts of the discussion. The chapters in Part I review theories and concepts within criminology relevant to the analysis of social policy. Chapter 1 deals with the extent to which criminologists should seek to integrate themselves in the policymaking process. Chapter 2 reviews four theoretical traditions about the relationship between crime and social policy, or, in the case of the fourth one, why there is no relationship. Chapter 3 pursues insights from social theory about how notions of class, 'race', and gender are embedded in popular discussions of poverty and crime. Part II reviews criminological research about major social policy areas. Chapter 4 deals with crime and housing policy, Chapter 5 with crime, health and education. Chapter 6 reviews research concerning unemployment and crime and Chapter 7 discusses family and youth policy. In Chapter 8, the focus is somewhat different. The chapter does not take up a social policy area but instead looks at the social policy implications of crime policies having to do with policing and prisons. Part III explores two larger issues concerning the conceptualisation of crime and social policy. Chapter 9 discusses the phenomenon of 'criminalisation of social policy' and Chapter 10 looks at the use of social justice as a guide to policy.

British criminology has always had a strong welfarist tradition. It is a tradition that advocates the 'welfare state solution', the expansion of social policy as the primary response to crime. There has never really been a voice from the right within criminology calling for more police and prisons (Garland and

Sparks, 2000: 194–5; Boutellier, 2004: 137–8). To challenge arguments for a 'criminal justice solution', British criminologists have addressed statements in policy documents advanced by political parties and their think tanks, or imported criminal-justice advocates from American criminology.

There is a nagging worry in recent years, however, that welfarist criminology may have become obsolete. In the present era, the themes familiar to academic criminology have been supplanted by political and media images advancing risk, safety, anti-social behaviour, surveillance and the like. The welfare state solution has faded in political imagination and criminologists have less influence over the policymaking process than before. The gap between what criminologists know and what policymakers do has widened. At universities, this shift has been experienced, in symbol if not in substance, by the drift of students from social policy to criminology. Modules in criminology and social policy have become popular. The question before criminologists is whether to adopt 'contemporary idiom' in an effort to close the gap. To be relevant, criminologists may need to re-invent themselves, to set aside traditional welfare concerns and engage policymakers in terms established by media and politicians. This is, as Garland and Sparks (2000) put it, the 'challenge of our times'.

My suggestion is for criminology to re-invent the welfarist theme. To facilitate this, I outline the parameters of 'criminology and social policy' as a field of inquiry. The discussions review staple themes and recent scholarship; I bring together material from criminology and social policy journals alongside evocative themes from other disciplines. While the focus is on the British situation, I make strategic use of theories and examples produced in the American and European contexts. My specific task is to inquire about what happens when social policy is applied to crime reduction. By 'what happens' I mean something other than 'what works'. Despite the summaries of research findings in various chapters, the most important questions to be resolved in this area are not empirical claims. Rather, the study of social policy in criminology brings moral considerations, political strategies, and concepts from social theory, as well as social-scientific research, to the policy response to crime. I like the idea of criminology as a reflexive policy science as described by Braithwaite (1993).

The larger objective here is to argue for re-thinking the question of welfarist criminology. Criminologists have tended to offer social policy as a conclusion rather than a problem statement, as a final destination rather than a point of departure. It is one thing to follow up a critique of some aspect of criminal justice with the suggestion that social policy affords a better response. It is another to interrogate this conclusion, to recognize that genuine dilemmas arise in carrying it out and real harms come about in getting in wrong. The convergence of crime and social policy merits scrutiny. In the present era, the justification for more and more social welfare programmes has been stated in the language of crime reduction. It is appropriate and important to ask whether the goals of crime reduction and poverty reduction can be successfully joined within the same institutional framework; how it is that the introduction of crime reduction as a justification for social policy leads to better social policy.

I set up this debate in the first two chapters and carry it through the policy chapters. Along the way, I introduce a number of concepts for understanding the impact of social policies on crime: racialisation of crime, unintended effects of social policies, politicisation of interventions, moral dilemmas in policymaking, and externalities of crime policies. I also offer a number of propositions: that social policies work as crime reduction measures when they are not seen in this way; that delivering social welfare to particular populations because they are thought to be dangerous and threatening is not an appropriate justification; that efforts to blend social work and policing become policing ... but I am getting ahead of the story. Criminology and social policy should investigate the possibility that making the welfare state into a solution for crime has diminished its capacity for improving social welfare.

This book would not have come together in the way it did without advice and support from several people. Colleagues past and present, Clive Norris, Kevin Farnsworth, and Peter Johnstone, commented on chapters in various stages. Caroline Porter at Sage steered the project in more promising directions than I had first proposed. No doubt the final product would have been better if I had followed their advice more often than I have done. I also want to thank Cathryn Knepper for enduring my commentary on virtually every aspect of this book and for helping me to be a better person while writing it than I otherwise would have been.

PART ONE

Theories and Concepts

PART ONE

The Role of Theory

Criminologists and the Welfare State

SUMMARY

- Criminology and social policy are concerned with different problems, but they share a common focus on policy and multi-disciplinary outlook
- Experimental criminology, crime science, critical criminology and left realist criminology imply a different role for criminologists in relation to the state
- Policymaking about crime reflects political, social, and cultural influences

---

The study of criminology and social policy has to do with the difference social policy can make in dealing with crime. Exploring the links between these two areas is about understanding social problems related to crime, about visions of a better response, and about strategies for making them happen. This book reviews criminological theories, research, and discussion about social policy.

The next two chapters review criminological theories suggesting a link between social policy and crime, and critique popular images of poor people. The following five chapters describe the findings of criminological research applied to social policy areas – housing, health, unemployment, family, and education – and document the social welfare impact of policing and prisons. The final two chapters take up questions of political strategy and broader vision: we will examine the criminalisation of social policy and the pursuit of social justice. Before we begin, we need to do some ground-clearing.

This chapter examines the relationship between knowledge and policymaking. It is divided into three parts, each of which takes up a question: What do we mean by the terms criminology and social policy? Should criminologists seek to integrate themselves in the policymaking process? To what extent does criminological research actually influence policymaking about crime? The first part explores the ways in which the concerns of criminology and social policy overlap, and where they differ, with a look at the history of these disciplines and the views of two key founders. The second part deals with four conceptions of the role of criminology in a welfare state: experimental criminology, crime science, critical criminology, and left realist criminology. The final part outlines influences on crime policy other than criminological knowledge.

Criminology and Social Policy

Ordinarily, criminology and social policy are thought of as separate disciplines. But during the past decade or so, a combined course of study has become available at British universities. This raises the question of what these two disciplines are about: how they are alike, where they differ.

Two Disciplines

Criminology and social policy share a common focus of concern and strategy of inquiry. Both disciplines concern themselves with 'action' rather than 'thought' (Halsey, 2004: 13). In sociology, the classical project has sought to build up a store of scientific knowledge of social activity. Sociologists make theory-guided conjectures about why things are as they are and test them against sociological data. Alternatively, the action disciplines concentrate on the relationship between ideas and activities; they translate theories of society into programmes for solving specific social problems. If sociology aspires to grasp the social world as it is, separate from idealised conceptions of how it ought to be, criminology and social policy seek to bridge universal ideals and society's more mundane concerns.

But of course, criminology and social policy concern themselves with a different set of problems. Criminology deals with the:

1 extent and distribution of criminal conduct in society; the
2 history, structure and operation of the criminal justice system; and the
3 social, political, and economic influences on changing definitions of criminality and criminal justice practices.

Or, to put it in a sentence: 'Criminology, in its broadest sense, consists of our organised ways of thinking and talking about crime, criminals, and crime control' (Garland and Sparks, 2000: 192). 'Crime policy' refers to the governmental response to crime. This includes the administration of criminal justice (police, criminal courts, and prisons) as well as broader programmes for crime reduction such as national strategies for crime prevention.

Social policy concerns the:

1 role of the state in distribution of resources and opportunities between rich and poor, workers and dependents, old and young; the
2 apportionment of responsibilities for this distribution to government and other social institutions – market, voluntary/charity sector, family and individual; and
3 an understanding of the social and economic consequences of different arrangements (Halsey, 2004: 10).

In a word – T.H. Marshall's – the objective of social policy is 'welfare' (quoted in Hill, 1988: 2).

The term 'social policy' also refers to the policies themselves, that is, an arena of public policy concerning social welfare. (And when this term appears in the chapters to follow, it almost always has this meaning.) Policy areas typically referred to as comprising social policy include social security,[1] unemployment insurance, housing, health, education and family. While these areas do not cover the widest range of social policy, they are consistent with the vision of the welfare state supplied by William Beveridge in 1942. The Beveridge Report called for an attack on the 'five giant evils' of want, disease, ignorance, squalor, and idleness. During the 1940s, legislation laid the foundations of the post-war welfare state: Education Act (1944), Family Allowance Act (1945), Housing Act (1946), National Insurance Act (1946), National Assistance Act (1948), National Health Service Act (1948), and the Housing Act (1949). Beveridge did not refer to the personal social services, but this area has since been incorporated into the welfare state.

As an academic discipline, criminology is linked with the Lombrosian project and the governmental project (Garland, 2002). The Lombrosian project refers to Cesare Lombroso's effort in the late nineteenth century to explain the difference between criminals and non-criminals. While he failed in his specific programme, he did manage to popularise criminology as the scientific study of criminal behaviour. The governmental project, developed several decades later, began with efforts to generate a practical knowledge for more efficient management of police and prisons. But in Britain, historically speaking, criminology did not extend from Lombroso. The first university lectures in criminology were given in Birmingham in the 1920s by prison medical officers to postgraduate students in medicine (Garland, 1988: 135). Criminology did not really become institutionalised in Britain until the years after the Second World War. Hermann Mannheim, a legal scholar and refugee from Hitler's Germany, offered the first sustained introduction to criminology in his lectures in the Department of Sociology during the 1930s. Mannheim became a Reader in Criminology at the LSE in 1946, the first senior post in the subject established at a British university (Hood, 2004: 481).

Social policy began with 'the social question' which had to do with explaining why poverty persisted in a time of advancing prosperity (Halsey, 2004: 9). Britain's industrial economy had made a quality of life possible for people at the end of the nineteenth century that could scarcely have been imagined in 1800. Yet it had also left many trapped in demoralising poverty, particularly in the cities. Beginning before the First World War, social investigators carried out social surveys with the aim of formulating an appropriate response from government. Social policy, or social administration as it was known originally, began at this time under the guise of training social workers. The universities of Liverpool, Birmingham, Manchester, and Leicester developed courses for social workers and probation officers before the Second World War. But like criminology, social policy did not become organised as a university discipline until later on. Richard Titmuss secured his position as Chair in Social Administration at the

---

[1]Now renamed 'work and pensions'.

LSE in 1950, the first academic post in social policy. His work as a historian of the Cabinet Office, culminating in his *Problems of Social Policy* (1950), led to his wide recognition as an expert in social policy (Halsey, 2004: 196–8).

Radzinowicz on Criminology and Social Policy

To explore the relationship between criminology and social policy further, it is worthwhile to compare the outlook of two founders. Leon Radzinowicz in criminology and Richard Titmuss in social policy have had great influence on their respective disciplines. Radzinowicz was born in Lodz, Poland, in 1906; he studied law in Paris, Geneva, and Rome. In 1936, he emigrated to England where he became Assistant Director of Research in Criminal Science at Cambridge, and in 1959, Wolfson Professor of Criminology. That same year, he became founding director of the Institute of Criminology at Cambridge, a position he held until his retirement in 1973.

The problem of crime, Radzinowicz taught, was intractable. Any attempt to isolate *the* cause of criminal behaviour was a wasted effort. He remained sceptical of abstract over-arching theories he considered pretentious as well as esoteric. Sociological approaches advocating a single explanatory structure amounted to 'unilateral approaches' leading to conceptual cul-de-sacs. 'The most that can be done is to throw light upon the combination of factors or circumstances associated with crime' (Radzinowicz, 1988: 95). Radzinowicz pursued a multi-disciplinary criminology, a vision expressed in the founding of the Institute of Criminology. The Cambridge Institute received the support of Lord Butler, who had become Home Secretary in 1957. He promoted the need for teams of sociologists, statisticians, psychiatrists, and legal specialists to carry out systematic investigations into criminal behaviour with a focus on intervention and prevention.

Radzinowicz believed in the use of empirical findings in social science as a means of bringing about humanitarian reform of criminal justice administration. He viewed criminology as a discipline that could provide a 'rational improvement' in the government's response to crime and criminals (Hood, 2002: 154). Reform of archaic practices in the punishment of criminals could only come about, he taught, by systematic research contributing to a long-term plan. Reforms should not follow swings in political expediency or popular emotion following particularly disturbing crimes. Radzinowicz was committed to British liberalism, perhaps because of his status as a European émigré. He endorsed the Howard League for Penal Reform: 'Being British,' Radzinowicz said, 'it was down to earth, practical, observant, critical and yet ready to accept reasonable compromises' (quoted in Cottee, 2005: 220). Yet the connection between scientific evidence in criminology and criminal policy should not be adhered to too closely, Radzinowicz insisted. He appreciated the influence of politics, in the form of an advancing welfare state 'with its emphasis on the protective and supportive functions of society as a whole', which he believed had a beneficial influence on criminal policy (Radzinowicz, 1964: 12).

Radzinowicz (1988: 95) took the position that 'the frontiers between social policy and criminal policy should not be confused or blurred'. Social welfare schemes, he explained, should be pursued as a matter of 'natural justice, of ethics, of economic and of political expediency' but not as a matter of crime reduction because 'social welfare schemes may not necessarily lead to a general reduction in crime'. He denied that social welfare represented the ultimate solution to delinquency and he worried about politicians turning crime into a political problem and exaggerating their power in response. Radzinowicz had seen how the positivism that had excited him as a student of Enrico Ferri had become distorted and abused by fascist regimes in the 1930s. The response to crime should remain tempered by the rule of law. He advocated the formation of a Ministry of Social Welfare so that some of the 'secondary responsibilities' of the Home Office could be hived off, allowing it to fall back on 'its fundamental and primary responsibility for law and order' (Radzinowicz, 1964: 24).

Titmuss on Social Policy and Crime

Richard Titmuss advocated a similar understanding of social policy but disagreed with Radzinowicz about social policy and crime. Remarkably, he was entirely self-taught. After the death of his father, a farmer, he found work with an insurance firm in London, and, using contacts with the Eugenics Society, landed a post with the Cabinet Office as official historian of wartime social policy. From his post in social policy at the LSE, he exercised a major influence on the subsequent development of the discipline during the 1950s and 1960s.

Titmuss laid the foundation for the discipline of social policy with his conceptualisation of 'social accounting', an analytical strategy for measuring the total amount of welfare benefits extended by government (Kincaid, 1984). Defenders and critics of social welfare alike erred in conceptualising social welfare in terms of direct services to the poor, unemployed, ill, and so on. Workers received substantial benefits via occupational schemes providing pensions, sick pay, and housing allowances that would otherwise appear as company profits and be subject to taxation. Substantial cash benefits provided via the tax system to the advantage of the better-off should also be regarded as welfare benefit. As an academic discipline, social policy represents 'a search for explanations of how and why state power affects the allocation of every type of financial, welfare and environmental resource' (Kincaid, 1984: 117–18).

And for Titmuss, this search was multi-disciplinary. Titmuss utilised the work of historians, sociologists, anthropologists, political scientists, economists, and medical doctors to address the roles and functions of social services. One cannot find in Titmuss a consistent theoretical or political position (Kincaid, 1984: 114). He did, however, reject economic imperialism, the application of economic analysis to non-market behaviour, and made strategic use of economic arguments to refute the work of the economists at London's

Institute of Economic Affairs. Titmuss avoided committing himself to any disciplinary perspective, but instead built up a repertoire of concepts that would enable him to tackle specific problems (Fontaine, 2002: 404–6).

Titmuss was a Social Democrat who regarded capitalism not only as economically wasteful but threatening social integration in driving out altruism (Welshman, 2004: 226). *Problems of Social Policy* established two principles. First, it was necessary to help all citizens, regardless of income and social class. The exclusion of the middle classes from social benefits encouraged contempt for recipients. Second, social policy should not attempt to means-test recipients; social benefits should be extended on a universalist rather than a contingent basis (Kincaid, 1984: 116–17). The 'Titmuss paradigm' expressed optimism about human nature, belief in universal services, and opposition to means testing (Welshman, 2004: 232). Essentially, Titmuss believed in the virtue of centralised state bureaucracies and the public ethos of working in them. He regarded the administration of social services as a benevolent activity.

Titmuss did not formulate a theory of crime. What he says on the subject must be pieced together from comments on the work of criminologists. Generally, he regarded crime as 'a social ill' or a 'social problem' that should be understood in relation to social activity and not individual pathology. Successive generations of social and economic upheavals stranded a portion of citizens in deprived areas of the city, a portion that turned to crime, Titmuss suggested, as the only available means of social mobility (Titmuss, 1954). Crime is a social problem originating within market inequalities, and because social policy seeks to iron out inequalities within the market, it makes sense to rely on social policy as a means of responding to crime. Titmuss, who read Mannheim's study of delinquency in inter-war England in 1939, agreed with Mannheim about 'faulty parenting' as *a* causal factor. But he insisted that 'overcrowding and bad housing conditions produce social misfits, frustration, petty delinquencies, and so on' (quoted in Welshman, 2004: 229). It follows that improvements in housing, by means of universal housing policy, would serve as a delinquency reduction measure.

Social Science and the State

The relationship between criminologists and politicians has never been easy. Some criminologists seek to integrate themselves in the policymaking process; others insist criminologists should criticise policies from a safe distance. Four different roles can be identified in relation to policymaking which differ according to beliefs about government and science.

Experimental Criminology

Experimental criminology sees the university-based research centre as a primary site for the production of criminological knowledge. Specialists in different fields work as a team to solve problems of interest to government authorities (who fund such research). This model came to prominence in the decade or so after the Second World War when national governments and international organisations solicited the advice of university researchers. Academics with expertise in criminology enjoyed wide-ranging influence (Walters, 2001). The Cambridge Institute of Criminology appeared in the 1950s, along with institutes of criminology at the University of California at Berkeley (1950), Melbourne University (1951), University of Oslo (1954), and the Hebrew University of Jerusalem (1959).

This tradition in criminology insists on science as the best, or at least the most reliable, route to planning sound policy. Experimental criminologists emulate the method of laboratory experiment used in chemistry and biology, in the belief that the more closely this procedure can be replicated, the more valid the results. In social affairs, experiments are conducted by means of randomised controls, meaning adherence to a methodology that divides research subjects into intervention and control groups and then measures the difference. Random assignment of subjects (and sufficiently large numbers of people in each group) makes it possible to disentangle the influences of other factors on the outcome of interest (Farrington, 2003).

Experimental criminology pursues a working relationship between criminologists and policymakers defined by a clear division of labour. Criminologists supply facts, policymakers make choices about values and priorities. From this point of view, researchers ought to remain indifferent to the content of policies. It is not the criminologist's job to advocate for particular policies but only to advise policymakers about which of their programmes work. 'What [criminology] cannot do is to decide what the *aims* of penal policy should be ... [but] given certain aims, criminologists can try and discover by research the best means of accomplishing them' (Hood, 2002: 162). Experimental criminology is associated with 'evidence-based policy', meaning that those crime-reduction programmes supported by research evidence should become policy, and those without such support should not. Evidence-based policy establishes the ideal of an 'ideology-free zone' consistent with a commitment to promote policy on the basis of social-scientific knowledge.

The most recent expression seeks to apply the model of medical science to the problem of crime. The Campbell Collaboration is an international group of social scientists promoting an evidence-based approach to policymaking in social welfare, education, and crime and justice. The Campbell Collaboration take their name from the American psychologist Donald Campbell, but their inspiration from British physician-epidemiologist Archie Cochrane. Cochrane insisted on the use of findings from randomised controls for making health care decisions. He taught that 'limited resources should be used to provide forms of health care that have been shown to be effective by properly controlled research' (quoted in Orleans, 1995: 634). His efforts led to the creation of Cochrane Centres worldwide for the maintenance and distribution of registers of randomised control research. The Campbell Collaboration, known to insiders as 'C2', aims to bring this approach to crime policy. Their network seeks to identify those policies with the greatest research support through 'systematic review' of evaluation findings (Farrington and Petrosino, 2001). The Jerry Lee Centre of Criminology at the University of Pennsylvania serves as an institutional home for the Campbell Collaboration Crime and Justice Group and the Academy of Experimental Criminology.

Experimental criminologists worry about the gap between what criminologists know and what policymakers do. Despite the success of criminology as an accredited discipline in the past few decades, fewer of its practitioners enjoy the status of government advisors. Wiles (2002) sees a connection between these two developments. The expansion of criminology has allowed criminologists to write for each other rather than engage the public. At the same time, criminologists have in striving to be external critics made the discipline into largely a private matter. Criminology, he argues, cannot merely be 'subversive of government interests' but must work with government to achieve the 'good society'; criminology should be practical in this sense, otherwise there is no point to it.

Crime Science

'Crime science', as the name implies, sees criminologists in possession of specialised knowledge of use for thwarting criminals. But there are important differences between the conceptualisation of science in this instance and that of the experimental criminology school. Crime science eschews purity as a model of scientific practice for research that is pragmatic and mundane; the focus is on *how* crime is committed and less on *why* it is committed (Clarke, 2004).

Crime science developed out of situational crime prevention which had been pioneered during the 1970s by researchers within the Home Office. Ronald Clarke, who directed the Research and Planning Unit, promoted simple, practical ways of reducing opportunity for criminal activity. Situational interventions make use of practical wisdom concerning the time, place, and circumstances of crime to circumvent would-be criminals. These interventions tend to be directed at specific occurrences of crime; involve management, design or manipulation of the immediate environment in a systematic and permanent way; and increase the effort and risks of crime and reduce the rewards of crime as perceived by a wide range of potential lawbreakers (Clarke and Mayhew, 1980: 1). Home Office researchers took this message to other parts of the world, with Clarke and others finding their way to American universities. Recently, a number of those formerly associated with the Home Office have re-organised around the Jill Dando Centre for Crime Science at University College London.

The difference between science, as understood in experimental criminology and that practised by the proponents of situational crime prevention, might be referred to as the difference between pure and industrial research. Some scientists work in university laboratories on projects without an application that is immediate or obvious as in the classic case of theoretical physics. The proponents of crime science are more like scientists who work for companies, the purpose of which is to come up with innovations of immediate use in industry. The advocates of crime science give the impression that they are not interested in theory-driven research dealing with crime prevention (Weisburd, 2002: 207). This understanding leads to opportunity-reduction projects, the most successful of which are often the least difficult to take up and maintain (Nicholson, 1995). In fact, there is no requirement that principles of crime science be advanced by government policy; crime science can (and has) been delivered on a micro-scale by shopkeepers, manufacturers, householders, and organisations with limited budgets.

Situational crime prevention has been equated with the Conservative political agenda of Thatcher's Home Office. Critics charge that crime science is short-sighted, ignoring the social and economic origins of criminal behaviour. Situational crime prevention not only offers a superficial and irrelevant response; it makes matters worse by diverting government resources away from addressing social inequality at the centre of the crime problem (Koch, 1998: 72). As Clarke (2000: 108–9) has acknowledged, there is a 'superficial fit' between situational crime prevention and conservative values, such as reducing the size of government and promoting individual responsibility. But he defends crime science as an alternative to 'dispositional' theories of crime prevention. He challenges the idea that no real improvements can be made in reducing crime without wide-scale and massive investment in schemes to tackle the 'root causes'.

Essentially, Clarke's argument extends to the British context an argument James Q. Wilson made in reference to anti-crime programmes carried out in the USA during the Kennedy–Johnson era (Clarke, 2004). Wilson, a political scientist, contended that criminologists insisting on attention to root causes had confused 'causal analysis' with 'policy analysis'. Causal analysis, of the sort favoured by sociologists, seeks to identify and understand the social processes behind human activities. Operating within this intellectual framework makes it difficult to develop feasible responses. 'If anything, it directs attention away from factors that government can control' and 'move[s] beyond the reach of social policy altogether' (Wilson, 1974: 47). Policy analysis, Wilson says, takes stock of the instruments at the government's disposal (such as measures to redistribute money, stimulate job creation, regulate alcohol, build detention facilities) and explores their impact on the level of crime. Such measures will not alter the root causes but may be able to make measurable differences in crime rates.

Critical Criminology

The 'critical tradition' in criminology[2] denies the possibility of an ideology-free zone from which to produce objective evidence for policymaking.

---

[2]Reference to the 'critical tradition' is meant to signify a stance toward policymaking implied by critical social theory; 'critical criminology' includes schools of thought ranging from socialism to postmodernism.

Criminologists, particularly those who work for government or carry out government-funded research, contribute to the larger politics of crime control. The critical stance rejects the ideal of a team of specialists working at a research institute in favour of the lone intellectual who remains sceptical and detached. The primary tool of the critical criminologist is not scientific procedure or data analysis, but rhetorical virtuosity, sophisticated rhetoric aimed at revealing the falsity behind political promises. Critical theorists champion the role of the outside provocateur who challenges claims to the 'truth' about crime and then questions the authority on which claims to such truth are made.

The critical perspective asserts that criminologists should question, challenge, and provoke from a location outside government. Or, as Christie (1981: 110) put it, criminology needs to be 'institutionally and intellectually protected against the embracement by authorities'. Criminologists employed in government research centres limit themselves to problems of interest to the state. This approach pursues a criminology incapable of addressing structural problems and renders the findings politically harmless. Christie encouraged criminologists to think of themselves as 'poets' rather then 'technicians'; poetic criminologists do not offer technical advice for use in running the state, but pose alternative questions within a broad cultural imagination. An iconic representative of this stance would be Antonio Gramsci, the founder of Italian communism, who was imprisoned in 1928 when fascist police smashed the underground organisation. He continued to oppose fascism while in prison through his writings, writings that have become increasingly important to generations of criminologists (and Italians) since the war.

In Britain, critical criminology emerged from the National Deviancy Conference (NDC) convened in 1968 at the University of York. The NDC served as a meeting place for sociologists, radical social workers, members of the anti-psychiatry movement, and others disillusioned with leftist politics. They broke away from the 'positivist methods' of Cambridge criminology and refused to engage in the practice of criminology as an 'auxiliary discipline' of governance. NDC members pursued a new paradigm for criminology, and within five years produced nearly one hundred books on crime, deviance and social control. The most influential of these, *The New Criminology* by Ian Taylor, Paul Walton and Jock Young (1973), proposed a 'fully social' theory of deviance. On the final page, the authors agreed with Christie that criminologists should be 'problem-raisers' rather than 'problem-solvers'. Crime required not piecemeal policy change, but political revolution, or something very close to it.

'The task', Taylor, Walton, and Young (1973: 282) wrote, 'is to create a society in which the facts of human diversity, whether personal, organic or social, are not subject to the power to criminalise'. Originally, this had been envisioned as an 'emancipatory' project derived from a worker–student alliance opposed to capitalism and the capitalist state. It reflected the idealism and utopianism that swept across universities in the years after the student revolts of 1968 (Taylor, 1999: 181). Utopianism made critical criminologists vulnerable to the charge that they were getting all dressed up with nowhere to go. Aside from 'grandiose calls for some sort of socialist reconstruction by largely unspecified means', wrote one critic, the new criminology offered 'nothing of policy or prescriptive value to contribute toward the more immediate and urgent debates about the nature of criminal justice in Britain' (Mungham, 1980: 29). It was all or nothing.

Yet, the new criminology spurred a re-direction of the criminological enterprise. The critical stance rejected criminology as the interrogation of working-class pathology and sought to relocate the usual suspects in criminological analysis from the underclass to the affluent. This has led to the study of white-collar and organised crime, leading to a broader understanding of social harm. Critical criminologists have studied such topics as workplace injury and illegal activities of multinational corporations (Tombs, 2005, for example). This approach turns social policy and crime on its head in the sense that the focus is on criminalisation of corporate practices and economic regulation rather than government assistance. The best response to injuries suffered by the poor is to prevent them from occurring in the first place.

Left Realist Criminology

Left realist criminology is the most closely aligned with social policy, defined in the first instance by commitment to particular political values. During the 1980s, Jock Young, John Lea, Ian Taylor, Roger Matthews and others proposed left realism as a response to the standoff between the crime policies associated with Thatcherism and the opposition to them expressed by critical criminologists. They encouraged their comrades to think through achievable goals in the area of crime reduction, and defend social welfare as a worthwhile policy response, rather than dream of a crime-free society.

Left realism has been described as the 'administrative criminology' of the left (Rock, 1988a: 197). Historically, it pioneered a new form of government patronage. As an alternative to the 'big science' model embodied in Cambridge criminology and Home Office sponsorship, left realists formed working relationships with progressive city councils, police monitoring units, and community safety committees. These organisations became the underwriters for victimisation surveys conducted in Islington, Broadwater Farm, Newham and elsewhere during the 1980s. This led to a realignment of academic criminology away from the ancient universities and toward the polytechnics. The Centre for Criminology, established at Middlesex Polytechnic (now University), became a major resource for left realist research and theory.

Clearly, the left realists believe that criminologists should integrate themselves in the policymaking process. They should be supplying knowledge, research findings, and theories leading government intervention toward specific ends. This involves a defence of the role of criminologists in the process leading to crime policy, but also of the role of empirical research. The victimisation survey represents a 'democratic instrument' with the potential of providing a 'reasonably accurate appraisal of people's fears and their experience of victimisation' (Young, 1992: 49–50). Left realism asserts a specific set of reforms aimed at 'democratic accountability' of policing, minimal use of prison and community crime prevention. The proponents also hope to spark a larger debate about whether a criminal justice system separated from other social institutions is desirable (Lea 1987, 364). They have argued for multi-agency responses to the problem of crime, which is bound up in the larger context of social exclusion.

Left realism is, relatively speaking, the most comfortable with political advocacy. Criminologists should participate in social movements to bring about greater social justice; they should align themselves with populations – workers, women, immigrants, youth – seeking inclusion and recognition. More to the point, criminologists should regard criminology *as* political advocacy. Criminologists not only bring a set of skills as social scientists, but a commitment to aiding the disenfranchised, the marginalised, and the excluded. If criminologists are not quite the conscience of crime policy, they are at least a counterweight to the excesses of political expediency.

Tony Blair's New Labour government invoked the 'left realist school' as the justification for a number of initiatives (Giddens, 2000: 8). The left realists became disillusioned with the effort and have sought to distance their criminological ideas from Blair's crime policies. Young and Matthews (2003) criticise 'team Blair' for ignoring local criminological talent. Not one criminologist in Britain supports prison expansion, and only a few believe that policing strategies can have anything more than a marginal effect on crime reduction. 'Government policies fly directly in the face of research evidence, and would seem almost wilfully to ignore expert opinion'. What is particularly troubling is the fact that it is a Labour administration that ignores criminologists. One might have expected as much from the Conservatives, who would 'turn to the saloon bar rather than the research centre for its inspiration' (Young and Matthews, 2003: 36).

Policymaking in Context

Criminologists have paid some attention to the matter of how policies to address crime are actually made. This area of theorising, informed by insights from sociology, tends to emphasise sources of crime policy other than criminological knowledge.

Politics

'Most developments in penal policy over the last decade have emerged not through the influence of criminological ideas or from the applications of findings from research ...' Hood (2002: 1) observes, 'but from ideological and political considerations fuelled by populist concerns and impulses'. Tonry and

Green (2003) refer to political influences as a set of 'filters' separating knowledge from policy. New policy ideas are filtered through prevailing crime policy paradigms and ideologies, as well as short-term political considerations. It is not uncommon, they suggest, for politicians to say in private that they support particular proposals but feel unable to take the risks politically.

Crime has become too important as a political theme for government to defer to university specialists. In the USA, the Republican Party introduced crime as a national issue during the angry politics of the 1960s. Richard Nixon countered Lyndon Johnson's 'war on poverty' with the need for a 'war on crime' and won the presidency for the Republicans. In the UK, Mrs Thatcher took the lead on crime and the Conservatives held office during the 1970s with a 'tough on crime' stance. Since then, members of the opposition parties have believed that it is impossible to win elections without appearing to be tough on crime, hence Tony Blair's (1993a: 27) often-repeated phrase that Labour 'should be tough on crime and tough on the causes of crime'. Conservatives and Labour have committed themselves to a bidding war in toughness, each wanting to appear to have a firmer grasp on issues of crime and safety (Downes and Morgan, 2002).

Haggerty (2004) argues that criminological expertise has been significantly devalued in the era of neo-liberalism. Whereas liberal governance relies on social welfare, neo-liberalism emphasises the individual as the agent of security, health, and happiness. Political power has detached itself from its previous need for academic legitimacy. Within crime policies, this has meant a movement away from governmental programmes, such as social crime prevention, to schemes that are more local and privatised. The proliferation of security technology has also led to multiple schemes for monitoring, detecting, capturing, processing, and detaining suspects. Whereas public safety was thought to be assured through provision of security by means of the welfare state, in the current era public safety is thought to rest on strategically placed CCTV cameras. Haggerty (2004) also observes, citing Jean-Paul Brodeur, that neo-liberalism has altered the definition of experts. Whereas experts were sought by government for envisioning and carrying out crime prevention schemes, experts are now sought for their advice on managing the symbols and images of safety. This 'new type of expert' specialises not in 'how things are' or 'how things are known' but on 'how things are perceived and mythologized for political ends' (Haggerty, 2004: 222).

The Social

In addition to the political climate at the level of national parties and philosophies of governance, policies operate in a broader social context. Translating any idea into policy subjects the idea to a political process the outcome of which is far from certain. Ideas can be hijacked by rival political parties and converted for use toward purposes remote from what was intended. But the larger issue here is that we simply do not know as much about how society works as we would like. Society cannot be made and unmade at will, even by governments.

The unforeseeable consequences of social action references a staple idea in sociology. Norbert Elias recognised that knowledge of the social structures or figurations in which they are bound up is always imperfect, incomplete and inaccurate. This is due to 'unintentional human interdependencies', which Elias said, 'lie at the root of every intentional human interaction' (quoted in Mennell, 1977: 100). He taught that unanticipated consequences are nearly universal in social life, essential to every theoretical model of social activity. Elias demonstrated that it is difficult, to explain individual action as a consequence of social structure, but more difficult, the other way around, to explain the social consequences of individual action. He offered the example of trying to predict the outcome of various games, from two-player to teams of increasingly larger size, as a way of showing the increasing complexity of human interaction.

The emerging study of how policies travel highlights the complexity of modelling social action. There is an increasing awareness that a significant portion of British policy ideas in the area of crime are not domestic but imported; examples can be found of 'transfer' or 'convergence' in the language and practice of crime policy. The USA is thought to be the largest exporter of policies. Analysts in the UK have noted a number of specific imports as well as a general similarity of themes (Tonry, 2004). At the same time, the mechanisms, directions, flow, and outcomes are much less understood than might be assumed. Policies change dramatically across political cultures, making it extremely unlikely that British crime control policy can be understood along the lines of what happens in the USA today will happen in the UK tomorrow (Sparks and Newburn, 2002).

Culture

Garland and Sparks (2000: 192) point out that criminology is not only located in the worlds of the university and government, but also in the 'world of culture – including mass mediated popular culture and political discourse'. The media in contemporary society cannot fabricate social problems out of nothing. But media coverage does help to define what people think about, which social activities are seen as problems, and the range of solutions to be considered.

Garland (2000) describes crime policy against a culture of insecurity. Politicians prior to the 1970s avoided crime as a political issue because they did not want to associate themselves with a problem that appeared unsolvable. But in the current era, high crime rates have come to be expected, part of a complex of fear, anger, and resentment. This change has come about as a result of media, primarily television coverage, of crime as a staple theme. Television, 'the central institution of modern life', presents its worrying stream of dramatic images suggesting the irrationality and unpredictability of criminal behaviour. This reinforces cultural sensibilities and beliefs about modern life as characterised by risk, unpredictability, and danger. And as people have come to believe that they can no longer trust government to maintain essential well-being, crime policy has become more diffuse and more symbolic. Cavender (2004) embellishes Garland's account, expanding the understanding of the American media in shaping policy responses to crime. He points not only to television, but newspapers, magazines, and film; his analysis includes not only news coverage, but drama series, reality television, and feature films. During the past 30 years, the presentation of crime across various media formats has reinforced a curiously singular message: crime is a feature of modern life, for reasons that cannot be grasped, and government by itself cannot protect the public.

Cultural sensibilities establish the parameters of policy innovation. And, generally speaking, the shift Garland describes means that appeals to law and order will have greater cultural meaning than appeals to rehabilitation. Cullen and colleagues argue 'it is clear that being right about crime – developing solid knowledge through "good" criminology – is not enough to influence public policy' (Cullen et al., 1999: 195). Policies do not hinge on what can be demonstrated empirically but on whether they make sense to people. Implementing a sustainable policy agenda requires that its advocates 'tell a good story', consistent with cultural sensibilities, about why crime occurs and what should be done in response. They argue that the criminologists who advocate social policy as an approach to crime have simply not been as effective at storytelling as have the advocates of changes in crime policy.

Conclusion

The role of criminologists in a welfare state is complicated. Some argue criminologists should join their cousins in social policy in building and strengthening the welfare state. Others insist that criminologists should engage the role of outside provocateur; external critics who challenge the government to do something more or something else. These arguments reflect differing beliefs about the value of social-science knowledge and political strategies for bringing about social change.

Questions for Discussion

1. *Are students of criminology and social policy concerned with 'the social question'? Should they be?*

2. *Would Leon Radzinowicz agree with New Labour's response to crime? Would Richard Titmuss?*

3. *Who worries most about the gap between what criminologists know and what policymakers do: experimental criminologists, crime scientists, critical criminologists, or left realists?*

4. *What influence do the theories and research findings of criminologists actually have on policymaking about crime?*

Further Reading

Michael Hill (2003) *Understanding Social Policy* (7th edn). Oxford: Blackwell.

NACRO (1995) *Crime and Social Policy*. London: NACRO.

Mick Ryan (2003) *Penal Policy and Political Culture in England and Wales*. Winchester: Waterside Press.

Michael Tonry (2004) *Punishment and Politics: Evidence and Emulation in English Crime Control Policy*. Cullompton: Willan.

Criminological Theory and Social Policy

2

SUMMARY

- Social disorganisation theory has traditionally emphasised community-based and local interventions as the best response to crime
- Strain theory affirms the importance of a national welfare system as an essential crime reduction measure
- Control theory can be interpreted as supporting the welfare state, but tends to emphasise family-centred and school-based interventions
- Routine activities theory insists that the problem of crime ought not be confused with provision of social welfare

Every theory of crime contains an argument about what should be done in response. While theories about the aetiology of crime do not always offer policy proposals as such, the theorised source of crime signals a preferred solution. A major distinction that applies, as we will see in this chapter, is the difference between individual and structural causes. Theories that identify social sources as the cause of crime tend to support social policy as a response, while theories built around psychological issues and individual choice do not necessarily lead in this direction. We will examine four theoretical traditions: two offering theoretical support for social policy, one that might make such a suggestion, and one suggesting that social policy has nothing to do with crime.

The theories to be considered in this discussion were all invented to explain crime in the United States. To what extent they can be meaningfully applied to British society will be discussed along the way. There are obvious and important differences between the UK and the USA. But as a number of criminologists have argued, the 'American Dream' is not peculiarly American. Ian Taylor (1997: 298) has written that post-war America represents a 'natural laboratory' for understanding the effects of market hegemony now underway in Europe.

The first part of the chapter reviews social disorganisation theory associated with the Chicago School and the 'New Chicagoans'. The second part takes up the strain/anomie tradition and recent innovations in social support theory and institutional anomie. The third part describes control theory and its policy implications. The fourth part reviews the routine activities approach and the argument that social policy does not matter.

Social Disorganisation

A good place to start looking for a theoretical explanation of the link between social policy and crime is in Chicago. Not that the Chicago School produced *the* explanation, but the concepts they proposed have been important to a number of subsequent explanations.

Zones of Delinquency

Social disorganisation theory is often referred to as 'the Chicago School' given its association with the Department of Sociology at the University of Chicago. Founded in the last decades of the nineteenth century, the Department became known for its theoretical and methodological innovations. The Chicago sociologists championed micro forms of sociological enquiry where the unit of analysis shifted from aspects of society to neighbourhoods, areas, and sectors within the city. Their commitment to 'theories of the middle range' allowed them to offer sociological analyses of numerous topics – gangs, delinquency, family, urban mobility, ethnic groups – important to criminology (Turner, 1988). Methodologically, they replaced the social survey with field research involving a combination of interviews, observation, and personal histories. And for their 'field', they looked no further than Chicago itself. By 1900, Chicago had become not only a leading railway hub and the site for expanding industries, but a major reception centre for waves of immigrants. Immigrants from Europe – Irish and German poor, peasants from southern Italy, Jews from Eastern Europe – poured in, along with African Americans from the southern United States.

Observing patterns of city growth led Clifford Shaw and Henry McKay (1969) to ask an important question about crime: Why did the same neighbourhoods remain 'delinquency areas' despite frequent turnover among residents? To find the answer, they turned to the work of their colleague Ernest Burgess who imagined the 'struggle for space' in the city using concentric zones. Burgess began with the central commercial district, the 'Chicago Loop', then moved outward in wider rings delineated by land use and residential type. The core contained banks, corporate headquarters, insurance companies, and government offices. The second zone he called the 'zone in transition' because it contained a factory zone that encroached on the homes of the city's poorest residents. Gangs, prostitutes, and drug addicts peopled the zone in transition, along with immigrants and ethnic minorities. The third zone was the 'zone of workingmen's homes', and outside it, the zones of the more affluent middle class, the 'commuters' and residents of 'satellite cities'. The newest arrivals took up residence in the zone in transition, and as each immigrant group acquired social standing, migrated to the zone of workingmen's homes and eventually to the commuter zone. Ethnic succession and related processes explained the 'pathological behaviour' of residents there.

Shaw and McKay (1969) mapped rates of delinquency and income for census tracts[1] within each zone. Their 'spot maps' revealed the areas of highest delinquency to be those adjacent to industry and commerce, those areas of lowest income status, and those areas with the highest concentration of European immigrants and Black Americans. Delinquency rates were highest within the zone in transition, Shaw and McKay reasoned, because relationships among the inhabitants had become too competitive and less cooperative, resulting in disequilibrium. Disequilibrium generated wide standards, from conventional behaviour to deviant, each of which offered opportunities for advancement, some legitimate, many illegitimate. This was consistent with Burgess's claim that disease, crime, disorder, vice, insanity, and suicide could be understood as 'rough indexes of social organisation'.

Shaw's sense of the source of delinquency led to community-based interventions as the solution. He initiated the Chicago Area Projects in 1932 to counteract the forces of social disorganisation and foster relationships important for informal social control. He established 22 neighbourhood centres in six areas. These centres mobilised community resources such as churches, schools, labour unions, industries, clubs and other groups addressing neighbourhood problems. They sponsored various programmes including camping, boxing, dramatics, handicrafts, printing, and club discussions (Snodgrass, 1976: 14). The Chicago Area Projects operated for more than twenty-five years, until Shaw's death in 1957. The projects inspired similar approaches in other cities and served as a prototype for the delinquency prevention and welfare programmes of the Kennedy–Johnson era. In that sense, Shaw established highly successful programmes.

Critics have argued that these community centres did little to alter the fundamental realities of Chicago politics and the economics of urban development responsible for the maintenance of slums (Snodgrass, 1976). Social disorganisation theory mistook the social fallout associated with capitalist production as 'natural' or 'spontaneous' processes in the life course of cities, the unfortunate by-product of organic processes of industrial development and urban sprawl. Shaw was not unaware of this. He realised how the presence of the community centres satisfied the consciences of philanthropists but did little about the system that allowed fortunes to be made from letting sub-standard housing. He had second thoughts about 'colluding with dishonest welfare organisations' and making friends of businessmen who 'knowingly misrepresent things because this makes a good story on the coast and helps to raise money' (Snodgrass, 1976: 15). He also worried about neighbourhood councils as a means of instilling community order. The techniques of informal social control they deployed resembled the coercive aspects of political control within authoritarian regimes (Snodgrass, 1976: 17).

---

[1]These are statistical areas with cities, designed by the Census Department, averaging about 4000 residents. Census tracts are meant to be small, stable areas reflecting neighbourhoods.

Smith (1988) observes that Chicago sociology expressed American liberalism. This belief regards the USA as the best expression of democratic society, a proper balance of individual liberty and the just community. Or, at least it would be, once a few wrinkles are ironed out. The Chicago sociologists regarded the city as a problem in need of solving for the American democracy to function properly. Using social maps, they visualised how the spaces of the city were connected by social pathologies and reasoned that these pathologies could only be addressed by neighbourhood interventions to cultivate the sense of community. In this way, they became 'market researchers of the welfare state', analysts with suggestions for improving its administration, but never questioning the overall governing apparatus (Smith, 1988: 18). (Chapter 4 discusses the application of the Chicago model to British cities.)

Collective Efficacy

By the 1950s, Chicago Sociology seemed antiquated and it surrendered its premiership to rivals. But during the 1980s, several sociologists revived the Chicago tradition with an infusion of new concepts and techniques.

Robert J. Sampson has built his conception of 'collective efficacy' on the foundation of social disorganisation. From Sampson's perspective, crime results from a community's inability to realise common values. The causal sequence begins with poverty, family disruption, and high residential mobility which bring about anonymity, the lack of relationships among residents, and indifference to community organisation. Because of this indifference, neighbours fail to exercise control over common areas, such as parks and streets, so these are frequented by criminals. Young people also have considerable freedom to act beyond neighbourhood control because anonymity means their friends are unknown to adults even though they may live a short distance from home. This results in higher crime within the area, regardless of the people who reside there. In the Project on Human Development in Chicago Neighbourhoods, Sampson and colleagues conducted a study of some 12,000 blocks in 196 neighbourhoods, combining interviews with government social statistics. They concluded that physical disorder and social disorder were associated with concentrated poverty and land use. Consistent with the idea of collective efficacy, there was less crime in neighbourhoods characterised by greater social cohesion and expectations concerning informal social control (Sampson and Raudenbush, 1999).

Sampson has argued that this work has implications for communities in British and European societies. He co-authored a study using information culled from British Crime Surveys conducted in 1982 and 1984. Sampson and Groves (1989) calculated crime rates and social indices for 238 localities across England and Wales. Three of the social indexes had been specified by Shaw and McKay as structural dimensions of social disorganisation: persistent poverty, ethnic diversity, and residential mobility. Sampson and Groves suggested two more: urbanisation and family disruption. They also proposed several 'intervening dimensions of social disorganisation' based on the prevalence of social networks within communities. They decided that communities differ in the collective capacity of residents to influence (control) one another based on differences in their ability to control 'teenage peer groups,' such as street-corner congregating, 'local friendship networks,' or social ties among residents, and 'formal and voluntary organisations,' such as committees, clubs, and local institutions. They affirmed the 'power and generalisability' of social disorganisation theory, concluding that 'Shaw and McKay's model explains crime and delinquency rates in a culture other than the United States' (Sampson and Groves, 1989). No single work, Lowenkamp, Cullen and Pratt (2003: 352) have remarked, did more to reinvigorate social disorganisation theory in criminology than this article. Lowenkamp and associates replicated the Sampson and Groves analysis with data from the 1994 British Crime Survey; they conclude that the processes described represent an underlying empirical pattern that has persisted over time.

Sampson's policy suggestions have to do with changing communities; he emphasises the need for 'changing places, not people'. Reducing social disorganisation and building collective efficacy are long-term propositions. Small successes accumulate to turn neighbourhoods around and this would lead to lowering crime in cities generally. These include: targeting specific neighbourhood sites known for frequent criminal activity; abating the 'spiral of decay' by removing rubbish and scrubbing graffiti from buildings; sponsoring youth activities to increase interactions between youths and adults; reducing residential mobility through programmes enabling people to buy their own homes; scattering public housing[2] across various neighbourhoods rather than concentrating it in poor neighbourhoods; ramping up urban services, including police, fire, and public health services (especially aimed at reducing teenage pregnancy and child abuse); and promoting volunteerism and community organisations (Sampson, 1995).

The Truly Disadvantaged

In the 1990s, Sampson teamed up with William J. Wilson, another representative of the 'new' Chicago sociology, to propose a theory about the overlap of inequality, urban location, and African American populations. 'The basic thesis,' they wrote, 'is that macro-social patterns of residential inequality give rise to the social isolation of the truly disadvantaged, which in turn leads to structural barriers and cultural adaptations that undermine social organisation and hence the control of crime' (Sampson and Wilson, 1995: 53). This explanation reflects much of Wilson's work in Chicago on the changing economic fortunes of Black Americans and the creation of the Black middle class. While new arrivals to the city faced various forms of racism, in schools and neighbourhoods, the expanding post-war economy brought economic opportunities for

---

[2]Housing built and operated by government agencies for low-income residents; multi-unit developments are colloquially referred to as 'the projects'.

Blacks that did not threaten Whites. This bifurcated the African American community; it allowed some Blacks to escape menial labour into skilled blue-collar trades and white-collar professions. The middle class did not remain in the city. Those who could afford better houses moved out to the suburbs, leaving behind a 'semi-permanent underclass' (Wilson, 1980; 1987).

Wilson referred to this underclass as 'the truly disadvantaged', individuals who experience long-term unemployment, who engage in street crime, and families in poverty and long-term welfare dependency (Wilson, 1987: 8). The same social and economic forces that allowed for the creation of the Black middle class now conspired against them. During the 1970s and 1980s, de-industrialisation and the loss of entry-level positions in factories meant that they could not pursue the same route to the suburbs the middle class had found before them. The departure of the middle class accelerated a downward spiral, the loss of contact with middle-class values and aspirations, and a deepening culture of despair. The Black underclass lost their 'social buffer,' their access to middle-class role models, to children who helped socialise neighbours into middle-class life, and members of professions who had supplied community leadership. The truly disadvantaged have responded by acting in deviant ways that deepen their isolation; they do not cling to families, insist on orderly schools, pursue employment, or resist alcohol and drugs (Wilson, 2003).

Wilson has departed from the orthodox Chicago School emphasis on community-based interventions to the extent that he sees a vital role for the federal government in instigating urban development projects. Wilson gave his support to the Clinton Administration's efforts to create universal health care, a national child care system, and national education standards. More than once, President Clinton remarked that he had been inspired by *The Truly Disadvantaged* and referred to 'the famous African American sociologist William Julius Wilson' when asked about how Black Americans stood to gain from New Democrat economic policies (Steinberg, 1997: 32). To address the problem of the city poor, Wilson (1996) has recommended reviving the Works Progress Administration (WPA). Wilson's WPA would follow along the same lines as the one established by President Franklin D. Roosevelt during the depression era. The new WPA would operate job centres not only to provide training but also to offer services such as organising car pools to bring individuals to places of employment. Not only would the new WPA improve the quality of life in impoverished neighbourhoods, but the jobs would also provide a conduit to permanent jobs by affording the opportunity to develop the 'soft skills' of employability.

Critics argue that Wilson's understanding of truly disadvantaged resembles neo-conservative thinking about the 'underclass', a term he has used (Bagguley and Mann, 1992; Wacquant, 1997). Essentially, his discussion places too much emphasis on the culture of poor people living in city neighbourhoods and not enough on the structure of society at large that leads to their impoverishment. Wilson has conceded that 'underclass' does have a pejorative meaning, especially when read in the columns of journalists and neo-conservative commentators. The term ought to be rejected, he suggested, because it had 'become a code word for inner-city blacks', because it brought about a public denunciation of poor people living in the city, and because it lacked sufficient value as a guide to social scientific analysis. He resolved to substitute 'ghetto poor' for 'underclass'. At the same time, he maintained that 'simplistic either/or notions of culture versus structure have impeded the development of a broader theoretical context' from which to investigate the impact of economic changes on the urban poor (Wilson, 1991: 1–4).

Strain Theory

Strain theory offers the most direct explanation for why social policy should be utilised for crime reduction. The strain/anomie tradition insists that crime is not brought about by poverty so much as *inequality*. In an economic system that prevents participation by some individuals, it is relative (rather than absolute) deprivation that pressurises them into criminal activity.

Anomie and Opportunity

The key question for strain theory is how to account for crime despite rising affluence. The United States is, by a number of measures, a wealthy country and yet it also has one of the highest rates of violent crime. For Robert Merton, who wrote the initial statement in the 1930s, the answer could be found in the difference between culture and structure. His essay, 'Social Structure and Anomie', remains among the most cited in criminology (Featherstone and Deflem, 2003: 471). Culture establishes the meaning of success; it specifies 'the goals', what things are worth pursuing, and the 'means,' the ways to go about obtaining them. Structure has to do with distribution of the means. In a well-ordered society, the goals and means are consonant. That is, society affords all of its members a reasonable expectation of achieving success during their lifetimes. But too many of those in American society experienced dissonance between the goals and means, Merton felt, because they had been led to desire a way of life social circumstances made it impossible to achieve.

'The cultural demands made on persons in this situation are incompatible,' Merton (1938: 679) wrote. 'On the one hand, they are asked to orient their conduct toward the prospect of accumulating wealth and on the other, they are largely denied effective opportunities to do so institutionally'. Living under conditions of strain requires adaptation by one of several strategies. 'Conformity', he suggested, was followed by all those who were reasonably comfortable with their position in society or at least confident of their ability to improve their position. They accept the cultural goals in the belief that they benefit from the means afforded by the prevailing structure. Members of the working class would be tempted to pursue another strategy, 'innovation'. Innovators accept the goals, but because the legitimate means are not available, pursue alternative means, which is to say illegal means, of obtaining them.

During the 1960s, strain theory was reformulated by Richard Cloward and Lloyd Ohlin. Their 'opportunity theory' extended strain logic to the problem of adolescent crime and gang affiliation. Like Merton, they wrote about the overemphasis in American culture on material success and the consequences of structural barriers for individual achievement. 'Pressures toward the formation of delinquent subcultures', Cloward and Ohlin (1960: 54) said, 'originate in the marked disparities between culturally induced aspirations among lower class youth and the possibility of achieving them by legitimate means'. But as Cloward and Ohlin pointed out, a young person who had decided to pursue an illegitimate route to success could only choose from those illegal activities available within the community. Whether to get involved in organised theft or burglary, the drug trade, or some other line of criminal work depended on the extent to which adults in the neighbourhood had already organised such enterprises. This aspect of their work has been referred to as the 'other side of strain'.

Opportunity theory informed the American experiment with social crime prevention during the 1960s. The solution to delinquency, Cloward and Ohlin argued, was a matter of expanding opportunities for young people. Make it possible for young people to succeed, by offering jobs and training for jobs, and they would turn their back on gangs, crime and drugs. The system needed fixing, not the youths. Their Mobilisation of Youth project, initiated in a poor neighbourhood within New York City, sought to increase employment opportunities, provide job-training and skill-development, and help minority youth overcome workplace discrimination. It became the model for numerous programmes carried out as part of President Lyndon Johnson's War on Poverty. Essentially, opportunity theory became a guide not only to delinquency prevention but poverty prevention in general.

David Downes (1998) has argued that Merton's theory works quite well in Britain. Merton had put his finger on the key question of how to account for rising delinquency despite growing affluence and welfare support. In focusing on rising expectations in the context of consumerism, Merton had identified a component of Marx's theory of political economy (rather than Durkheim's concept of anomie as Merton framed it) and distilled a theory of deviance from it. Downes's research in London's East End during the 1960s led him to conclude that if non-skilled young men were to be denied the chance of contributing to and benefiting from technological society as it was being built, the price would be high. He feared that erosion of the welfare state initiated by the Thatcher government in 1979 would lead to American-style crime policies of mass imprisonment (Downes, 1998: 107–8).

Social Support

The emergence of social support theory in the 1980s rekindled strain theory. Francis Cullen (1983) distinguished two meanings of strain in Merton's writing – individual (psychological) and societal (structural). Strain, experienced by individuals at the psychological level, would produce anger, frustration, and anxiety and lead to deviant behaviour as an expression of this frustration. But strain also represented a rational choice in the context of limited opportunities. The criminal, under conditions in American society, did not need to experience any special stress or pressure to become deviant. Deviance and crime occur when illegitimate routes to success become the 'technically most effective procedure'. Cullen avoided the word 'strain' as a characteristic of such theories and replaced it with 'structuring'.

Cullen's theory of crime centres on the concept of 'social support', an idea implicit in sociologies of crime going back to the Chicago criminologists. Cullen contends that people avoid crime to the extent that communities and neighbourhoods meet their material and psychological needs. 'An important key to solving the crime problem', Cullen (1994: 552) has stated, 'is the construction of a supportive social order'. If enough resources flow to areas of need, people will commit fewer crimes and there will be much less need for harsher measures of government crime control. At the same time, government should prevent crime by means of social policy rather than crime policy generally. Social justice expresses criminology's highest ambition. Or, as Cullen put it, 'good criminology' pursues the 'good society'. Progressive strategies should nurture a culture of supportive concern for others and discourage the values of individualism and competitiveness (Cullen, Wright and Chamlin, 1999: 198–203).

Social support theory is consistent with research in the USA about the impact of government benefits on crime. Hannon and DeFronzo (1998) examined welfare assistance across 406 metropolitan counties and found increases in welfare payments to be correlated with lower levels of crime. They conclude that welfare assistance mitigates what would otherwise be a strong relationship between disadvantage and crime rates. This finding is consistent with anomie/strain theory, they suggest, as welfare assistance appears to allow poor individuals to legally obtain culturally defined goals, lessening the anger and frustration that would otherwise lead them to crime.

There is some disagreement among the proponents of social support theory about whether government can truly stand in for families and communities when they fail to provide nurturance, shared values, aid and comfort. Government programmes offer a soulless alternative to the experience of solidarity within a community. Cullen's model proposes, however, that most people need all the support they can get from all sources. Social support should be delivered at the local level through early intervention and community-based programmes. It should be delivered at the national level through government assistance to persons in need and indirectly through federally funded programmes. Cullen suggests that social support can also be delivered within the criminal justice system, by such means as prisoner rehabilitation and re-entry (Pratt and Godsey, 2002: 590–1).

Crime and the 'American Dream'

In 1994, Steven Messner and Richard Rosenfeld published a major restatement of Merton's work that has been called 'institutional anomie' theory. They attribute high levels of criminal violence in American society to the 'American Dream' defined as a 'broad cultural ethos that entails a commitment to the goal of material success, to be pursued by everyone in society, under conditions of open, individual competition' (Messner and Rosenfeld, 1994). This cultural ethos generates strong pressure for acquiring wealth, but does not contain sufficient prohibitions about the means of achieving that fortune.

Messner and Rosenfeld, as Bernburg (2002) explains, depart from Merton in their portrayal of the structural sources of anomie within the cultural sensibilities of the capitalist market economy. The values engendered by market society, the pursuit of self-interest, accumulation of wealth, and individual competition, have become exaggerated relative to the values related to the family, education, and even politics. Messner and Rosenfeld point to the overwhelming influence of economic institutions in American society. Other institutions – family, school, and even politics – tend to be overwhelmed by the market. These other institutions would be instilling cultural beliefs about the importance of playing by the rules, that family is important, and so on. These institutions are important for 'socialising' members into accepted social standards. For Messner and Rosenfeld, the market not only shapes the cultural definition of success and the distribution of labour, but also limits the effectiveness of other social institutions in their ability to address the imbalance (Bernburg, 2002: 733).

Messner and Rosenfeld make several policy recommendations aimed at reducing the influence of money in American life. Pro-family policies, such as family leave for workers, job sharing, flexible work schedules and employer-organised child care would give parents more time to devote to their families. Severing the link between educational credentials and employment (by de-emphasising the high school diploma as the qualification for work) would allow students motivated to work to begin a job, and students interested in learning to pursue an education. They would lobby for creation of a national service corps to engage people in the ways that emphasise collective goals rather than individual material success. And, they advocate cultural transformation generally – American culture should be steered toward mutual support and collective obligations and away from individual rights, interests, rewards, and privileges (Messner and Rosenfeld, 2006).

While Messner and Rosenfeld entitled their work to reflect their critique of American society, they have extended this critique beyond its borders. The threat posed by the American Dream is not peculiarly American, because market hegemony is actually a planetary phenomenon. Drawing on Karl Polanyi's framework, Messner and Rosenfeld (2000: 13) stress the 'fundamental issue confronting all capitalist societies: the need to restrain the market and prevent the economy from dominating other institutional realms'. In *The Great Transformation* (1944), Polanyi offered an account of the progress of industrial capitalism during the nineteenth and early twentieth centuries. One process in this transformation involved the expansion of the market as the mechanism for centring economic activity. The other involved counter-moves to prevent the market from undermining social order altogether. This was necessary because market exchange is 'disembedded' from other social relationships. To allow the market to expand unchecked would prove disastrous because it would undermine the cultural and moral foundations of human existence.

Capitalist societies staved off the worst effects of the market by constructing welfare states, essentially a strategy for *re*-embedding (Messner and Rosenfeld, 2000). The difficult task confronting market societies is thus to 'nurture cultural orientations' that sustain market exchange, but, at the same time, instil 'considerations of collective order and mutual obligation'. While markets promote the values of individual rights and liberties, it falls to government to supply counter-balancing political and social values.

Market dominance promotes high rates of crime through both structural and cultural processes. Messner and Rosenfeld suggest that crime rates in advanced industrial states vary with the extent and scope of welfare provisions. Globalisation, the 'confluence of social and cultural changes that loosen the constraints of geography on the actions of individuals and collectivities', threatens to elevate crime rates unless governments take steps to mitigate its impact (Messner and Rosenfeld, 2000: 18). Savolainen (2000) took a look at cross-national homicide rates to examine the welfare state effect. He surmised that homicide rates would differ by nation depending on the strength of the welfare state in mitigating the impact of economic inequality. Consistent with institutional anomie theory, he found economic inequality to be a strong predictor of national homicide rates in nations with under-developed welfare structures. He suggested that homicide may not be a function of inequality so much as the size of an economically marginalised population; nations most resistant to the effects of economic inequality are those with tiny or nonexistent underclass populations.

Control Theory

Control theory presents an unlikely explanation for the link between social policy and crime. It is frequently classified as rational choice theory, meaning that individual choice is more important to the explanation of crime than social conditions constraining that choice. But control theory can be read in different ways, leading W. Byron Groves and associates to argue that it should be regarded as a radical theory consistent with Marx's theory of political economy (Lynch and Groves, 1989; Groves and Sampson, 1987).

The Social Bond

Travis Hirschi decided that most criminological theories start with the wrong question. Rather than asking what is it that leads some people to break the law, Hirschi invites criminologists to ask: Why is it that most people abide by the law? If inequality pressurised society in the way strain theory says it does, then the real mystery would be why *more* people are not involved in crime. His answer, in the form of social bond theory, has ranked as the most popular explanation of crime among American criminologists (Walsh and Ellis, 1999).

Most people, Hirschi (1969) reasons, have motivations other than fear of arrest and imprisonment for behaving themselves. They have made investments in society, 'stakes in conformity', that would be jeopardised by an adventure into lawbreaking. They are bonded to society to an extent sufficient to render them unwilling to break the rules. The social bond can be understood as the rewards that accrue from participation in conventional social activities; it is comprised of the relationships, ambitions, and moral beliefs that commit people to law-abiding behaviour. Delinquents engage in anti-social behaviour and crime because their ties to conventional order have been weak or broken. He identified four elements of the social bond: attachment (sensitivity to the opinions of others), commitment (pursuit of conventional behaviour), involvement (time spent in conventional activities), and belief (accepting that people should obey the rules).

In other words, law-abiding behaviour must be *purchased*; it must have some payoff for individuals (Lynch and Groves, 1989). If this sort of reward system fails, crime can be suppressed only by coercive measures such as punishment and threat of punishment. To make conformity attractive, society must offer something to its members – something of use for meeting human and culturally defined needs. The moral of the control story, then, is grasping the structures and processes by which these rewards are unequally distributed so that social bonds are not the same for everyone (Lynch and Groves, 1989: 79–80). It is easy, given this reading of control theory, to see how the social bond varies in proportion to social exclusion: the greater the experience of social exclusion, the weaker the social bond. This reading of social bond theory explains its popularity among self-described liberal criminologists in the USA who think of broken social bonds in terms of unfair economic opportunities and lack of educational opportunities (Walsh and Ellis, 1999).

'Eight Simple Rules'

Control theory has been classified as a conservative approach because of the tendency to read it alongside Hirschi's later work. *A General Theory of Crime*, co-authored with Michael Gottfredson (Gottfredson and Hirschi, 2002), sets out self-control as the explanation for criminal behaviour, and since its publication, interpreters have tended to project the Hirschi of self-control onto the Hirschi of social bond. In this way, 'control theory' becomes an unlikely place for social policy. Jock Young (1999) places Gottfredson's and Hirschi's approach on the 'right of the political spectrum' and suggests that they champion an individualist explanation of crime consistent with a criminal justice response. Yet as Taylor (2001: 374) points out, Gottfredson and Hirschi clearly reject long-term imprisonment and aggressive policing as a primary response: 'Because offenders are oriented to the short-term, manipulation of the criminal justice system, the ancient and popular solution to the crime problem, should have little or no impact on their behaviour' (Gottfredson and Hirschi, 2002: 295). While *A General Theory of Crime* does not explicitly deal with issues of inequality, there is no theoretical bar to why programmes aimed at helping the poor and disadvantaged would not contribute positively to parents' ability to teach self-control.

Gottfredson and Hirschi (2002) explain that their self-control theory is a 'choice theory'; a theory that assumes rational decision-making on the part of the criminal. This leads them in the direction of situational crime prevention. Programmes or practices that reduce opportunities, or make it more difficult or complex to enjoy criminal pleasures, will be most effective. Increasing the cost of alcohol or prohibiting its availability in particular settings offers a low-cost method of crime control. Generally, crime policies should address specific crimes rather than attempt to deal with all crimes, or the most serious of crimes. For this reason, control theory counsels against placing greater authority for crime control with the federal government. Local authorities, particularly those responsible for schools and closest to the community where they can aid families in distress, should take the lead in crime prevention.

Gottfredson and Hirschi (2002: 298–301) propose 'eight simple rules' for crime reduction. Policymakers should not attempt to reduce crime by incapacitating adults, rehabilitating adults, promoting proactive policing, or increasing severity of criminal penalties. Rather, policymakers should support programmes providing alternatives to unsupervised activities of teenagers and providing early education and effective childcare. Policies are needed that promote and facilitate two-parent families and that increase the number of caregivers relative to the number of children.

Routine Activities

Like control theory, routine activities theory seems an unlikely entry in a conversation about social policy and crime. One of the primary advocates of this theory, Marcus Felson, declares that welfare provision has no impact on crime rates. Routine activities theory does, however, offer a sociological explanation for crime leading to the conclusion that criminal justice is not the solution.

The Chemistry for Crime

Routine activities theory arrives at its iconoclastic statements about the welfare state from an intriguing starting point. Rather than ask why some people commit crimes, routine activities theory asks why some people become crime victims. Since the first victimisation surveys were carried out in the 1970s, criminologists have become aware that people differ in their risk of becoming victims of crime. Individuals who are young, unmarried, and who live in cities run a higher risk of being victimised. And, one of the groups in society with the highest risk of victimisation consists of those persons who have been victimised before. To explain these patterns, criminologists have looked at the lifestyles or 'routine activities' of persons on the assumption that how people act, and with whom they interact, places them at greater or lesser risk of being victimised.

Felson (2002) explains this 'chemistry for crime' with reference to convergence in time and space of three elements. In order for a crime to occur, there must be a willing offender, a suitable target, and the absence of a capable guardian. The model does not seek to understand what makes an offender willing; it only assumes that a crime could not occur unless someone was willing, for whatever reason, to break the law. The term 'target' is preferred over victim because the victim might be completely absent from the scene – the owner of a television set is usually away when the burglar nicks it. Guardianship does not refer to uniformed security or police but to anybody whose presence discourages the would-be criminal. The fact that 'someone is at home' inhibits burglary even though that somebody is not intentionally engaged in security. This line of reasoning leads to two initial conclusions. First, patterns of routine activities and lifestyles are assumed to create a criminal opportunity structure by enhancing contact between potential criminals and victims. Second, the subjective value of the victim as a 'target' and its level of accessibility related to 'guardianship' determine the choice of a particular victim (Miethe and Meier, 1990: 245). Or, as Felson (1987: 914) phrases it: 'Although the fox finds each hare one by one, the fox population varies with the hare population on which it feeds'.

Cohen and Felson (1979) outlined the routine activities approach in 1979 in an article dealing with crime trends in the USA in the decades after the Second World War. Many theories of crime did not seem to fit. If poverty, unemployment, and urbanisation explain crime rates, then crime should have decreased. But crime *increased*. They surmised that changes in the lifestyle of many Americans had made them more vulnerable to household crimes. More homes were left unguarded as women entered full-time work and more families could afford weeks away on holiday (by travelling on the newly built 'interstate'). At the same time, the diffusion of transistors and plastics generated new categories of portable goods that could be stolen. Property crime was an unintended effect of the dispersion of activities away from family and household settings. Felson contends that this reasoning still represents the best explanation for the rise in burglary in the USA and Western Europe during the 1960s and 1970s. The best predictor of annual burglary rates, he points out, is the weight of the smallest television set sold each year.

Much of the empirical study of crime that makes use of the routine activities framework is conducted in the USA. But studies of developments in the European context have begun to appear. Tseloni and others (2004) examined factors related to burglary in the UK, USA, and the Netherlands based on victimisation surveys conducted in these countries during the 1990s. They conclude that burglary of American households displayed more idiosyncratic patterns than European households, but that some cross-national patterns support the application of routine activities theory. Wittebrood and Nieuwbeerta (2000) carried out an innovative study in the Netherlands using information culled from life histories data rather than victimisation surveys. They affirmed the usefulness of the routine activities perspective in explaining repeat victimisation: individuals who have once been victimised suffer a higher risk of subsequent victimisation.

The Welfare State Fallacy?

Although Felson's theory has been taken as theoretical support for situational crime prevention, there is an argument for sociological intervention on a macro scale. When Felson talks about situational crime prevention, he has in mind 'natural social control' maintained through relationships among passers-by, neighbours, and family members (Felson, 1987: 912). He is decidedly unenthusiastic about the 'unnatural' social control carried out by police, courts and prisons.

Felson is also unenthusiastic about social policy as a means of crime prevention, going so far as to refer to the 'welfare state fallacy'. He is sceptical of the claim that the USA is a world-leader in crime rates because it refuses to deliver more than a minimalist welfare state. America certainly offers less in the way of welfare benefits than European welfare states, but this does not translate into higher crime. The welfare state neither causes crime nor reduces crime – 'crime variations in industrial nations have nothing to do with the welfare state' (Felson, 2002: 12). Felson points out that according to victimisation surveys, the USA does *not* have a higher crime rate than Europe. He cites the work of Van Kesteren, Mayhew, and Nieuwbeerta (2001), who coordinated victimisation surveys in 17 industrial countries, and found the USA to rank eleventh in overall victimisation. Countries with generous welfare benefits – Netherlands and Sweden – were found to have *higher* overall criminal victimisation than the USA (Van Kesteren, Mayhew, and Nieuwbeerta, 2001: 38).

As is always the case in comparative criminology, finding appropriate points of comparison is difficult. The weakest link in Felson's argument is that victimisation surveys provide better information about property crime than about violent crime. The Netherlands, for example, falls into the 'high' band of overall victimisation along with Australia, England and Wales, and Sweden. But much of this is a function of higher rates of petty crime, such as bicycle theft and car vandalism, which account for half of all reported victimisation (Van Kesteren, Mayhew and Nieuwbeerta, 2001). In other words, the Netherlands does have a high rate of crime when it comes to bicycle theft and the USA has a high rate of crime when it comes to murder. That said, the point Felson wants to make is that policy rhetoric about social welfare should not be confused with that of crime reduction. One can believe the welfare state will bring about poverty reduction without believing that it will also bring about crime reduction.

Tham (1998) reports on an interesting 'natural experiment' to test the welfare effect on crime. He compared crime rates in the UK and Sweden during the 1980s, following the Conservative victory in the UK of 1979 and a victory for the Social Democrats in Sweden in 1982. The differing approaches to crime during these years should have, according to the logic of the welfare state, led to differences in crime. But in carrying out his analysis, Tham could not point to evidence showing that 'welfare-state policies actually might have diminished crime' in Sweden. Similarly, Bondeson (2005) observes that crime rates have increased in all the Scandinavian countries (Sweden, Finland, Denmark, Norway) since the 1960s. Similar trends can be observed for crimes of theft and assault in the Scandinavian countries and in Austria, England and Wales, Germany, and the Netherlands. The welfare model, she proposes, has not lessened crime but has softened the criminal justice policies in the welfare states.

Conclusion

In this chapter, we have seen how four questions about crime lead to different conclusions about the impact of social policy. Why do 'high crime' areas of cities persist despite turnover among residents? How is it that a wealthy society also has high rates of crime? Why do most people living in conditions of social inequality not turn to crime? How is it that some people are victimised by crime much more than others? At the policy end, this translates into emphasis on community-based and local programmes, affirmation of the welfare state, programmes targeting parents and schools, and efforts to redirect the social activities that comprise everyday life. Criminologists working within each of these frameworks agree that conventional methods of policing and prisons will be ineffective.

Questions for Discussion

1. *The UK government plans to redevelop blighted areas of East London in preparation for the 2012 Olympic Games. Will rebuilding this area achieve long-term poverty reduction?*

2. *Does pursuit of the American Dream explain crime in British society? Is the 'British Dream' slightly or significantly different?*

3. *Is it fair to say that police and prisons are short-term solutions to the problem of crime and that social policy presents a long-term solution?*

4. *Is it appropriate to justify social policies with reference to their (potential) crime reduction qualities?*

Further Reading

Robert Lilly, Francis Cullen, and Richard Ball (2006) *Criminological Theory: Context and Consequences* (4th edn). Thousand Oaks, CA: Sage.

Wayne Morrison (1995) *Theoretical Criminology: From Modernity to Post-Modernism*. London: Cavendish.

John Tierny (2006) *Criminology: Theory and Content* (3rd edn). Essex: Pearson.

Rene van Swaanigen (1997) *Critical Criminology: Visions from Europe*. London: Sage.

Poverty, 'Race' and Gender

3

SUMMARY

- Policy terms such as 'underclass' and 'social exclusion' activate racialised and gendered images of poor people
- Popular concerns about the welfare state have focused on issues of welfare dependency and scrounging and have overlooked implications for victimisation of women
- Reactions to urban riots and immigrants have invoked the belief that poor people are dangerous and violent

One of the working assumptions of critical enquiry in criminology is that social problems are seldom what they seem. Critical criminologists demonstrate how the response to crime is about more than reducing victimisation. Crime represents a site for the construction of a number of social projects principally tied to popular anxieties about the poor. News headlines about surges in crime rates and the emergence of new types of criminality convey messages consistent with the popular beliefs that poor people are prone to violence and are addicted to welfare benefits.

Popular discussions of crime and poverty often invoke racialised and gendered images of criminality. Portrayals reference the idea of a criminal underclass, a subset of people distinguished by the persistence of their criminality and the hopelessness of their poverty. The image of the rioter is an immigrant, linking violence with 'blackness' or 'asianness'; the image of the welfare 'scrounger' is a woman, cheating the system. While the text is about crime and poverty, the subtext is about blackness and whiteness, masculinity and femininity.

This chapter pursues insights from critical criminology into ulterior aspects of crime and social policy. We will examine three recent policy discussions with the aim of revealing the messages for 'race'[1] and gender. Part one

[1] 'Race' appears in inverted commas to draw attention to its meaning as a sociopolitical construction. I capitalise Black and White because these terms reflect group identities in society and not divisions of humankind based on skin colour (Knepper, 1996: 2001).

considers underclass and social exclusion as explanations for crime, pointing to their effect in racialising crime. Part two critiques the idea of welfare dependency and crime in diffusing ideas about women and welfare provision. Part three examines the 'threat' of the poor; the notion that poor people are prone to violence.

From Underclass to Social Exclusion

The language of underclass and social exclusion has entered British policy debates about poverty and crime. While these conceptions do invite discussion of serious and worthwhile issues, they also represent unsavoury projects in relation to ethnic and cultural minorities.

The Underclass

For several decades, underclass terminology has been overheard in popular discussions of poverty. Dahrendorf (1987) and Field (1989) popularised this term in the 1980s as a commentary on the public's indifference to the victims of economic transformation. The British economy threatened to create a category of persons with an economic standing so low in the class structure that they stood outside it. The underclass lacked the requisite vocational skills and educational qualifications to become working class, and, without strategic government support, would withdraw both culturally and politically to become a permanent class of outsiders. Yet attitudes toward the poor expressed themselves in a growing indifference.

By making use of the underclass terminology, Dahrendorf and Field were, as Lister (1996: 10) has argued, playing with fire. 'Underclass' has always been more of a journalistic term than a social science concept (Westergaard, 1992) and reflects a political judgment rather than the language of social-science measurement (Lister, 1990). It has had the greatest currency in America, where media-led investigations during the 1970s and 1980s into the problems of the cities linked it with African Americans.

In American policy debate, underclass has been understood as referring to not merely the poorest of the poor, but to people characterised as poor, Black, and criminal. A cover story in *Time* magazine for 1977 defined the underclass as 'people who are more intractable, more socially alien and more hostile than almost anyone had imagined'. To avoid leaving any ambiguity about who was being referred to, the article went on to explain that although members come from all 'races' and live in different places, 'the underclass is made up mostly of impoverished urban blacks who still suffer from the heritage of slavery and discrimination' (quoted in Marks, 1991: 447). A decade later, *The Atlantic*, a more 'serious' literary magazine, updated the popular criminology of the underclass with an article clarifying its origins. The author explained how almost every aspect of ghetto life was the consequence not of slavery but the migration of Black Americans from rural areas of the South to northern cities following the Second World War. 'It appears that the distinctive culture is now the greatest barrier to progress by the black underclass, rather than either employment or welfare' (quoted in Marks, 1991: 451).

The term amounts to a code word for urban Blacks, enabling journalists to diffuse demeaning stereotypes under cover of civic-minded social investigation. Inniss and Feagin (1989) pointed to serious conceptual problems with underclass analysis by noting its usage as a pejorative for Black residents of impoverished areas in American cities. Poor people in Liverpool, they began, suffered from the same economic forces as poor people in Chicago, New York and Atlanta, but 'few US scholars would seriously discuss these white, formerly middle-income families and individuals in Liverpool as some type of "underclass" ... ' (Inniss and Feagin, 1989: 14). As it happened, one American scholar, Charles Murray, did just this. In a pair of *Sunday Times* editorials, he warned of an emerging British underclass. He defined the underclass not by a changing economic situation, but by behaviour of underclass members, much of it against the law, and claimed that it had more to do with the welfare state than 'racial' minorities in British society. Murray's use of the term illustrates its use as a stigmatising label. Seeing the poor as a class apart makes it easier for the working and middle classes to write off poor people as beyond the bonds of common citizenship (Lister, 1990: 24–6).

In the British context, underclass terminology is not linked to blackness as it is in the American context, but it continues to operate in much the same way in relation to cultural minorities and crime. Vanderbeck (2003) unpacks media discussion surrounding the conviction of Tony Martin, a Norfolk farmer, for the murder of sixteen-year-old Fred Barras, a gypsy traveller, in 1999. Barras broke into Martin's farmhouse and Martin killed him with a shotgun blast. Newspaper journalists made use of the event as an occasion to vent anxieties about Travellers, locating them within the underclass. Descriptions of Barras's life included the signifiers of underclass membership: experienced educational failure, grew up on a deprived council estate, raised by a single mother, and connived with Travellers. 'Fred Barrass', said *The Sunday Times*, 'was an underclass criminal who became the victim of his own offending'. In fact, *The Sunday Times* used the Martin trial to introduce a section of readers' letters entitled 'A Violent Underclass is a Threat to Us All' (quoted in Vanderbeck, 2003: 373).

Hayward and Yar (2006) provide a further example in their discussion of the 'chav' phenomenon. The chav lifestyle is thought to be reflected in baseball caps and tracksuits, gold chains, excessive make-up and sun-bed tans, binge drinking and hip-hop music. As a label for a group of people, the word is clearly meant to convey scorn and derision. Chav is said to mean 'Council Housed And Violent' or 'Council House Vermin'; chavs are believed to represent 'Britain's new burgeoning underclass'. The word has a long association with marginalisation and exclusion. In Romany dialect, a small child is known as a *chavo* or *chavi*. Its current meaning appears to have emerged from North

Kent in the southeast of England, a destination frequented by gypsy travellers since the nineteenth century. Chavs became a national concern following the decisions of major shopping centres, such as Bluewater in Kent and Elephant and Castle in south London to ban baseball caps and hoods. Hayward and Yar (2006) suggest that popular discourse about a criminal underclass has metamorphosed into discussion of chavs, a population increasingly seen as threatening and menacing.

Social Exclusion and Crime Prevention

In the simplest sense, 'social exclusion' was meant to be less demeaning than underclass, to highlight the victimhood of poor people. It was also meant to signify a moral commitment to helping the poor with a comprehensive programme, consistent with the idea of being tough on the causes of crime. The phrase began to appear in UK policy documents after the 1997 election of the Labour government. The Social Exclusion Unit, set up in Whitehall the following year, signalled the priority attached to reducing economic and social divisions in the country. The official definition explains social exclusion as:

> A short-hand label for what can happen when individuals or areas suffer from a combination of linked problems such as unemployment, poor skills, low incomes, poor housing, high crime environments, bad health and family breakdown. (Social Exclusion Unit, 2000: 1)

The phrase found its way to Britain from France via EU anti-poverty programmes. Originally, *exclusion sociale* referred to groups left out of the social insurance scheme. The French government had made policies that excluded categories of persons from receiving social insurance on the basis of explicit criteria; to be included, persons needed to have a job or be married to someone who had a job. There were some eleven categories of excluded persons (in 1974): physically and mentally disabled, the 'suicidal', aged invalids, abused children, chemically dependent, delinquents, single parents (sole mothers), multi-problem households, 'marginals', 'asocials', and 'social misfits' (Peace, 2001: 19).

Social exclusion remains a contested term. MacDonald and Marsh (2001: 375–6) do not offer an unqualified endorsement, but recognise the language of social exclusion has some advantages in comparison with underclass. It points to how aspects of disadvantage cluster together, suggesting the need for multiple kinds of support. It implies a process whereby some people become *in*cluded and some people do not. And, it suggests the importance of locality, the difference in levels of disadvantage across geographical areas. Other scholars believe the social exclusion paradigm should be jettisoned because it adds nothing to our understanding of inequality. Ratcliffe (1999) says that its use leads to oversimplification of complicated social, economic and political processes and can lead to pathologisation of communities. When used to refer to cultural exclusion, for example, it is problematic given the difficulty of defining the cultural mainstream, the crude dichotomy involved, and the implication of powerlessness as a starting point. The dangers of this phrase, Ratcliffe concludes, mirror those of the underclass.

Saris and Bartley (2002) discuss Ireland's experience with the social exclusion model and how it has led to the spacialisation of social problems. They studied Gallanstown Housing Estate in Cherry Orchard, a western suburb of Dublin following the Hallowe'en riots of 1995. This estate had come to resemble a 'national park' for the socially excluded, complete with 'park rangers', specially trained police and welfare workers, to manage park residents. This spacialisation contributed to the conflation of 'street culture' and criminality in a way that reinforced estate inhabitants as a distinct population, almost a sub-category of whiteness. The wearing of tracksuits, sovereign rings, and particular hairstyles were taken as the signs of a category of persons prone to violence and crime (Saris and Bartley, 2002: 15).

When taken as the source of crime, social exclusion is problematic because its solution, social inclusion or *integration*, is about more than crime reduction. This can be seen in a look at the French effort to use social inclusion as a means of crime prevention. Shortly after the election of François Mitterand in May 1981, riots occurred in Lyon and other French cities. The government chose to see these events as symptomatic of a decline in French citizenship. Riotous behaviour occurred among groups that experienced 'exclusion' from French life and participation in key social, educational, cultural, and political institutions. Mitterand established a commission of mayors, chaired by Gilbert Bonnemaison, to formulate a plan of action, and the commission's report, *Dealing with Delinquency: Prevention, Repression, Solidarity* (1982), outlined what became known as the Bonnemaison model. Generally speaking, the model proposed that government should rely on social policies, rather than law enforcement and punishment, to alleviate the causes of crime (Bonnemaison, 1992). The rationale derived from the belief that the purpose of social policy should allow every individual the 'chance to become integrated' within French society.

The French model attracted the attention of the international community, including Home Office authorities. Crawford (2000, 26) argues that 'British criminologists have been seduced by the language of "social exclusion"' in official French discourse. British endorsements neglect to mention that crime rates have increased in France since the 1980s despite the Bonnemaison programme, and further, the projects put in place during the 1980s failed to circumvent a recurrence of rioting in several French cities during the 1990s (Crawford, 2000a: 27).[2]

But the primary problem is not an argument over its effectiveness. Crawford argues that British observers have overlooked the ways in which social crime

---

[2] In November 2005, riots broke out in African and Arab areas of several French cities, including Paris, Toulouse, Strasbourg, and Nantes.

prevention contributes to French politics. The inclusion effort expressed in French criminal law 'is blind to social difference and the reality of cultural pluralism in France' (Crawford, 2000a: 28). The concept of *solidarity* conceives of the French people as homogenous. Like the French ideal of *citoyen*, 'citizen', it does not recognise divergent ethnic identities. All French people are presumed to work toward the fulfilment of national goals, despite ethnic and cultural differences. The idea of *integration* refers to the process by which individuals at the margins of French nationhood are understood to require incorporation. The failure to incorporate such groups represented by immigrant populations is seen as the central problem confronting the French state, and therefore the strategy targeted marginal youths, particularly those of North African origin, for inclusion into French society. Questions should be asked, Crawford says, about the meaning of social inclusion as a remedy: Inclusion into what? Inclusion on what terms?

The Welfare State, Crime and Dependency

In the 1990s, the idea of welfare dependency emerged as a cause of crime. This discussion took place as governments in the UK and USA pursued restructuring of welfare in the direction of workfare.

Welfare Dependency

Charles Murray provoked discussion in Britain about welfare dependency with his *Sunday Times* editorials. Britain's emerging underclass, he said, had resulted from 'incentives to fail' within the benefits scheme (Murray, 1996a).

Murray acknowledged that the USA had higher rates of violent crimes than the UK, but claimed that Britain was caught up in the same criminogenic trend. It was just that America had reached the future first. Murray predicted that rival interpretations of the crime figures would fade against the reality 'that England is indeed becoming a more dangerous place to live' and insisted that this process was not occurring everywhere, only in those neighbourhoods in which the underclass was taking over (Murray, 1996a: 36–7). Murray did not see social policy as the solution, but part of the problem. Welfare had done at least as much harm as good, proven more expensive than anticipated, and had many negative side-effects, including illegitimacy, voluntary joblessness, fatherless families, and crime. Murray expressed his belief in 'limited central government' and urged those concerned about the problem of persistent poverty to 'stop thinking as engineers' (Murray, 1996b: 90–1).

Murray's argument is inconsistent with research in the USA into the effects of welfare assistance on rates of crime. DeFronzo conducted a series of studies in the 1980s and 1990s comparing crime rates and welfare assistance across urban areas. He has found higher welfare expenditures to be associated with *less* rather than more crime, specifically homicide, rape and burglary (DeFronzo,

1983, 1996, 1997). Other researchers have reached similar conclusions. Cao, Cao and Zhao (2004) examined the effect of welfare on family structure and delinquency to test the welfare dependency argument that households headed by women led to greater delinquency. The female-headed households they studied in the State of Washington experienced neither greater prevalence nor frequency of delinquency.

The idea of a causal link between welfare dependency and crime is also inconsistent with what welfare recipients say about themselves. Luck, Elifson and Sterk (2004) interviewed 61 welfare recipients in Atlanta, Georgia, to learn about the lives of women drug-users within the welfare system. They report that the women saw no correlation between their status as welfare recipients and drug use. The researchers conclude that welfare dependency and drug use are both symptoms of the women's position in society. The women wound up using drugs and receiving government assistance as a result of lack of education, few job skills, the absence of employment and affordable childcare, and restricted geographic mobility. But the argument about welfare dependency has never really represented an empirical claim so much as a polemic related to welfare reform.

The Politics of Benefits Fraud

The debate about welfare dependency and crime took place within a larger discussion about replacing welfare with workfare. In this larger discussion, the issue of benefits fraud acquired significance beyond its economic impact.

In Britain during the 1980s, benefits fraud served as one of the key rationales supporting the Conservatives' effort to reform the welfare state. Loveland (1989) points to wider cultural forces in shaping attitudes toward fraud in the housing benefit scheme. Drawing on his analysis of enforcement in three authorities during the 1980s, he showed how fraud policy is to a large extent dictated by what is perceived as the need to respond to public feeling against 'scroungers'. The Thatcherite ethos demanded able-bodied citizens to be self-sufficient in the labour and housing markets. Not to be so expressed a form of deviance. Benefits are not seen as rights of eligible claimants, but of the beneficence of taxpayers who make them available to those who deserve them. Preventing abuse became a major concern among welfare administrators consistent with public anxieties about 'loony left' councils unable or unwilling to administer the housing benefit properly. Mass media presentation of benefit abuse imposed dividing lines between the immorality of the 'scrounger' and the criminality of the fraudster.

Cook's research (1987, 1989) shows how the attention to benefits fraud is principally (and ideologically) concerned with issues of poor women, especially single mothers. The welfare scheme, as envisioned by Beveridge, assumed the normality of the traditional family: husband at work, wife at home. It did not contain provision for lifestyle changes at the end of the century in which a large portion of women claiming supplementary benefit are single mothers. Cook argues that the Conservatives' attention to welfare fraud reflected deep suspicions about single mothers as deviants from the family ideal. They targeted single mothers as bad household managers and breeders of bad children, and in this way diverted responsibility of the State for social problems. Cook tells how the media coverage of supplementary benefit fraud assisted in promotion of this ideology through denunciations of 'scroungers'. The scrounger story involved essential aspects of the stereotype of women's deviance: unjust enrichment, excessive drinking, and sloppy sexuality. In newspaper accounts from the 1980s, scroungers appeared as 'Black' and 'Irish'. The accounts portray fraud in a way that makes women's crime not so much defrauding the government, but violating gender expectations concerning proper self-presentation, family propriety and femininity.

Benefits fraud re-emerged as a public issue in the 1990s, when governments in the UK, as well as the USA and former Commonwealth nations, announced their intention to move persons in receipt of government assistance into the labour market. Chunn and Gavigan (2004) describe how in Ontario, Canada, the commitment to crack down on 'welfare cheats' became the centrepiece of the government's welfare policy, a systematic linking of poverty, welfare and crime. In this public discussion, welfare fraud came to include all forms of overpayment, whether administrative errors or formal fraud convictions. Although there was no evidence that fraud in the social assistance system was greater than in the tax system or unemployment assistance system, welfare fraud became emblematic of problems within the welfare system as a whole. Discussions of 'zero tolerance', 'snitch lines', and 'permanent ineligibility' reinforced the determination to deny assistance to the 'never deserving' poor. Public discourse became restructured in such a way that 'welfare fraud became welfare as fraud' (Chunn and Gavigan, 2004: 220).

The greatest change in this direction was brought about by President Bill Clinton who pledged to 'end welfare as we know it'. The legislation he signed in 1996 ended Aid to Families with Dependent Children (AFDC), an entitlement programme that had been in place since the 1930s. In place of AFDC, the legislation established Temporary Assistance to Needy Families (TANF), which established time limits on receipt of aid and put in place welfare-to-work provisions. Several observers have pointed out how 'welfare reform' was caught up in racialised images of welfare recipients, particularly African American women. The Civil Rights movement of the 1960s opened up the welfare rolls to African Americans, and as AFDC became associated with Black people, Americans (in general) became increasingly indifferent and (some) hostile. Political discussions became increasingly fused with degrading images of Black womanhood, the characterisation of the typical welfare recipient as an irresponsible, lazy, lone mother (Jordan-Zachery, 2001). Peffley, Hurwitz and Sniderman (1997) attempted to sort out the racial stereotypes in White Americans' views of Black Americans in the context of welfare and crime. They analysed the responses of 1841 White Americans to varying scenarios involving welfare mothers, welfare recipients, and drug suspects. They affirmed the importance of negative stereotypes in shaping political opinions, and determined that achieving meaningful welfare reform was difficult given a political rhetoric that discussed welfare and crime in racially coded terms and media coverage that depicted welfare recipients and criminal suspects as Black.

Women, Crime and Victimisation

There is a connection between the welfare state, crime and dependency, but not the dependency Murray has in mind. Researchers have shown how the restructuring of welfare provision in North America includes a particular risk for women. Domestic violence is a common reason for the initiation of welfare support, and rather than ending dependency on the State, the reforms increase what Scott, London and Myers (2002) call 'dangerous dependencies'.

Scott, London and Myers (2002) explain how an unintended outcome of Clinton's welfare reform initiative involved increased risk of battering and domestic assault. In their study of women in Cleveland, Los Angeles, Miami and Philadelphia between 1998 and 2001, they explain how the move to push women into the labour market may drive them into relationships with men who have been, or are currently, abusive to them. They interviewed women who had come to rely on men for income because they believed they had few other options. Further, the failure to find employment, combined with the loss of welfare income, may lead women into the underground drug economy and the market for prostitution. Postmus (2004) assessed the impact of the Family Violence Option in New York. This measure gave states the option of implementing exemptions in welfare regulations for battered women, including waiver of work requirements and time limits on welfare receipt. She found that the provision did not have the impact that was hoped for due to inconsistencies in implementation. Several of the women she interviewed did not disclose their victimisation because they worried that their children would be taken into state care by the Department of Social Services. Some feared being judged or questioned by social workers about the abuse; others doubted the ability of social workers to maintain confidentiality, thus increasing the risk of further subsequent abuse.

A similar outcome has been described as occurring in Canada. The provinces of Ontario, Alberta, and British Columbia saw cutbacks in health and social services during the 1990s, including services for victims of domestic violence such as transition houses and community-based victim assistance programmes. Morrow, Hankivsky and Varcoe (2004) argue that while the rationale was cost-savings, the effect has been to create larger economic and social costs. Because the new measures create barriers and obstacles for women who attempt to leave violent situations, they increase economic costs to the State. When Alberta trimmed social services by 19 per cent in the early 1990s, some 4000 women were turned away from shelters (Morrow, Hankivsky and Varcoe, 2004: 367–8). Shelter-workers reported women arriving at shelters with more severe injuries and of relinquishing children to partners because their partners had money for food and clothing and they did not.

The withdrawal of welfare benefits can be seen alongside the 'criminalisation of female poverty' and the increasing willingness to see women as risky, dangerous, and threatening. Hunter and Nixon (2001) describe a British pattern related to gender in prosecutions of anti-social behaviour. Drawing on their analysis of 67 nuisance cases, they determined that women-headed households appear to be particularly vulnerable to losing their homes as a result of anti-social behaviour. They found the perpetrators of serious or prolonged anti-social behaviour were more likely to have dependent children, and women-headed households were disproportionately represented in the sample. In other words, the problem of anti-social behaviour has an unmistakable gender dimension. While women are not necessarily engaged in the behaviour, they are held to account for it. Hunter and Nixon conclude, consistent with Campbell (1993), that the punitive approach taken by social landlords and the judiciary is directed at women who fail to control their boyfriends' and teenage sons' behaviour. As Campbell (1993: 303) explained, the policy rhetoric about criminal behaviour within economically marginalised communities transformed the problem from 'one of a *masculine* response to an economic crisis, to the failure of *mothers* to manage the men'.

Pantazias and Gordon (1997) found a similar pattern in the prosecution of television licence evasion. Beginning in the 1980s, a growing number of women entered the criminal justice system for a relatively trivial offence – television licence evasion. Pantazias and Gordon surmise that this has occurred because the real level of the licence fee has risen above the ability to pay, given the growth in poverty during the 1980s and 1990s. Women have been poorer than men. But women are also more likely to be criminalised owing to the method of enforcement. The vast majority of evaders are identified through computer database searches that match postcode addresses with records of licences held. Because poor women are more likely to be unemployed, or employed within their homes in childcare, they have more of a chance of being interviewed by the television licence enquiry officer as the 'responsible householder'.

The 'Threat' of the Poor

The popular language of poverty and crime invokes the suspicion that poor people are dangerous. The 'threat' of the poor can be seen in media understandings of urban violence and political responses to immigrants.

Racialisation of Crime

The riots that occurred in Britain during 1980–1 seemed to confirm, as far as public dialogue was concerned, the link between extreme poverty and spontaneous violence. Violence erupted in several areas of London (Brixton, Southall) and in parts of Liverpool (Toxteth) and Manchester (Moss Side) as West Indian and Asian youth clashed with White police authorities.[3] Explanations of the violence also linked this danger to blackness, and specifically the inability of Blacks to assimilate into British society. Neal (2003) shows how journalistic accounts of Britain's 'race riots' in the 1980s included the fear of collective violence rooted in social exclusion and racial identity. The *Mirror* predicted that 'Bloody race riots threaten to destroy our society if Blacks are not given a chance' and the *Mail* asserted that 'deprived Blacks must get a better deal than Whites over the next few years if Britain is to avoid a racial holocaust' (Neal, 2003: 63).

Some observers, such as Brake (1983), assert that the poor are potentially violent. Such violence does not result from their criminality, but occurs in response to their isolation and marginalisation. Brake's account highlights how community leaders referred to the violent clashes of 1980–1 as 'uprisings' while the media and police insisted on calling them 'riots'. This represented a means of criminalising the violence; converting revolutionary, or potentially revolutionary activities into apolitical and de-racial, illegal acts committed by ungovernable hooligans. Brake goes on to explain how these events originated in immigration policy; discrimination in housing, education, and employment; poor police–community relations; and development of a politically aware youth culture.

Brake's analysis draws on the conceptual scheme of Frantz Fanon who saw the poor as a source of revolution. The 'pimps, the hooligans, the unemployed, and the petty criminal' represented a concentration of spontaneous violence. For Fanon, this was a struggle against 'racialisation', a word he used to signify the construction and re-construction of racial meanings during the historical period of de-colonisation. The disenfranchised class of humanity had nothing to lose and everything to gain by turning to collective violence; they could redeem themselves through revolutionary struggle. Resistance to racialisation necessarily means violence, because the colonised states had been created and maintained by violence and the threat of violence. *Negritude*, or black power, emerged as the antithesis of colonialism, an attempt to restore the psyche of those throughout the African Diaspora (Fairchild, 1994).

Others have shown how the belief that poor people are prone to violence contributes to the construction of racial identities. Solomos (1993) situates the imagery of poverty and violence against the background of efforts to link criminality with blackness. During the 1970s, police authorities and news journalists had linked 'the younger generation of West Indians' to mugging. The word, referring to robbery, had been imported from New York. It symbolised the problems of life in ghetto areas, the drift of young Afro-Caribbeans into a life of crime and poverty. By 1978 or so, 'mugging' and 'black crime' had become synonymous, and Black youth in Britain had become a suspect community, not only because of perceptions about their involvement in crime, but

---

[3]Riots occurring in British city areas during 1991–2 did not involve high proportions of minority youth; the vast majority of rioters were 'White' and British-born (Power and Tunstall, 1997).

because of their style of dress, social manner, and leisure pursuits. Solomos (1993: 129) points out how political rhetoric in the aftermath of the 1980s riots reinforced social constructions of 'black criminality'. The Metropolitan Police released figures, not previously published, showing 'disproportionate involvement' of young Blacks in street crimes such as mugging, purse snatching, and robbery from stores.

The process Solomos (1993) writes about has been described as the 'racialisation of crime'. When understood as a socio-political process in which racial and criminal identities become fused, racialisation of crime can be seen as a social phenomenon occurring in the 1990s and 2000s as well as the 1980s. In researching the question of 'Asian crime' in Yorkshire in the 1990s, Goodey (2001) came to describe young British Pakistani men as the new urban 'folk devils'. The relationship between Asian communities and crime was caught up in an 'incident of public disorder' in Sheffield and a 'riot' in Bradford in which race-specific explanations of crime evoked negative stereotypes. Alexander (2004) shows how the vocabulary of 'the riots' of 2001 in Oldham reflected understandings of racial identities. Newspaper stories compared the violence, in which Asian youths confronted police and National Front demonstrators, to the riots of 1980–1. The *Guardian* described 'the same combustible mix: race, poverty and a distrusted local police force' (Alexander, 2004: 528). She describes how this discussion contributed to the 'Asian gang' as a symptom of a 'Muslim underclass' that had chosen to isolate themselves. While Asian youth had been invisible in racialised public speech, they became linked with images of dangerousness and rebelliousness associated with Black youth cultures.

From a policy perspective, it is important to see how racialised images of violence corrupt the rationale for intervention. It is one thing to frame the need for intervention in poor areas with reference to social justice, and quite another to argue for it as a means of pacifying a population seen as threatening. This sort of logic, of extending social benefits to groups of people out of fear of what they might do otherwise, presents an inadequate and inappropriate basis for social policy.

The New Immigration

Racialisation of crime has occurred in the context of immigration. In France, the popular imagery of the *banlieues*, peripheral areas of large cities where large numbers of immigrants live, portrays a permanent class of outsiders engaged in continuous criminality and episodic collective violence. While this characterisation has been challenged by the findings of social research, it remains a fixture in national discussions of the issue, reinforced through novels and films. The setting for *La Haine*, 'The Hate', a film released in 1995, is a housing estate in the suburbs of Paris. A North African youth has been beaten during police questioning, and as news of the youth's critical condition spreads, young people take to the streets. In the clash with police, the youth centre burns to the ground. The three central characters in the film, immigrants of Jewish, Black, and Arab origins, are all unemployed. They survive by petty crime and drug-dealing. In fact, the film opens with archive footage of an actual riot in the estate, in the western suburbs of Paris at Chantelouples-Vignes (White, 1997: 19).

Morris (1994) explains how the desire for entry by 'outsiders', by invitation and by illegal migration, has come to be seen as the creation of an underclass. Nation-states have sought to benefit from immigrant labour without diluting their resources and culture in general and without commitment to full social welfare benefit in specific. During the 1950s and 1960s, the industrialised economies of Europe welcomed migrants to fill the demand for low-skilled workers. Britain, France and the Netherlands drew on colonial and former colonial populations; West Germany, Switzerland and Belgium relied on guest worker schemes. The most recent wave of immigration, beginning in the 1980s, has taken place against the background of EU policy. This immigration has occurred as member states have transferred their sovereignty to the EU. It reflects a new geography, different economic context, and migrants with varying legal statuses. This new migration includes asylum seekers, who, due to the length of governmental procedures, are kept in suspension for some time while the decision is made about whether to grant permanent residence status. It also includes undocumented or illegal immigrants who entered on temporary visas and stayed or who otherwise crossed the border illegally (Moore, 1994: 155).

The Netherlands provides a poignant example. The analysis Engbersen and Van der Leun (2001) provide could be replicated in a number of countries in Western Europe. During the decades after the Second World War, the Netherlands welcomed migrants for the purpose of low-skilled work. This policy reached its peak in the 1980s with years of open borders when it remained easy for migrants to find employment in at least some sectors of the Dutch economy (agriculture). There began, however, debates about 'the Netherlands being "full"', raising concern about illegal stay of temporary workers and asylum seekers. By the 1990s, migrants came to be regarded with much less sympathy, being increasingly associated with abuse of public provisions, disruption of the labour market, and particularly with crime. Notwithstanding issues of illegal entry and, quite possibly, organised migrant trafficking, there has been little empirical evidence to document the equation of illegal immigrants with crime. Drawing on information they obtained about illegal migrants in four Dutch cities, Engbersen and Van der Leun (2001: 55–6) conclude that the majority of illegal migrants are not criminally active.

In Italy, the popular vocabulary of job-stealing and immigrant crime has contributed to an emerging debate about immigration policy. Angel-Ajani (2001) shows how such concerns reflect the cultural politics of 'race'. The notion of 'race' links particular forms of criminality to gender and national origin, as if the potential for criminality could be predicted by cultural background or nationality. Much of this is directed at immigrants of African origin;

blackness becomes *the* marker of otherness. Italy's other marked groups include Jews and *Nomadi*, 'gypsies', along the lines of Nazi antisemitism. Terms such as *Marocchini*, 'Moroccans', and, less crude, *extra-comunitari*, meaning people from non-EU countries, are in frequent use. She explains that *Marocchini* is a racial shorthand used by Italians to refer to all immigrants of colour, regardless of their national background (Angel-Ajani, 2001: 339).

Thinking about the current situation in Europe, Melossi (2003) points to the danger of a racially defined underclass forming along the American and French varieties. He refers to migration as the 'crime of modernity' as immigrants in all parts of Europe experience criminalisation and racialisation. There is, however, an important difference between the experiences of migrants across parts of Europe. In former colonial countries, such as the UK and France, immigrants from non-White ethnic backgrounds have been legally incorporated but socially excluded. In Southern European countries – Spain, Greece and Italy – there is a high level of undocumented migration created by the impossible task of legal immigration for purposes of work. In these countries, the criminal justice system represents the only system of government 'care' available to 'criminal' migrants. Melossi (2003: 378) writes that 'Rather than *substituting* for welfare, the penal system constitutes the *only* system of welfare available, *lato sensu'*.

While in Britain the focus in recent years has been on 'Black criminality' and a 'Muslim underclass', this is in some sense a continuation of historic anxieties about immigration. Swift has shown that the increase of Irish immigration to England during the nineteenth century contributed to the imagery of 'Irish criminality'. He explains that the 'widespread belief in the innate criminality of the Irish – and, more particularly, of the Irish poor – formed an integral component of the negative side of the Irish stereotype' during the late Victorian Era (Swift, 1997: 399). 'Irish criminality' invoked interrelated categories of drunkenness, disorderly behaviour, and assault, and to a lesser extent theft and vagrancy. In British eyes, the terms 'drink' and 'Irish' were synonyms, reinforcing the belief in 'Irish criminality'. Drink was the Irishman's weakness, and drunkenness was the precursor of crime. Further, the image of 'Irish criminality' was established in the public mind earlier in the nineteenth century, even before the influx of Irish during the famine of the 1840s and 1850s (Swift, 1989: 167).

During the late Victorian and Edwardian eras, 'Jewish criminality' emerged in popular discussion. Beginning in the 1880s, as thousands of Jews poured into London, politicians, journalists and other antisemitic agitators aroused fear and concern with portrayals of crime and vice. In the debate leading up to the Aliens Act (1905), racialist MPs and journalists claimed that immigrant Jews were perpetrating a crime wave and prominent British Jews in Parliament were engaging in a conspiracy to cover it up. While the anti-social behaviours of the English centred on excessive beer-drinking were understandable and controllable, the sexual and social conduct of immigrant Jews, located around 'disorderly houses' and gambling, were said to conceal crimes, the full extent of which would only become known in future (Knepper, 2007).

Conclusion

Public discussions of the relationship between inequality and crime have been hampered by the idea of the criminal poor, a distinct class of persons who revel in their ability to survive outside conventional society. We have seen how images of this population convey particular messages about 'race' and gender. Discussions of the underclass and social exclusion, scrounging and benefits fraud, riots and immigrants convey a racialised and gendered understanding of poverty and crime.

Questions for Discussion

1. *Is there a British underclass? Is 'social exclusion' another way of saying 'underclass'?*

2. *Is welfare dependency a real or imaginary problem? Are men engaged in 'scrounging'?*

3. *There will be a recurrence of riots in British cities if immigrants continue to be isolated. True or false?*

Further Reading

A.L. Beier (2005) 'Identity, Language, and Resistance in the Making of the Victorian "Criminal Class": Mayhew's Convict Revisited', *Journal of British Studies* 44: 239–42.

Catherine Jones Finer and Mike Nellis (1998) *Crime and Social Exclusion.* Oxford: Blackwell.

Robert MacDonald (1997) *Youth, the 'Underclass', and Social Exclusion.* London: Routledge.

Lydia Morris (1994) *Dangerous Classes: The Underclass and Social Citizenship.* London: Routledge.

PART TWO

Policy Areas

Crime and Housing Policy

SUMMARY

- The impact of housing policy on patterns of crime can be understood along the lines of housing class, residential community crime careers, residualisation, and spill-over
- Crime on the 'problem estate' has been explained by architectural design, spiral of decline, estate culture, allocation hypothesis, demonisation
- The problem of crime in social housing areas has been addressed through polic ing, designing-out crime, anti-social behaviour orders, and tenant associations

The issue of housing policy and crime deals not so much with how crime relates to a social problem but how it relates to government efforts to solve a social problem. In exploring patterns of crime in cities, criminologists have emphasised the difference housing makes, and particularly the location and characteristics of council estates. Crime and social housing represents, as Robert Sampson (1990, 526) has noticed, an example of what might be called 'crime effects of non-crime policies'.

This is a theme criminological theorising has yet to fully appreciate. Understanding the crime that results from previous attempts to solve the crime problem, or from government efforts to solve some other social problem, calls attention to the sense in which criminologists are like archaeologists excavating ancient ruins. In their effort to learn the secrets of the ancients, they must distinguish aspects of the site left by the ancients themselves from alterations to site left by everyone else who wanted to learn the secrets – previous expeditions, grave-robbers, efforts to shore up the site, and so on. Patterns of urban crime cannot be fully mapped without taking into account the impact of housing policy.

This chapter explores criminological research dealing with the 'housing effect' on crime. Part one addresses the significance of housing policy in accounting for patterns of crime in cities. Part two reviews five explanations of crime on the 'problem estate'. Part three concerns four strategies for reducing the victimisation of council housing residents.

Crime and the Housing System

Compared to the Chicago theory of social disorganisation, the urban landscape in Britain is significantly different owing to more than a century of government provision of housing. Attempts to take the impact of housing policy into account have led to a re-thinking of the Chicago model and this effort has introduced a number of concepts related to housing policy and crime.

Crime in the British City

The Chicago criminologists portrayed residential neighbourhoods characterised by deteriorated, overcrowded housing as production centres for delinquency and crime. Shaw and McKay did not claim that sub-standard housing led directly to crime but that it served as a marker for social disorganisation. The residential population of high-crime areas was constantly changing as a consequence of larger sociological processes associated with urbanisation – an expanding industrial economy, influx of immigrants, and upward class mobility – while the area itself remained high-crime. They thought of residential neighbourhoods as 'natural areas' determined by the relationship between individual property-owners and tenants within a virtually unregulated real estate market.

Any attempt to apply this analysis to a British city confronts the obvious fact that social housing has been developed on a much wider scale in the UK than in the USA. The first social housing, referred to as 'council housing' because it was built by the local housing authority or council, appeared in the 1880s. After the First World War, local housing authorities across the country began construction of low-cost housing to meet the needs of a working-class population. The trend accelerated after the Second World War, when massive housing estates went up as a means of replenishing housing stock destroyed by the Luftwaffe and as part of slum-clearance initiatives. This larger role for government in the provision and control of housing means that the UK has something better described as a 'housing system' rather than a 'housing market' (Malpass and Murie, 1999: 6).

Morris's (1958) study of Croydon, the first systematic effort to apply the Chicago model in Britain, pointed to the location of council estates in accounting for the geographic distribution of crime. Using statistics for 1952, Morris mapped delinquency areas along the lines of Shaw and McKay but found little correlation between neighbourhood deterioration and high delinquency as predicted by the concentric zone model. Delinquency tended to cluster around housing estates rather than residential areas adjoining commerce and industry. He learned that Croydon's housing authority had followed a practice of 'segregation', of building residences for the poor within relatively small areas rather than distributing them throughout the city. This tended to create enclaves of 'problem families' with children prone to delinquency. While the housing authority did not intend to create high-delinquency areas, the practice of segregation did allow for containment, allowing other neighbourhoods to avoid the effects of these young people (Morris, 1958: 183–9).

In 1976, John Baldwin and Anthony Bottoms published their research of crime in the city of Sheffield, very likely the most extensive study of urban crime patterns since Shaw and McKay (Baldwin and Bottoms, 1976). Overall, they demonstrated that the distribution of crime in the city followed patterns of housing tenure. They mapped crime across three categories of British housing stock: (1) owner-occupied (including mortgaged properties), (2) privately rented housing, and (3) housing rented from the local authority. They found crime in owner-occupied areas to be much lower than areas of privately rented and council housing. Baldwin and Bottoms also noted the importance of distinguishing 'criminal area' from 'crime area', the difference between where offenders live and where offenders carry out crimes. For some crimes, such as auto-theft, offenders travel some distance from their homes, but much crime, including violent crime, occurs within a short distance of the offender's residence. Offenders residing on council estates tend to prey on their neighbours (Bottoms and Wiles, 1998: 4; Bottoms and Wiles, 1986: 158–60).

To explain their findings, Baldwin and Bottoms (1976) drew in part on Rex's (1968) critique of the Chicago model. Rex theorised that the basic process in urban social interaction occurs as a result of competition over scarce and desired housing (suburban housing). In this process, even people who share a common relationship to the labour market are distinguished from one another by their strength in the housing market, or within the system of housing allocation. He distinguished seven 'housing classes' ranging from outright ownership of large houses and mortgaged houses in desirable areas to tenants in slum housing on the verge of being razed and lodgers in rooms. The difference in housing class, he suggested, had implications for social behaviour generally.

Another strand of theorising about housing and crime begins with making an effort to understand the extent and impact of 'private crime and public housing', that is, the overlap of housing patterns and violence against women (Renzetti, 2002). The familiar image of fatherless youth who become delinquent, emanating in part from the Chicago tradition, is only partly true. The majority of tenants in social housing are women and demographic, economic, and geographic factors combine to bring about a high incidence of violent victimisation of women in these settings. When DeKeseredy et al. (2003a) surveyed public housing residents on six estates in a Canadian city about criminal victimisation, alcohol consumption, and drug use, they turned up results consistent with social disorganisation theory. The housing estates they studied in Eastern Ontario did experience higher rates of these activities as well as predatory crimes. But, they add that households in public housing settings are likely to include 'male guests', whether short-term or long-term. And the factors that lead to higher rates of crime generally – economic change, labour market exclusion, social isolation, and stress – combine with larger forms of patriarchy to make it more likely that women living in public housing will become victims of male violence. The feminisation of social housing is important for understanding patterns of crime in the city (DeKeseredy and Schwartz, 2002).

Council Estates

During the past 30 years, the image of the high-crime, 'no go' area has centred on large housing estates at the edge of the city. In a sense, the problem estate has replaced that of the Victorian slum as the criminal area to be explained in the urban environment.

Neild and Paylor (1996) examined crime in Colne, a small industrial town in northeast Lancashire. Prior to 1978 or so, the Chicago model would have provided a plausible explanation for Colne's crime problem, as the town's criminal area was Exchange Street, an area of run-down terraced housing near the town centre. But Colne's criminal area shifted to Glenroy Avenue, an attractive residential neighbourhood on the other side of town. From a social disorganisation standpoint, this should not have happened. But as Neild and Paylor (1996) explain, this pattern emerged in the wake of a change in the housing market. A redevelopment scheme introduced in the town centre led to resettlement of families from Exchange Street to the Glenroy Avenue site. Borrowing a typology of working-class families proposed by Bottoms, Mawby and Xanthos (1989), the Colne researchers argue that this resettlement involved the introduction of a number of 'rough' and 'problem' families from Exchange Street to Glenroy Avenue which had been inhabited for the most part by 'ordinary families'. Glenroy Avenue has remained a criminal area since then as a result of the local housing authority's unofficial allocation policy (Neild and Paylor, 1996: 759).

It is important to keep in mind, however, that council estates are not categorically criminogenic. There are marked differences between estates in the amount and type of criminal activity. Jones and Short (1993) compared five areas of social housing in Dundee and found significant differences in recorded statistics of, and residents' concern about, housebreaking. Bottoms and associates have looked at 'pairs' of council estates in Sheffield to figure out why some estates become criminal areas while others do not. They have studied two similarly situated housing estates – both built in the 1920s, with comparable residential populations, and 'crime-free' in the early years – but with very different crime rates in later decades. One estate, Stonewall, retained its crime-free reputation, while the other, Gardenia, became a criminal area in the 1940s. Neither estate bordered a mixed-use area and neither consisted of a transient population as would be expected from the Chicago paradigm. Bottoms and associates attribute the difference to direct and indirect consequences of allocation. Once the two estates had diverged in terms of crime, housing allocation practices tended to reinforce the difference by routing residents to the estates with different propensities to engage in criminal behaviour (Bottoms and Wiles, 2002: 635–7).

Bottoms and Wiles (1986) have proposed 'residential community crime careers' to explain how whole communities can over the course of time shift from respectable to deviant, as well as the other way around. They have insisted that two areas of similar social class composition can, as a function of housing allocation practices, have different crime careers. Bottoms and Wiles (1986: 123) also insist that community crime careers of council estates cannot be understood apart from the context of housing allocation processes. If an estate begins as respectable, remains sought after, and there is nothing to alter this sought-after reputation, then it is likely to enjoy a safe reputation over an extended period of time. Some estates, however, acquire a bad reputation early on, sometimes as a result of the housing department's 'dumping' of tenants regarded as problematic. Others undergo a 'tipping process' when original tenants transfer to more desirable estates elsewhere, leaving the estate to become categorised as the place for 'problem families'.

This process is not as straightforward as the idea of dumping by council housing managers suggests. At the national level, the allocation process is shaped by the process of 'residualisation', a term which refers to the historical trend for council housing to become less affluent, catering disproportionately to lower-income groups, older persons, and those outside the labour market. While these trends have been observed throughout the twentieth century, they have accelerated in the 1980s and 1990s as a result of the widening economic inequality and the frequency of active tenure transfers, especially through the sale of council houses. Not all estates are changing at the same rate, or along these lines, but as very little new council housing has been built since the 1980s, the less-popular and least-attractive estates become the primary domain of housing let by the local authority (Murie, 1997: 27–9).

The point of residualisation is significant in theoretical terms because one of the theoretical difficulties with applying social disorganisation theory to an understanding of the effect on housing policy on crime concerns the boundaries. It is too easy to conceptualise a council estate as a 'community' or 'neighbourhood' with the implications that the sociological processes responsible for crime occur within its geographic boundaries. This conceptual image reinforces the idea of council estates as construction sites for social problems, the problematic aspects extending only as far as the residents themselves.

The Political Context

Thirty years ago, Baldwin and Bottoms (1976: 173) observed: 'The political control of the housing stock of the city may have important repercussions on criminality for the areas concerned'. Subsequent research has confirmed the importance of the political context of housing policy for distribution of crime in British cities but also in American cities. The clustering of economic disadvantage and crime on social housing estates has been perceived as a 'British problem', but similar trends are visible in Northern Europe and North America (Coles, England, and Rugg, 2000: 21; Sampson, 1990: 526).

The first public housing built in the USA went up during Roosevelt's New Deal. The primary purpose of this programme was not so much to provide housing for the poor as to relieve unemployment and these early developments went up as symbols of jobs and hope. After the Second World War, federal policy shifted and public housing went up as part of slum clearance programmes. Public opinion turned against public housing, and community groups organised to pressurise housing officials to keep developments out of their neighbourhoods. In Chicago and elsewhere, government practices located projects among residents least able to resist them, in African-American neighbourhoods (Hirsch, 1983). This resulted in 'massive, segregated housing projects that have become ghettos for minorities and the disadvantaged' (Sampson, 1990: 528–9).

The political context of housing and crime can be seen in research concerning 'spill-over', the spread of criminal activity from public housing projects to adjacent residential neighbourhoods. There is research to suggest that spill-over effects are not nearly as pronounced as feared when the plans for these public housing projects are announced. Research comparing crime across city blocks adjacent to public housing in Cleveland, Ohio, found that spill-over effects, where present, were rather small in magnitude. Such effects appear to be related to the size of housing projects (Roncek, Bell and Francik 1981).

At the same time, research in Atlanta, Georgia, demonstrated significant overlap of public housing, 'race', and disadvantage. McNulty and Holloway (2000) suggest that the 'race'-crime relationship in criminology is geographically contingent: the higher crime rates reported for African-American communities are a function of the political placement of public housing. Their research in Atlanta supports the 'distance-delay spread effect', meaning that Black neighbourhoods in close proximity to public housing developments exhibited the highest crime rates while those farther away from public housing were no more likely to exhibit high crime rates that White neighbourhoods. They also examined the crime impact of Techwood Homes, the first federally funded public housing project in the USA. This project was explicitly sited in a transitional area in order to create a buffer between Black and White residential districts of the city. They found that crime associated with residents of public housing does transcend the boundaries of housing projects, but does not spread uniformly across urban spaces. Spill-over from public housing inhabited by African Americans did not affect White neighbourhoods but did affect Black neighbourhoods, a finding explained by the on-going reality of racialised Atlanta: White Atlanta and Black Atlanta comprise discrete urban spaces. Or, in other words, the distance-delay spread effect is mediated by social factors characterising regions of cities, such as racial segregation (Holloway and McNulty, 2003).

The Criminology of the 'Problem Estate'

In the UK, the 'problem estate' became a national worry in the aftermath of riots in several social housing areas during the 1980s and 1990s. Episodes of wide-scale destruction and violence prompted a number of social investigations into the social milieu of council housing. The criminology of the problem estate in the British context also benefits from research on crime in public housing conducted in other countries, including Australia, Canada, South Africa and the USA.

Architectural Design

The idea that some architectural designs are more criminogenic than others became prominent following publication of Alice Coleman's study of design and layout of council housing. Based on surveys of design aspects of council housing in two areas of London (Tower Hamlets and Southwark) and in Oxford (Blackbird Leys), she found poor design to be the most glaring feature of modern problem estates. Bad design, or 'design-disavantagement', made it a struggle for residents to achieve conventional standards of decency and civility; it encouraged litter, graffiti and vandalism, and contributed to higher levels of stress, mental illness, and crime. She identified 15 aspects of council estates to be particularly problematic, most of which had been combined in the 'failed utopia' of massive high-rise complexes. Too many storeys, along with misplacement of overhead walkways, interconnecting exits, and entrances had 'tipped the balance sufficiently to make criminals out of potentially law-abiding citizens' (Coleman, 1990: 22).

Coleman's work built on principles of 'defensible space' outlined by Oscar Newman in the 1970s (Newman, 1973). Newman offered a theory about the role of the built environment in promoting, or in the case of high-rise public housing, thwarting, the sense of community among residents. Community-enhancing designs promoted 'territoriality' and 'natural surveillance', allowing people to satisfy their urge to mark out and defend their space through observing and monitoring of semi-private spaces and being aware of those who do not belong. A good design made it clear which spaces belonged to whom – some would be private, some shared with permission of the owner, and some public. He established links between high-rise schemes and crime rates: the high-rise buildings' inner elements – lifts, fire escapes, roofs, and corridors – led to elevated levels of crime because they were isolated from public view and engendered anonymity. When Newman (1973: 47) compared two public housing projects in New York City, he found the high-rise development had recorded crime rates as much as 50 per cent higher than the low-rise project. Newman's ideas inspired a series of follow-up studies pointing to the architecture of social housing projects as the chief source for criminal activity within them (Holzman, 1996).

The proposition that crime on problem estates can be explained primarily as a feature of the built environment is reductionist. Crime-in-the-design thinking neglects cultural, political, and economic aspects of the social milieu. The Jan Hofmeyer council estate in Johannesburg, South Africa, is notorious for high incidences of crime and suicide. Gruesome crimes and public violence occur more often than such a small community ought to warrant. Unlike the designs Coleman and Newman indicted, the Jan Hofmeyer scheme is quaint and suburban. Built originally for 'poor whites' in the 1930s, it has become home to a significant portion of 'coloured' residents in post-apartheid years. The units are free-standing, built of red brick, with corrugated metal roofs. Each stands on its own plot, separated from the next by a wire mesh fence. Streets are tree-lined and short, with bends and curves, and most properties overlook grassy spaces; all streets are tarred and kerbed. The estate even boasts a community hall. The designers did everything right, it would seem, and yet there is crime (du Plessis, 2004).

The attention to architectural design does, however, incorporate a significant social feature that has been under-appreciated by sceptics: *perceptions* of the image and stigma of particular housing. Cozens, Hillier and Prescott (2002) carried out an interesting study of the subliminal and symbolic messages embedded within housing designs common to British cities. They presented two depictions (well-maintained, poorly maintained) of five estate designs (high-rise flats, low-rise/walk-up flats, terraced housing, semi-detached housing, and detached housing) to three groups (convicted criminals, planning professionals, and police). They found broad agreement among the groups concerning expectations of crime and deviancy and how the level of maintenance contributed to these expectations. Uncollected rubbish, boarded-up windows, abandoned cars – the visible signs of decay – are 'undefendable' regardless of design (Cozens, Hillier and Prescott, 2002: 133). This research coincides with the notion of 'signal disorders'. Innes (2004: 341) theorises that the significance of unpleasant urban scenes, such as vacant houses and unkept lots, 'lies in how they encode messages about levels of unwanted risk and social control in an area'.

Spiral of Decline

Crime is frequently understood as a result of structural deficiencies within society at large, deficiencies that become more visible and acute in the context of social housing. Dramatic shifts in the housing market and changes in social housing have left council estates with ever poorer and problematic residents who are in possession of ever fewer traditional means of controlling them.

Crime from the spiral-of-decline perspective is understood as a consequence of multiple and overlapping social problems. Elisabeth Burney (1999) provides an effective summary: children below poverty line; unemployed, and unemployable young adults; single parent households; single adults, especially those formerly in institutional care; ethnic minorities, including refugees. These areas become characterised by instability and change: rapid turnover of households, decline of labour market, loss of services and transportation, and visible deterioration of buildings, as well as radical physical alteration, such as demolition and construction of housing stock. The crime profile typically includes young men engaged in vandalism, auto crime, burglary, drug-dealing and gang-related violence (Burney, 1999: 54–5).

The idea here is that informal ways of dealing with unpopular behaviour within neighbourhoods are less frequently available now than in the past. Structural deficiencies pressurise family life on estates, leading to tensions between neighbours and high turnover, as residents are unable to cope with their vulnerability to crime and overriding fear of crime. As Burney (1999) explains, this fear of crime becomes even more significant as trust between neighbours breaks down. Fear of crime involves fear of the 'stranger', the unknown other, but in some neighbourhoods the 'stranger' lives within the same housing block, next door and across the street. New systems of order-maintenance seeking to assert formal control are the result of the perception than informal controls have weakened. Foster and Hope (1993) discuss this perspective in their assessment of the Priority Estates Project (PEP) in Hull, a Home Office initiative to turn around problematic estates. 'The reality of life on high crime estates,' they observe, 'is that "community" is socially fragmented ...'. They found that established families tended to keep themselves apart from vulnerable residents, especially troublesome minorities. 'In the light of this study, it would seem unrealistic to expect many residents to be able or willing to exert much direct influence over the behaviour of those involved in crime and disorder on the estate' (Foster and Hope, 1993: 85).

In their study of Meadowell, an archetypal 'sink estate' near Newcastle upon Tyne, Barke and Turnbull (1992) outline the processes contributing to crime. Economic deprivation is at root. Many large estates are located on the economic fringe of cities, isolated from mainstream economic activity. Jobs are hard to find and hard to get to; public services are strained because of high levels of demand on limited budgets. Long-term unemployment leads to poor health, declining schools, and low motivation and achievement. Concentrations of low-income households amount to limited access to jobs and lack of choice in the housing market; they contribute to a lack of political voice, over-stretched public services, and stereotypes reinforcing isolation. Murie (1997: 30) agrees that 'these [structural] pressures result in a spiral of decline and despair' but adds two important qualifications:

1. The spiral of decline represents only one side of the coin, applicable to *some* council estates. The other side of the spiral of decline emphasises the remarkable ability of council families to survive and bounce back; despite the pressures of life on the problem estate, many do not become criminals.

2. Decline and despair do not operate exclusively in social housing. The concentration of the poor in the private rental sector may be just as noticeable. Overemphasis of the spiral of decline on council estates serves to reinforce stereotypes in the public domain and contributes *in itself* to spiral processes.

Estate Culture

By 'estate culture' is meant that problem estate does not describe a place of economic deprivation but also a state of consciousness, the tendency of economic irrelevance to become a source of identity. Beatrix Campbell (1993), in her study of council estates that became the scenes of riots in 1991–2, described neighbourhood hierarchies in which assertive groups of young men had become the prevailing power, intimidating residents into 'looking the other way'. They had become Goliath, the boasting giant who had intimidated the army of King Saul; they had replaced conventional authority in civic society with their display of actual and symbolic power. Campbell suggested that the problem with problem estates was not that they were disorganised, but that in such areas residents were not able to organise themselves to confront common problems. Instead, they hunkered down, concentrated on their own individual survival, and turned to acquiescence as a defence against the violence around them. The main survival strategy is to 'mind your own business' and refuse to acknowledge or report the surrounding crime.

In a study for the Rowntree Foundation, Page (2000) carried out interviews and focus groups with residents and public service workers in three large council estates: one in a northern industrial area suffering from the loss of traditional industries, one in a medium-sized city enjoying its share of rising national prosperity, and one in a London borough encompassing both rich and poor. Residents did not perceive high rates of joblessness or disrepair on the estate as significant problems, nor did they think of themselves as poor or socially isolated. The biggest single issue identified was the anti-social behaviour of young people, including crime, vandalism, and drug use. They spoke of an estate culture which tolerated crime, drugs and anti-social behaviour and 'estate norms' that differed from mainstream society in which residents accepted low personal achievement and educational attainment.

Several reasons have been suggested for the formation of estate cultures conducive to crime. Many large estates were sited on the fringes of cities or were planned as enclosed, separate, and distinct areas. This tended to isolate residents from mainstream population centres and reinforced an inward-looking mentality (Power, 1989: 210). Under-enforcement of the law, whether based on police reluctance to venture into these 'semi-private' spaces or resident mistrust of police based on fear of racial harassment, allows the wrong role models to emerge. With traditional brakes on their power absent, the claims of neighbourhood toughs achieve an exaggerated importance (Burney, 1999: 63). Estate cultures might also come about as an unintended consequence of the wider struggle of poor people to make it in a success-oriented society, an instance of classical *anomie*. Activities such as stealing money from the pre-payment box linked to the electricity meter and purchasing stolen household furnishings come to be seen as a plausible way of fulfilling needs and, therefore, not particularly wrong. In the same way, violence could be regarded as a method of dealing with domestic problems (Bottoms and Xanthos, 1981: 213).

The Allocation Hypothesis

It is possible that the housing aspect of problem estates is unimportant to the explanation of crime in the sense that council estates occupy the receiving-end of social problems produced elsewhere in society. It is not the estate itself that affords or encourages criminal behaviour, but rather that the decision-making process responsible for the letting of council housing concentrates crime-prone individuals. This explanation for problem estates has been referred to as the 'allocation hypothesis'.

Don Weatherburn and his associates in Australia advance this explanation. Their research in Sydney has led them to accept the 'view that the public housing allocation process is largely, if not entirely, responsible for the association between public housing and crime' (Weatherburn, Lind, and Ku, 1999: 270). When they looked at differences in youth crime within postcodes across Sydney, they found the influence of public housing, as measured by regression analyses, to be very small. Or, in other words, the crime attributed to public housing is an artefact of the concentration of economically disadvantaged individuals, not a consequence of design features of public housing. Their findings coincide with earlier research in Sydney along the same lines. This research showed that people in public housing were more likely to commit crime in the first instance due to their lower socio-economic status. Once statistical controls were introduced for factors as related to socio-economic status, the association between quantity of public housing and crime decreased in magnitude (Matka, 1997).

The most intense and direct form of a problem-estate manufacture by this method has been called 'dumping'. This would refer to a situation in which housing managers make a conscious effort to concentrate problem tenants together in one place. Gill (1977) described the creation of a problem estate in 'Luke Street', Crossley, near Liverpool. This estate enjoyed a favourable reputation, at first. But as it contained large houses, it became the estate for large families, families with multiple difficulties, and families known to police. These characteristics spoilt the reputation, leading to a decision on the part of the council to utilise parts of the estate to 're-house the town's problem families'. Families regarded as suitable for Luke Street by housing officials were those they described as the 'poor type family', 'rough type of family' and families judged 'NSNP', meaning 'not suitable for new property' (Gill, 1977: 25–6).

The allocation processes responsible for high-crime estates do not reflect the biases or preferences of individual housing managers, but organisational and bureaucratic procedures reflecting larger social and political pressures. High-crime estates result from decision-making practices that separate the respectable from the rough; respectable families are routed toward the staid, stable estates so as not to put these estates at risk, while the rough and non-respectable, including a disproportionate number of minorities, are channelled toward problem estates on the theory that they will not make them any worse and because they are the least likely to refuse offers on such estates (Murie, 1997).

Demonisation

Council estates, like individuals and families, acquire reputations. Some estates, even those comprised of well-built, pre-war houses with attractive gardens and views of the countryside, fall into the 'difficult to let' category as a result of stigma attached to them. Their unpopularity sometimes derives from their association with slum-clearance; their original residents brought with them associations of crime, poverty and disarray (Power, 1989: 210). In other cases, the arrival of even one or two 'problem families' has been enough to affect their desirability, as estates with perceived problems tend to become estates with actual problems (Burney, 1999: 44). When this happens, the process of demonisation has run its course.

The stigma attached to estates has an intensely local flavour. In their study of four new housing association estates, Cole and colleagues (1996) found that views of new estates were seen through a lens reflecting widely held beliefs about social housing: residence of last resort, awkwardly designed, rife with crime and vandalism. It is often contingent on the classification given it by local journalists and rumours about the 'type of people' the council was moving in. Damer (1974) described this process some thirty years ago in his 'sociology of a dreadful enclosure,' a small, slum-clearance estate in Glasgow known as Wine Alley. He told about how a local newspaper contributed to vilifying the tenants as part of a larger scapegoating campaign. A series of articles and editorials took the side of Glasgow residents who resented that houses on the estate, which they had hoped to acquire, had been allocated to 'outsiders' from a distant slum. The families moving into this small estate in the 1950s became stigmatised for hard-drinking (to the extent of distilling their own liquor) and other anti-social behaviours. So intense and powerful was this process that the dreadfulness of Wine Alley not only became common knowledge across the city but permeated the estate itself, leading residents to regard their neighbours with suspicion and hostility.

Jacobs, Kemeny and Manzi (2003) describe the demonisation of council housing in the political rhetoric surrounding anti-social behaviour in Britain. While crime is ubiquitous, anti-social behaviour is thought to occur exclusively on council estates. The UK television progamme *Neighbours from Hell* disparaged life on council estates with regular examples of boundary disputes, dumping of rubbish, and noise disturbance. The underlying message was clear: council estates represented an undesirable form of housing peopled by dysfunctional families unable to form a community. The stigma attached to council housing in recent years is a direct consequence of government policies beginning in the 1980s; policymakers sought to portray council estates as undesirable residences as a means of justifying privatisation strategies under the Housing Act 1988 (Jacobs, Kemeny and Manzi, 2003: 441).

Johannesburg's Jan Hofmeyer estate provides a telling example of the impact of stigma. Current and former residents use the phrase 'to grow up in Jan Bom', a term conveying affection despite the estate's reputation for poverty and crime. It appears to have originated with the estate's poor Whites who had been settled there because their families could not afford to pay rent. Saying that one has grown in up in Jan Bom refers to strength of character; it is to say that one has made it against the odds (du Plessis, 2004: 895).

Crime-Reduction Strategies

One definition of problem estate, as Rock (1988b: 101) observes, is that it 'causes problems for authorities'. Concerns about elevated levels of crime in council housing areas have led to a number of proposals for reducing crime.

Policing

Until relatively recently, lack of policing was a regular feature of estates. Policing occurred only in response to emergency calls and police authorities ignored or delayed their response to residents who contacted them. Policing of social housing residents became the subject of intense interest following rioting in Brixton, Tottenham, and other cities during the 1980s, Ely, Meadowell and Blackbird Leys estates in the 1990s, and Bradford and Oldham in this decade. In the aftermath of these spectacular failures, more has been said about what went wrong with policing rather than the way forward, which might be said about policing problem estates generally.

Short-term, intensive law enforcement actions rarely succeed where police have disengaged from ordinary policing. Aggressive, militaristic police interventions have been identified as the immediate source of riots. The riots on the Meadowell estate were touched off by the death of a young resident who died in a stolen car, being chased by police. Graef (2004), who filmed life on the estate over the course of a year, reports that while police officials have made extensive efforts in recent decades to develop ordinary and positive relations with residents of council estates, tensions remain high. Residents viewed the death of this 'joyrider' as a police murder, not an accident provoked by the young man himself, who challenged the police to chase after him. The father of the boy complained that the police had targeted him unfairly; he was 'a good boy, just an ordinary honest burglar, who did nothing wrong' (Graef, 2004: 27). Graffiti on walls around the estate socialised the youngest residents into this interpretation of events long after the riots had ended.

For 'community' or 'neighbourhood' style policing to work, there must be a community. Police interventions, such as dispersing youths from congregating in common areas, may be described as undertaken on behalf of 'the community', but to actually be a part of community life residents and police must identify with a common purpose. Graef (2004) contends that in places such as Meadowell, where loan-sharking, drug-dealing, and fencing stolen goods involve a substantial number of residents, residents view property crime as youthful time-wasting, survival strategies, and 'shopping in other people's houses'.

Police are the enemy because of their hostility towards and suspicion of any resident. Meadowell remains typical of estates where grassing is considered worse than burglary, robbery, or violence (Graef, 2004). A 'grass' refers to someone who provides information to police about ongoing criminal activities.[1] This ethos comes about from residents' belief in the potential for reprisal, as well as entrusting personal safety to family and kinship networks rather than police and council authorities. The 'no grassing' rule makes police and crime prevention activities difficult. Even where police and community work together to build trust, hostility toward the criminal justice system remains, and residents are unlikely to assist in prosecution of local youth causing problems (burglary, car theft, vandalism) due to intimidation of witnesses (Evans, Fraser, and Walklate, 1996).

Perhaps the greatest challenge is overcoming the sense that police are powerless to have any real impact on the problems of the problem estate. Foster (2000: 324) notes that the police she interviewed concerning a housing estate in the North East of England had a 'surprising degree' of sympathy for the residents; the sheer weight of problems related to social exclusion meant an awareness of the inadequacy of a tactical response as a solution.

Designing-Out Crime

'Secured by Design' (SPD), a police initiative launched in the UK in 1993, certifies new housing developments with the SPD logo if they meet certain minimum security design criteria. This initiative is one aspect of the designing-out crime movement pursued by police, surveyors, planners and policymakers in Australia, Canada, Netherlands, USA as well as the UK.

Designing-out crime is based on the idea that certain design and management interventions in the built environment can make a difference in terms of crime prevention by reducing the opportunities for criminal activity and improving policing. In the context of housing, designing-out strategies correspond to the idea that the layout of estates can attract criminals by making it easier for them to avoid detection and minimize risk of arrest. Safe-design principles lead to evaluation of residential space in terms of its capacity to create perceived zones of territorial influence; provide surveillance opportunities for residents; project isolation and stigma; and contribute to 'safe zones' consistent with, or in juxtaposition to environmental and socio-economic characteristics. Application of these principles to council estates has led to designs aimed at reducing the size and height of blocks, reducing the number of residences sharing a single entrance, arranging residences to encourage social interaction among inhabitants, making public areas visible from dwellings,

---

[1]The word originates in Cockney rhyming slang used in the criminal underworld of the 1920s; someone close to a 'copper' was called a 'grasshopper' (Evans, Fraser and Walklate, 1996: 365).

and ensuring that front windows face the street or shared access area (Wilson, 1980).

Designing-out crime can be counter-productive if taken too far or in isolation. When Green, Gilbertson and Grimsley (2002) explored the fear of crime among 407 residents of 21 tower blocks in Liverpool, they found that improved security measures as part of architectural design were associated with lower levels of fear, but that feelings of safety within fortress-like spaces did not extend to walking neighbourhood streets. Provocatively, they suggest that security measures produce a feeling of safety while *inside* at the expense of feeling unsafe while *outside*. Planners and designers need to resist, these authors point out, the creation of a divided society wherein the better-off exclude the less-privileged by privatising what were formally public spaces. Apart from the moral question raised by this project, this polarization of space can raise levels of fear and mutual suspicion.

One extension of designing-out crime principles points to the creation of 'gated communities': residential areas with a restricted access through some barrier such as a fence, wall, security guardhouse, or electronic gate. Blandy (2004–5: 30) reports that there are some 1000 gated communities in England, mostly in London and the Southeast. Although the popularity of these communities rests in part on their ability to enhance the safety of residents, this has not been demonstrated as yet. There is little evidence that gated communities provide an adequate response either in terms of physical security or collective efficacy.

Anti-Social Behaviour Orders

The anti-social behaviour order (ASBO) came about in response to troublesome behaviour in social housing. It was meant to provide a legal means of dealing with persistent behaviour considered too trivial to be dealt with by police but serious from the standpoint of residents who live in fear and intimidation.

The Crime and Disorder Act of 1998 introduced the anti-social behaviour disorder as a civil order backed up by criminal penalties for breach. An ASBO can be obtained by a local authority or police against a person whose conduct might cause 'harassment, alarm or distress' to persons not living in the same household. The Anti-Social Behaviour Bill (2003) introduced measures, including fixed penalties, to deal with noise, truancy, parental irresponsibility, and graffiti. In the realm of social housing, it included measures to improve the operation of injunctions and evictions, and removed the 'right to buy' for anti-social tenants. In Scotland, the Anti-Social Behaviour Bill included similar provisions to that of England, but also extended the functioning of ASBOs, such as arrest without warrant for breach of order (Brown, 2004: 203–4).

Despite recent legislation, anti-social behaviour remains a vague, elastic term that encompasses a range of behaviours from the traditionally or potentially criminal to acts that do not offend the criminal law but do break social conventions. The Home Office day-count of anti-social behaviour in September 2003 identified thirteen categories: litter/rubbish, criminal damage/ vandalism, vehicle-related nuisance, nuisance behaviour, intimidation/harassment, noise, rowdy behaviour, abandoned vehicles, drinking in the street and begging, drug abuse/misuse and dealing, animal-related problems, prostitution and sexual acts, and hoax calls (Hough and Jacobson, 2004: 37). This ambiguity raises questions about the ASBO as a solution to problem estates (Scott and Parkey, 1998: 327). As it does not concern crime, there is no legal interest in motivation or intention, which explains why control of anti-social behaviour is unconcerned about mental health problems, addictions, social pressures and other legal excuses (Brown, 2004: 206–7).

The government's focus on anti-social behaviour may represent an instance of greater social control over the poor. Squires (2006) argues the case against ASBO enforcement. It represents the 'blurring, widening and masking' of control mechanisms; the dispersal and diffusion of disciplinary relationships throughout policy arenas. He spotlights the fact that the ASBO is purely about behaviour. Intention, the essential legal element of criminal activity, is irrelevant. In this way, the ASBO blurs the traditional distinction between civil and criminal law, neutralising the conventional legal protections afforded to those suspected of crimes. Anti-social behaviour does not become a category of criminal behaviour, but of *sub*-criminal or *nearly*-criminal activity. Flint (2002) argues that restricting housing benefits as a consequence for anti-social behaviour has led to creation of a new law enforcement profession. The ASBO has made housing managers into a key element of government crime control policy, civilian investigators who apply their own interpretation of social codes. This development can be taken as an example of what Foucault called governmentality, the 'deliberations, strategies, tactics and devices employed by authorities for making up and acting upon a population' (Flint, 2002: 620).

Others argue that it represents a means of empowering the poor. The case for enforcement of ASBOs in the social housing context rests on the argument that someone's right to housing is balanced by an obligation not to abuse that housing. Social order practices not only reflect the needs or interests of employers, elites and ruling classes, but also reflect the interests and actions of other social divisions who feel the need to seek or defend a quality of life. From this standpoint, critics of 'authoritarian landlordism' fail to acknowledge that 'tenants themselves are disempowered by violent, racist or criminal neighbours' (Harrison, 2001: 103).

Tenant Associations

The significance of tenant associations follows from the importance of voluntary associations generally in sustaining social cohesion within neighbourhoods. Saergert, Winkel and Swartz (2002), who surveyed residents of 487 buildings providing low-income housing in New York City, emphasise the role of tenant associations in preventing crime in low-income housing. Basic participation in tenant associations proved highly effective in reducing in-building crime across both high-crime and low-crime neighbourhoods. The presence of tenant pro-social norms and formal leadership activities also proved to be important, depending on neighbourhood context; pro-social norms reduced in-building crime in high-crime neighbourhoods and formal leadership led to lower levels of building crime in low-crime neighbourhoods. Their research suggests the need for housing policies that provide funds and training for tenant organisers in low-income housing; ownership and transfer of buildings to limited-equity coopera-tives; and recognition by police agencies of the resources that tenant associations can provide (Saergert, Winkel and Swartz, 2002: 222).

Based on their research of crime in Canadian public housing, DeKeseredy et al. (2003b: 24) conclude that active tenant associations should be encour-aged as a means of reducing social disorganisation in public housing areas. In the six estates within Eastern Ontario they studied, residents rarely partici-pated in activities with neighbours; the people resided in 'severely distressed households', making social disorganisation more likely. They also note that while local, community-based crime prevention schemes such as tenant asso-ciations are important, they should not be taken as substitutes for larger eco-nomic strategies and public spending to reduce contributory factors such as joblessness.

Conclusion

Political attention to the problem of crime and social housing can result in the infusion of resources needed for reducing victimisation and improving the well-being of residents generally, although the focus on a few notorious estates threatens to exaggerate and distort the crime problem. From a criminological perspective, the council estate represents a meaningful social space, to be understood not only by looking at the attitudes and behaviours of residents but the way in which the larger social context of housing impinges on their lives.

Questions for Discussion

1. *Does the Chicago model of social disorganisation explain patterns of crime in British cities?*

2. *What is the best explanation for the problem of crime on the 'problem estate'?*

3. *In what sense is crime on council estates an unintended effect of government efforts to solve inequalities in housing?*

4. *Is the ASBO the best strategy for reducing crime in social housing areas?*

Further Reading

Elisabeth Burney (1999) *Crime and Banishment: Nuisance and Exclusion in Social Housing*. Winchester: Waterside Press.

Criminology and Public Policy (2003) 3(1). Special section concerning public housing and violence.

John Flint (ed.) (2006) *Housing, Urban Governance and Anti-Social Behaviour*. Bristol: Policy Press.

Alan Murie (1997) 'Linking Housing Changes to Crime', *Social Policy and Administration* 31: 22–36.

Violence Against Women (2001) 7(6). Special issue devoted to public housing and violence against women.

Crime, Health and Education

SUMMARY

- Biologistic criminology, self-control theory and social discipline theory suggest a link between health and crime
- Regarding crime as a health problem raises questions about criminalisation of unhealthy behaviours and placing medical doctors in the role of crime-fighters
- Theorised links between education and crime include educational disaffection, sociology of adolescence, and the cultural reproduction of violence
- Much of the concern with educational policy and crime focuses on the issue of school exclusion

In recent decades, crime has become increasingly defined as a safety issue. Boutellier (2001) describes the emergence of a 'safety state' in which new forms of safety policy are developed whereby the line between social policy and crime policy becomes blurred. Criminal victimisation is seen as a category, or sub-category, of threat to healthy living alongside illness, accidents, incivilities, addictions, and conflict.

The concern with safety, particularly the safety of children, has enlisted new agencies in the suppression of crime. Health and education have come to be seen as important sites for crime prevention; adopting the right policies in areas of health and education would bring about crime reduction as well as improve body fitness and enable a more rewarding lifestyle. One of the primary premises of the public health approach to crime prevention and school-based crime prevention programmes is that increased knowledge and awareness of the dangers of particular activities provides for successful negotiation of the harm involved.

This chapter explores health and education in relation to crime. We will look at the various ways criminologists have perceived the relationship between health and crime, and between education and crime, and the implications of overlapping concerns in these areas for policy. The first half of the chapter looks at three versions of the link between illness and criminality and critiques of the depiction of crime as a health issue. The second half reviews three ways of thinking about the link between schools and crime, and discusses the dilemmas involved in pursuing education policy for purposes of crime reduction.

Illness and Criminality

There is a relationship between illness and criminality according to several strands of criminological enquiry. The way this relationship is understood depends on the conceptual framework in which it appears.

Biologism

'Biologism' proposes a direct link between biology and behaviour. Essentially, the proponents of biologism in criminology believe the source of criminal behaviour to be located within the body itself. Arguments from this perspective include claims about a genetic basis for alcoholism and neuro-chemical imbalances leading to hyperactivity in children (Rose, 2000). Securing reliable information in this area is difficult owing to the relative scarcity of credible scholarly work and the abundance of popular wisdom. Mistrust of artificial ingredients and anxieties about secret additives in common foods provide a perennial source of urban legends and conspiracy theories. In Britain, 'blue smarties' have been rumoured to trigger hyperactivity in children and in America 'red M&Ms' have been said to have this effect.[1] Nevertheless, there are some studies about how particular substances, or lack of them, lead to both illness and crime.

In the 1940s, maverick nutritionist Hugh Macdonald Sinclair suggested that a poor diet precipitated anti-social behaviour in young people. He convinced the wartime government to supplement the diet of children with cod-liver oil and orange juice as a matter of delinquency prevention. Prior to the war, he had written fifteen scientific papers advocating an integrated approach to human physical and social well-being, and surmised that among other ills, inadequate nutrition brought about aggressive and inappropriate behaviour. But Sinclair received severe criticism, and eventually lost his post at Oxford, for failing to adhere to accepted standards of scientific methodology in his nutrition studies (Ewin, 2002).

Sinclair's argument about links between poor nutrition and delinquency has received some support. Neugebauer, Hoek, Wijbrand and Susser (1999) carried out research, in a retrospective cohort study, to see whether severe nutritional deficiency during pregnancy led to anti-social behaviour in children. During 1944–5, a period known to the Dutch as the *Hongerwinter*, 'hunger winter', Hitler's army blockaded food supplies. The people of Amsterdam, Haarlem,

---

[1]Nestlé Rowntree announced in May 2006 it would be replacing the blue smartie with a white smartie.

Leiden, Rotterdam, Utrecht and The Hague ate tulip bulbs and sugar beets to survive. The researchers examined the impact of starvation on the children born to women pregnant during this period using psychiatric examinations given (at 18 years of age) for military registration during the 1960s. They concluded that 'severe nutritional deficiency in first or second trimester of intrauterine life is associated with risk of development for ASPD [anti-social personality disorder]' (Neugebauer, Hoek, Wijbrand and Susser, 1999: 461). Prenatal nutritional deficiency could lead to anti-social behaviour through general nutritional deficiency or through deficiency of a specific micronutrient.

Another study has explored this possibility, and specifically the idea that if there is a causal relationship between micronutrient deficiencies and anti-social behaviour, then supplementing the diet with vitamins to resolve these deficiencies should lead to improved behaviour. Gesch and others (2002) gave commercially available vitamin supplements to an experimental group of 231 men within a British prison. Compared to prisoners not receiving the supplements, the experimental group committed significantly fewer disciplinary incidents, with the greatest difference observed for violent incidents. This research suggests that 'supplementing prisoners' diets with physiological dosages of vitamins, minerals, and essential fatty acids caused a marked reduction in antisocial behaviour to a remarkable degree' and with similar implications for those eating poor diets within the community (Gesch et al., 2002: 26).

Other researchers point to poisons in the environment, such as lead, as an explanation for varying rates of crime across populations. Exposure to lead is associated with brain dysfunction, an aspect of which may explain criminal behaviour. According to the neurotoxicity hypothesis, exposure to lead alters neurotransmitter and hormonal systems in ways that may induce aggressive and violent behaviour. Needleman and associates (1996) investigated clinical reports of aggressive behaviour in children recovering from lead-poisoning. They found higher bone lead levels in a sample of 301 boys in primary schools within Pittsburgh, Pennsylvania, identified by parents, teachers, and the boys themselves as more aggressive and prone to anti-social behaviour. The researchers noted that lead levels are generally higher in disadvantaged and low-income populations and that delinquency is associated with minority status, poverty, and family dysfunction. Stretesky and Lynch (2004) explored this connection in a national study. Their comparison of airborne lead levels across 2772 counties in the USA suggests a direct connection between lead levels and crime rates and the role of resource deprivation in this connection. The populations most at risk of lead poisoning are the least likely to receive resources required to prevent, screen, and treat the illness.

Self-Control

For Gottfredson and Hirschi (1990), the connection between crime and health is a feature of self-control. In popular imagination, crime is the work of exceptionally clever individuals or those who have perfected illicit skills. This may be the case for some white-collar crooks, Hirschi and Gottfredson (2000) insist, but not for the kinds of crime that bring most people to criminal courts. Most crimes are trivial, mundane activities requiring little planning or skill. Crime represents 'acts of force or fraud taken in pursuit of self-interest' by those who never learned to restrain their impulses.

They contend that early childhood socialisation represents the single most important explanation for subsequent criminal activity. Most people obey the law, particularly with regard to serious offences, out of a habit learned early in life. Most crimes, then, can be attributed to those persons who failed to learn self-control (Hirschi and Gottfredson, 2000: 56). Low self-control explains both criminal and 'analogous acts', such as dangerous driving, drinking to intoxication, irresponsible sex, and an unhealthy diet. People who tend to be impulsive, insensitive, sensual, risk-taking, short-sighted and non-verbal are likely to find themselves not only in trouble with the law, but also in poor health.

Research in this area has produced mixed results. Low self-regulation does not lead to illness. In an analysis of information from their longitudinal survey of 411 males in south London, Shepherd, Farrington and Potts (2002) found those likely to have experienced an injury (industrial, sports, assault, motorbike, and home) were also those with anti-social personalities (characterised by lawbreaking, drug use, heavy smoking, heavy drinking, unprotected sex and unstable employment). Illness in general was not related to anti-social personality, although those who had experienced a respiratory tract disease (colds, flu, asthma, bronchitis) were less likely to be anti-social, or to put it the other way around, those in poorer health tended to be less anti-social. They surmise that, among other factors, respiratory tract illness may be a protective factor because it limits outdoor activity and visits to pubs or because it undermines fitness needed for more anti-social behaviour associated with adolescent daring and masculine risk-taking (Shepherd, Farrington, and Potts, 2002: 543).

On the other hand, low self-regulation has been linked with greater likelihood of injury due to accidents. Research conducted in the Netherlands ties risky behaviour of drivers in traffic to criminal behaviour. The researchers took a random sample of 1000 traffic accidents registered with police in The Hague during 1994. They identified those accidents attributed by police to risky driving behaviour and then determined the portion of risky drivers with criminal records. Taking into account exposure to traffic situations and alcohol use, they found that risky traffic behaviour was related to criminal involvement, particularly violent crime, vandalism, and property crime. The results are consistent with the idea of a common factor underlying both risky behaviour in traffic and criminal behaviour. This common factor may be defined as a trait referred to as risk-taking, impulsiveness or lack of self-control (Junger, West and Timman, 2001; see also Junger and Tremblay, 1999).

Thinking about a common origin for criminality and poor health in personal dispositions tends to reify personality traits and has the potential for personalising social problems. That said, it also contains the basis for re-thinking public policy. If health risks attributed to personal cost–benefit calculation actually result from a habit of conduct (more unconscious than rational), then deterrence-based strategies and public awareness campaigns will have little impact.

Social Discipline

Foucault (1975) portrays medicine as a mechanism of social discipline. In a series of books dealing with the asylum, the clinic, and the prison, he describes the practices by which people become classified in modern bureaucratic society. Medicine no more reveals humanitarian impulses than penology and psychiatry, but contributes new techniques for regulating, universalising, and economising discipline. The observation that many people seek medical attention is but an aspect of 'subjectification', the practice of tying individuals to particular identities. Medical practitioners share with prison-managers in the manufacture of power and knowledge; this knowledge divides people up through continuous surveillance and discipline (Timmerman and Gabe, 2002).

Foucault's analysis does not offer a critique of policy responses to crime and illness. He does not see crime and illness as problems to be solved but opportunities for the concentration and exercise of power on the part of bureaucratic elements in society. His analysis spotlights how certain practices become legitimated by suppression of others. Following Foucault, Timmerman and Gabe (2002) conceptualise the relationship between criminality and illness as 'the medico-legal borderland' comprised of sites – clinics, prisons, public health offices, crisis intervention centres, and police – that link medical knowledge about criminality for social control purposes. They contend that:

> The borderland between crime and health care is populated and guarded by a number of professionals engaging in processes that contain both the criminalisation of contested medical interventions and the medicalisation of criminal danger. (Timmerman and Gabe, 2002: 507)

From this perspective, health policy and crime policy can be seen as two competing cultures – medicine and law enforcement – and the relationship between them, the scene of struggle in which a fight for supremacy occurs, each attempting to redraw the borders to its advantage. Such a struggle might lead to criminalisation of actions previously considered medical and the medicalisation of issues formerly under legal jurisdiction.

The case of 'Typhoid Mary' illustrates the relationship between illness, crime, and power. In 1938, Mary Mallon died after spending nearly two decades in confinement. Although she had never been convicted of any crime, the New York City Department of Health had detained her on evidence that in pursuing her employment as a cook, she had caused at least 53 cases of typhoid fever. The creation of Typhoid Mary rested on the bacteriological theory that healthy persons could become carriers of typhoid organisms, and at a time when public health sought recognition, she became emblematic of the need to cede police power to health officials. While the state was satisfied with occasional surveillance of other typhoid carriers known to them, they assisted in the creation of the Typhoid Mary identity within the press. Mary Mallon was likely singled-out for such treatment owing to her 'Irishness', and her stubborn refusal to acknowledge the authority of medical and legal authorities. In later years, she turned down the opportunity for release having reconciled herself to a life of imprisonment required by the Typhoid Mary persona (Hasian, 2000).

Public Health and Crime Prevention

In recent decades, the public health and crime prevention establishments have found one another. Those concerned with public health and those concerned with crime prevention have decided that there is, or should be, substantial overlap in their strategies.

Health Promotion and Crime

Public health, as traditionally practised, consists of a medical specialisation focused on the health of populations rather than individuals. It originated with the Victorian interest in good sewerage and clean water as a primary means of disease prevention. At that time, public health practitioners sought government intervention in housing conditions, food supply, sewage disposal, and working conditions to improve the 'sanitation' of the physical environment. Even before the First World War, public health authorities could point to significant successes. They had reduced to insignificance the threat of some diseases (Keithly and Robinson, 1999: 68).

Following the Second World War, a new public health model has emerged, stressing health promotion rather than disease prevention. The post-war public health lobby concerned itself with admonishing the government to carry out its alleged responsibility for advising people on personal tastes and habits. This more comprehensive approach considers 'patterns and conditions of living, eating, playing, working ... most of which lie outside the realm of the health sector and are not consciously health directed' (Green and Kreuter, 1990: 319). During the 1950s and 1960s, public health authorities moved away from the service-oriented public health ethos of the inter-war years toward a new type of 'healthism' symbolised by concern about smoking. By the 1970s, the anti-smoking campaign had moved from a matter of advising smokers about health dangers to seeking prohibition as a means of eliminating the threat of 'passive smoking' to 'innocent victims' (Berridge, 2003).

This new emphasis on conceptual and empirical links between health and social behaviour includes a concern with crime. Crime affects health directly and indirectly (Goodwin, 2004). 'Direct effects' include physical injury, disability and death resulting from violent assaults and abuse. Victims of intimate partner violence, for instance, experience multiple physical and mental health problems including chronic pain, sexually transmitted disease, depression and post-traumatic stress disorder (Campbell, 2002). The less obvious, 'indirect effects' include the impact on victims' health resulting in time off work, financial losses, and changes in circumstances with families. Indirect effects also include fear of crime; there is evidence to suggest that some people change their behaviour as a result of being victimised (Goodwin, 2004: 27–8). In London, as many as 100,000 women per year seek medical treatment for injuries received from men living with them. Physical injuries include cuts, bruises, burns, scalds, concussion, broken bones and puncture wounds (from knives and other objects). Permanent injuries such as damage to joints, loss of hearing, disfigurement also result. There are also long-term health problems, especially arthritis, hypertension, and heart disease, as well as debilitating conditions accruing from stress and depression (Abbott and Williamson, 1999: 85).

Health authorities have become increasingly aware of the impact of crime on provision of health services (Robinson and Keithley, 2000). Dealing with the direct and indirect effects of crime creates significant costs for the National Health Service. One recent report estimated the total costs associated with the annual number of bed days relating to crime and disorder at somewhere between £1.1 and £2.3 billion, comprising 3 to 6.5 per cent of the hospital, community, and family health services allocation for England in 2002–3 (Goodwin, 2004: 31). Not only victims, but the perpetrators of crime, require significant medical resources. Individuals with extensive criminal histories experience more frequent health problems overall, and accordingly, greater frequency of emergency room use and hospitalisations. This connection between criminal involvement and elevated use of medical resources is attributed to that portion of lawbreakers engaged in extensive consumption of alcohol and illegal drugs (Mateyoke-Scrivner et al., 2003).

Health authorities have also become aware of crime as a result of violence directed at NHS staff (O'Beirne and Gabe, 2005). Some 116,000 NHS staff were reported as being victims of violence and aggression in 2002/03 (Goodwin, 2004: 30). A 2002 survey of 697 general practitioners in south-east England (including south London and the south-east coast) found that nearly four-fifths had been victims of violence during the previous two years (Elston et al., 2002). Nurses working in general hospitals throughout the UK do appear to be at higher risk of assault – more than four times – than workers generally. But it is difficult to know whether violence directed at nurses (and other health professionals) has increased in recent years or whether the 'increase' reflects greater attention to a problem that has always been there. Public health rhetoric about an 'epidemic' of violence suggests greater vulnerability of those in 'front line' occupations and there has been an alarmist quality to some writing in this area. The risk to nurses, according to an article in *Nursing Times,* can be compared to that of bouncers (cited in Wells and Bowers, 2002: 231).

A significant question about the public health approach to crime has to do with whether health policy should be regarded as an analogy or instrument. It is one thing to say that crime is *like* a disease in its impact on society. This way of thinking suggests that public health techniques can be adapted for use in forestalling crime, such as planning crime prevention programmes along primary, secondary and tertiary lines. (See Chapter 7). It is another thing to say that crime *is* a disease in the sense that both originate in the same source, such as the human body. This way of thinking has led to eugenics, the idea that human beings can be managed to 'breed out' criminality, alcoholism, and poverty. The British eugenics movement of the early twentieth century advocated restrictive immigration laws, compulsory sterilisation laws, and imperialist foreign policy to safeguard the British 'race' (Paul, 1984).

Crime as a Health Issue?

The public health perspective brings the language of medicine to crime policy. It concerns 'intentional injuries', not 'crimes', reflecting values inherent in the commitment to minimise disease and disability and extend health protection to vulnerable populations. The public health view shifts policy away from identifying 'bad' and 'dangerous' individuals who merit punishment to 'at risk' populations in need of essential social benefits. It seeks to reorient the response to crime away from retribution for crimes committed toward steps to prevent them. Or, as Shepherd and Farrington (1993) put it: 'it is surely better to prevent violence through the positive aim of promoting health than through the negative aims of conviction and punishment'. .

Whether the public health establishment can repeat its success in preventing contagious diseases with non-traditional 'diseases' such as homicide and domestic violence has been questioned. Ruttenberg (1994: 1903) argues that recent successes the public health establishment has had in altering the behaviour of individuals in the contexts of driving with safety belts, drink driving and cigarette smoking were accomplished by altering perceptions of the cost–benefit analysis of the behaviour in question. Presumably, fewer people smoke cigarettes because of greater awareness of the health consequences of smoking which had not been understood before. Ruttenberg concludes that public-health experts have failed, however, to convince working class and the poor to quit smoking in the same numbers as the affluent. The public health approach 'works' for the middle and affluent classes in the same way that the criminal justice approach 'works' for them. Berridge (2003: 63) points out that public health campaigners succeeded in altering the social profile of smoking, that is, by making it a lower-class activity. The main cultural change in the UK since the Second World War concerning smoking has been increased marginalisation of smoking and association with poorer groups in society.

One of the most contentious issues in this context concerns the criminalisation of health risks. An element of the public health sector, the Alcohol and

Other Drugs or 'AOD' movement, seeks to convince legislators, the media, and the public that alcohol should be considered a drug and not a beverage. Leaders of this movement, which began in Canada and the USA in the 1960s and 1970s, feared the issue of alcohol abuse had been ignored, and encouraged health officials to see alcohol as a more serious threat to youth than illicit drugs. By the 1980s, this approach had expanded to become 'ATOD' – Alcohol, Tobacco and Other Drugs (Marquis, 2005). Recognizing the health consequences of legal drugs was intended as a means of garnering more resources for public health and the logic of seeing drug abuse as a health problem should have meant diversion of resources from criminal justice to public health. What actually happened is the reverse: alcohol became a criminal problem rather than an under-appreciated health problem.

The American public health lobby pushed for and won something akin to 'zero tolerance medicine' in regard to alcohol consumption among young persons. During the 1980s, campaigners succeeded in raising the minimum age for alcohol consumption to 21 in all states; minimum age drinking laws, depending on the state, had specified 18, 19 or 20 years of age. The rationale for raising the age had to do with the aim of reducing traffic crashes among young drivers, and research carried out by the National Highway and Traffic Safety Administration did find that increased minimum age drinking laws resulted in a 13 per cent decline in youth motor-vehicle deaths (Mosher and Jernigan, 2001: 278). But rather than seek one or other means of minimising driving under the influence of alcohol, a crime for licensed drivers of any age, this public health campaign had the effect of criminalising alcohol consumption altogether for young adults. It shifted law enforcement resources away from catching heavily intoxicated drivers to criminalising the behaviour of young drinkers (Wolfson and Hourigan, 1997).

Another contentious issue has to do with diverting medical resources from health to crime-fighting. The public health approach offers a 'new platform' for use in inquiry into crime from which to launch interventions. This new platform includes 'the engagement of physicians and health practitioners lodged in emergency rooms, private offices and schools' (Moore, 1995: 257). From this vantage point, medical practitioners are positioned to see aspects of crime, such as family violence, that may never come to the attention of police. They are available to intervene in less-formal and potentially supportive ways. But it is worth considering what health resources are worth diverting to crime control; physicians already have a long list of social problems on their remit. The addition of smoking and alcohol and drug abuse to the public health agenda already consumes a significant portion of budgets. This takes public health funds away from the traditional focus, such as ensuring safe water and preventing spread of communicable diseases. 'Medicalisation' of crime relieves some of the responsibility for crime reduction on the part of police, and perhaps more importantly, politicians and other government officials, who receive public resources precisely for this purpose (Sidel and Wesley, 1995: 155). Fitzpatrick (2001) argues for establishment of a clear boundary between politics and medicine so that doctors can leave the well alone and concentrate on the sick.

Using the clinical setting to achieve political or policy goals raises a controversial point. In addition to treating wounds, doctors can alleviate the suffering of crime victims. By acknowledging to women who are victims of violent men in domestic settings 'that it is not their own fault but a social and political issue in a patriarchal society, doctors would play a powerful role in empowering women' (Abbott and Williamson, 1999: 84). At the same time, a clinical effort to regulate behaviour rather than treat injury and illness can lead to a politicisation of the doctor–patient relationship and prohibition of 'unhealthy' lifestyles. The relationship between a doctor and a patient is unequal; patients are arguably more inclined to follow a doctor's advice than a politician's advice about making behavioural changes (Sidel and Wesley, 1995). Also, there is a distinction between practising medicine and engaging in crime-fighting. The doctor–patient relationship has been historically guided by medical ethics requiring respect for the privacy and integrity of patients. Physicians have been reluctant to become agents of the State in the investigation and apprehension of criminal suspects, but making the reduction of criminal victimisation a medical issue would appear to change this.

Education and Crime

Criminologists have long suspected that solving problems related to education is key to solving the problem of crime. There are, it might be said, three ways of thinking about the connection between education and crime: problems *at* school, problems *around* schools, and problems *with* schools.

Educational Disaffection

One of the longstanding theories of delinquency proposes that children who have problems at school are more likely to engage in delinquency. Educational disaffection or 'educational deficiencies' include academic underachievement, truancy, and disciplinary problems while at school. Ball and Conolly (2000), in their study of school-based information used by the youth court, affirm the 'well established' links between educational disaffection and delinquency. They collected information for a sample of 522 school-age defendants in four cities across England (London, the Midlands, Yorkshire, and the North East) who had been sentenced in 1995. According to information in pre-sentence reports, some 85 per cent were perceived to have problems at school and 25 per cent had chronic multiple difficulties. At the time the report had been written, only a minority of defendants were currently attending school; 25 per cent of these were truanting and 22 per cent of these had been excluded (Ball and Conolly, 2000: 603).

A similar picture emerges from the USA. A study comparing 5000 delinquents with the same number of non-delinquents in Florida found that delinquents experience a combination of educational deficiencies as compared to their non-delinquent counterparts. Delinquent students were more likely to have lower grade point averages, have poorer attendance records, be retained more often in the same grade, and receive more disciplinary actions (Wang, Blomberg and Li, 2005).

Perennial explanations for the link between educational disaffection and delinquency have involved references to individual factors such as low intelligence (Crocker and Hodgins, 1997) and low self-esteem (Donnellan et al., 2005). While these explanations retain currency in educational settings, they have been, and continue to be, criticised by criminologists and others. Simpson and Hogg (2001) argue that statements such as 'children with lower IQs are at higher risk of delinquent behaviour' are misleading and unhelpful because they fail to convey the complexity of the relationship. 'There is a level of intellectual functioning below which the prevalence of delinquent and criminal behaviour declines' (Simpson and Hogg, 2001: 403). There is an emerging area of research insisting that *high* levels of self-esteem are conducive to crime. Baumeister, Smart and Boden (1996) argue that when individuals with inflated self-esteem face negative external evaluations, they may react violently. As these researchers put it, 'threatened egoism' is a major source of violent behaviour. It helps explain gender differences in school discipline problems and youth crime generally.

The Invention of Adolescence

The idea of adolescence, of a period in life between childhood and adulthood, is a recent invention. During the late nineteenth and early twentieth century, academics and social reformers reconstructed the image of childhood. They portrayed adolescence as a developmental stage with distinct needs and interests, no longer children but not quite yet adults. Throughout the twentieth century, economic, cultural, and technological changes extended the period of adolescence to include more persons, which led to the proliferation of specialised social institutions meant to respond to the predicament of those in their 'teenage' or 'in-between' years (Ainsworth, 1991).

Felson (2002) discusses the consequences of this process for crime. Essentially, late modern society must structure its social institutions to stave off adult interests of persons considered to be in children's bodies. Whereas in the early nineteenth century, the daily activities of 16-year-olds would have been taken up by farming, marriage, homemaking, factory work and other adult responsibilities, the situation now is how to address the increasing expansion of leisure (playtime). In other words, teenagers have more occasions for drug-taking, drinking, standing around, sex, shopping, lounging about, and vandalism. This is why, Felson argues, the greatest number of juvenile crimes occurs during the after-school hours in areas around schools, not within them.

Terrible incidents of violence at schools, such as shootings, have made school violence a political issue. But the majority of school incidents, Felson insists, are small thefts and truancy. The greatest risk of young people engaging in crime occurs when school lets out, when young people are on the way home and no longer in supervised and organised activities. One study in South Carolina showed that as much as five times more violent delinquency occurred during the hour immediately after the school day than a hour in the middle of the school day. 'This evidence flies in the face of most of the publicity about violence *inside* the school during school hours' (Felson, 2000: 86).

This way of thinking suggests the importance of after-school programmes. Aside from their child-care and supervision benefits, such programmes are intended to assist in building skills in youth, making them more resilient and resistant to criminal behaviour. Gottfredson et al. (2004), who evaluated 14 such programmes in Maryland, concluded that they do have potential as delinquency prevention tools. Specifically, they found that participation in after-school programmes reduced delinquency for middle-school but not for elementary-school youths. For older children, programme participation led to a reduction in delinquency due to increased resolve on the part of individuals not to use drugs and through positive peer relationships rather than by providing constructive alternative activities per se.

Cultural Reproduction of Violence

There is an unspoken sense in much analysis of school violence that it is an alien and foreign element in schools. Larger troubles in society, embodied in students, walk through school doors and create assorted crime problems in classrooms and corridors. But there is a strand of theorising, drawing on the ideas of Pierre Bourdieu, that emphasises the ways in which schools generate violence.

Herr and Anderson (2003) point to school violence as a consequence of the cultural reproduction of social inequality within the educational milieu. Bourdieu described subtle and unconscious mechanisms through which dominant groups exercise their hegemony through 'pedagogical work'. The primary means of pedagogical work is accomplished through child-rearing and social institutions outside the family, such as formal schooling. In this process, the students become the victims of 'symbolic violence' directed towards them in the form of denial of the cultural capital they bring with them. Educators inculcate students with a 'cultural arbitrary' which advances the institutionalisation and legitimation of the majority's economic, political and social interests. In an empirical analysis of 'critical incidents' at one school, Herr and Anderson (2003) show how unequal social relations are reproduced through social institutions.

Osler and Starkey (2005) offer examples of the cultural reproduction of violence from media portrayals in Britain and France of school crime. In France, the government refers to the problem of *la violence à l'école*, 'violence at school'; discourse tends to be about incivility, making a moral judgement implying anti-social behaviour. In the UK, the term is 'disaffection,' which is used for a variety of behaviours, including low attainment, persistent disruption, truancy and self-exclusion. Although this term implies a reaction to the school as an environment, it tends to be problematised as occurring within individuals rather than populations. Osler and Starkey (2005) argue that policymakers have been reluctant to acknowledge the presence of institutional barriers, in the form of structural racial discrimination. In Britain, as well as France, young people from minority ethnic groups are over-represented in disadvantaged schools, but rather than taking steps to correct this, educational authorities pursue policies to address the symptoms of the inequalities, that is, violence and disaffection.

The cultural reproduction of fear has been theorised to occur not only along ethnic/racial lines, but gender as well. Goodey (1995) discusses the gender basis of fear within a comprehensive school on a council estate outside a northern British city. She examined the differences in fear of being victimised in a public place expressed by 663 boys and girls who completed the survey. She found that amongst young persons between the ages of 11 and 16 years of age, fear is gendered; girls expressed greater fear of 'people' when outside and of men in particular. One implication of this finding is to understand the role of the school environment in reproducing gendered fear in girls which may become normalised in women. Stanko (1990) has described 'climates of un-safety', the ways in which women negotiate their lives in circumstances to manage vulnerability. Women negotiate work, home, and public places to maintain a sense of personal well-being. These climates of un-safety can be thought of as a form of gender control, leading women to curtail some activities and pursue various strategies to minimise danger.

Education Policy and Crime Prevention

Education represents the single most important social policy investment in overcoming social disadvantage. But making crime reduction a goal of educational policy necessarily raises a question of priorities.

The Education Effect

Education affords a bundle of social benefits, not least of which is discouraging crime. Those persons who pursue an education are not only more likely to succeed in various aspects of life but are also less likely to run into trouble with the law. Hansen (2000) collected self-report information from young men between 16 and 25 years of age in England and Wales, comparing those who left school at 16 with those who stayed on past the school-leaving age. She found clear differences between the groups in characteristics related to labour market, family relationships, and neighbourhood situation that contribute to an individual's decision to stay on at school as well as get involved in crime. The education–crime link is clear enough: for those who stay on at school, criminal activity is almost non-existent by the age of 25, but for those who left school at 16, there is no decline in the crime rate from the age of 22 onwards (Hansen, 2000: 9). The most straightforward policy implication of this finding, Hansen concludes, is to encourage youths to stay on at school. The introduction of the educational maintenance allowance for those staying on at school should encourage young persons, particularly those from low-income backgrounds, to continue their education (Hansen, 2003: 156–7).

Feinstein and Sabates (2005) evaluated the impact of the educational maintenance allowance on crime. This Department for Education and Skills programme, originally piloted in 15 local educational authority areas (LEAs) in 1999, became a national scheme in 2004. The scheme provides for payments of up to £30 per week to young persons from families with low incomes (less than £30,000). Feinstein and Sabates compared conviction rates of youth (16 to 18 years of age) for burglary, theft and violent crimes from 1996 to 2002. They found that youth burglary and theft offences fell in the 15 LEAs that piloted educational maintenance allowances compared to the rest of England, although this did not occur for violent crime. They conclude that 'educational policies could have substantial external effects and could complement direct interventions for crime prevention' (Feinstein and Sabates, 2005: 25).

As clear as the link between educational success and crime reduction appears to be, translating the anti-crime properties of the educational process into policy has been problematic. The Labour government of Tony Blair expressed an understanding of the importance of educational policy in an overall criminal prevention strategy. Education Secretary David Blunkett explained in 1999 that New Labour had taken on the challenge of educational disengagement:

> [O]ne of our greatest challenges is to tackle disaffection and disengagement by those in the 14–19 age group who are outside education and work, and so often outside our society – forgotten until they become the concern of every one of us, on our streets and in our prisons. (Quoted in Blythe, 2001: 569).

The government introduced target-setting for local educational authorities to reduce unauthorised absence and exclusion, introduced new legal powers to pressurise parents to enforce school attendance, and expanded funding for programmes to improve behaviour and attendance. The Blair government also kept in place initiatives introduced by the Conservatives such as policies to encourage competition between schools (Blythe, 2001).

The Labour government also continued the Conservative initiative in the area of school-based drug education. For two decades and longer, UK governments have seen schools as a medium for confronting increasing levels of drug use among youth, and during the 1990s, drug education was deemed appropriate for inclusion in the primary curriculum. The statutory order for national curriculum science (in 1991) obliged schools to deliver elements of drug education in key stages 1 through to 4. Consistent with New Labour's interest in 'joined-up' responses, teachers have been encouraged to collaborate with police officers and youth workers in delivering anti-drug curricula.

Allot, Paxton and Leonard (1999) observe that drug education is based on the assumption that providing students with knowledge about the consequences of drug use will promote a negative attitude toward drugs and bring about a reduction in consumption, but research findings from evaluations of such programmes do not support this assumption. In fact, providing young people with knowledge alone can increase drug use and promote a positive attitude toward drug use (Allot, Paxton and Leonard, 1999: 494). Part of the problem is that drug education, unlike traditional curricula, is more ambiguous and open to interpretation. There is a danger of mixed or contradictory messages evidenced by confusion in policy documents about whether the meaning of 'drugs' includes alcohol and tobacco. Further, appropriate collaboration among teachers and police officers in delivering drug education is difficult to achieve. In her study of collaborative efforts in the north of England during the late 1990s, Harris (2003) found teachers willing to rely on the police to carry out instruction in this area. Whereas the national science curriculum has to do with how drugs affect body organs, police-led instruction has centred on the appearance and harmful effects of illicit substances.

What priority should be assigned to crime reduction alongside the goals of imparting knowledge of language, maths, history, science, etc. in education policy? This is an important question particularly when crime prevention has been proposed as a goal for education policy because the anti-crime effects of education have more to do with the attainment of qualifications in language, maths, history, science and so on than specifically anti-crime curricula such as drug education. While drug education and other crime prevention curricula are visible politically, such efforts are less effective as crime reduction measures than academic and vocational educational pathways enabling successful transitions to adulthood.

School Exclusions

The goals of crime policy and education policy do not overlap precisely as can be seen in government policy concerning school exclusions. Exclusion from school on a temporary or permanent basis can have short-term and long-term consequences for youth including the increased risk that the young person will embark on a criminal path.

During the 1990s, the government sought to reduce the number of school exclusions as a means of curtailing crime. A Home Office study *Young People and Crime* (1995) identified school exclusion as the chief reason for an upsurge in youth crime. The study explored self-reported delinquency among some 2500 young persons (between 14 and 25 years of age) across England and Wales. The report declared that three-fourths of the male students and nearly half of the female students who had been temporarily excluded (suspended), and all of the males and over half of the females who had been permanently excluded (expelled), were offenders (Graham and Bowling, 1995: 42). Following the 1997 general election, the Labour government issued its report *Truancy and School*

Exclusion, which made an explicit link between school exclusion and criminal behaviour. The report warned that young people excluded from school 'are in danger of becoming tomorrow's criminals and unemployed' (Social Exclusion Unit, 1997: 1). The government sent a clear policy message that schools should not use exclusion or condone extended absence as a routine means of dealing with troublesome students.

The discouragement of exclusions is consistent with theorising that a strong school bond constitutes a significant protective factor for children at risk of engaging in delinquency. Children from troubled families may become bonded to school because staff show an interest in them and because they experience a sense of connectedness not experienced at home. The sense of connectedness inhibits violence through concern about jeopardising relationships that are emotionally and developmentally important. From this perspective, zero tolerance policies that exclude problem children by means of suspension and expulsion are counterproductive because they weaken school bonds and undercut school as a protective factor (Sprott, Jenkins and Doob, 2005: 72). And, from a cost–benefit perspective, school exclusion is a costly policy. Pritchard and Cox (1998) calculated the financial costs of school exclusion as a means of dealing with individuals associated with educational and behavioural personality disorders. They scanned police records for a cohort of 227 adolescents in one county in England who had been in 'special educational provision' and 'excluded from school'. The subsequent criminality of this cohort was 'far worse' than expected of the general population. Within this cohort, 143 had been convicted of a criminal offence; this population had an average of 7.4 offences each, with about a third having a conviction for a violent offence. Based on estimates obtained from the Home Office, Audit Commission and Department of Health, Pritchard and Cox (1998: 617) calculated this group of 143 adolescents cost the public purse £4.16 million over a period of six years.

On the other hand, there is evidence to suggest that the relationship between school exclusion and criminal careers is not as clear as the 'minimise exclusions' policy assumed. Hodgson and Webb (2005) note that statements in government reports about school exclusions leading to crime have not received the scrutiny with which government claims are ordinarily met with by criminologists. They located 56 young people for interview who had been subject to a fixed-term or permanent school exclusion. They heard some surprising things: the overwhelming majority (90 per cent) said that their criminal behaviour commenced *prior* to their first exclusion, and nearly the same portion (84 per cent) said that being excluded from school did not have an impact on the likelihood of them offending. More than half said that they were *less* likely to engage in crime during the exclusion period, which is understandable, Hodgson and Webb (2005: 18) point out, because the majority experienced stricter parental control (grounding during the evenings as well as school hours).

In practice, there has been a shift in the government's policy after 2000. The government made it easier to exclude young persons from school leading to an increase in the number of exclusions. This change occurred in the wake of growing concern about the problem of indiscipline at schools, and particularly reports from teachers that pupil behaviour had deteriorated. In 2000, 13 teachers across England and Wales brought civil actions against the authorities for violence and intimidation directed at them by students and the National Union of Teachers threatened industrial action if headteachers did not exclude students who needed to be physically restrained. Physical restraint, the union argued, should not be seen as a normal or regular activity in schools (Harris, 2002: 71). The desire to minimise school exclusions in the interest of crime prevention should be balanced against the need to provide a safe working environment for teachers and a safe learning environment for students in the interest of pursuing educational goals.

Fear at School

Fear of victimisation at school is a serious issue for a significant portion of young people and their parents. The Department for Education and Employment estimates that one-third of girls and a quarter of boys have at some time feared attending school because of bullying (Furniss, 2000: 9). Noakes and Noakes (2000), who surveyed year 9 students in a South Wales valley community, found that about a third of boys and girls worried about victimisation within the school setting. More than a quarter of boys and girls reported having been bullied during their time at school; boys experienced name-calling, threats, hitting and pushing and girls tended to be victimised by gossip-spreading, name-calling and threats. The typical response, in the UK and elsewhere, has been the setting up of anti-bullying legal guidelines that schools must observe (Ananiadou and Smith, 2002).

Some have challenged this response: perceiving bullying as a school problem fails to recognise the detrimental and serious impact it has on its victims. Furniss (2000) argues for the criminalisation of bullying in situations where the school disciplinary measures are unable to tackle the problem and in cases where the bullying is too serious to be dealt with by school authorities alone. She argues for a changing perception of bullying along the lines of domestic violence and child abuse which have come to be regarded as problems requiring a criminal-justice response. An effective anti-bullying response could be seen as a meaningful part of an educational policy directed at crime reduction. Andershed, Kerr and Stattin (2001) carried out research among 14-year-olds in Sweden showing that the same people are involved in bullying in school and violence on the streets. In other words, bullying is part of a larger pattern of aggressive and violent behaviour in society and not the product of the school environment alone.

It is also possible that reducing bullying would contribute to a reduction in educational disengagement, truancy and early school-leaving and criminal careers associated with this population. MacDonald and Marsh (2005: 52), who interviewed 'disconnected youth' in Teesside in the northeast of England, found the majority had been victims of bullying. For some, 'getting tortured' explained their disengagement from education. This suggests that reducing the victimisation of students in schools not only improves the learning environment, but contributes to the goal of crime reduction.

Conclusion

Health policy and education policy have emerged as opportunities for advancing the goal of crime reduction, particularly within the language of ensuring 'safety'. But the overlap of these areas has been seen in different ways and leads in a number of situations to undesirable outcomes. Directing health and education resources to further goals of crime policy can lead to criminalisation of unhealthy behaviours and diminished learning environments within schools. Policymaking needs to be supported by clear thinking about the relative priority of crime reduction in social policy areas.

Questions for Discussion

1. *Do impoverished living conditions corrupt moral character as well as physical health?*

2. *Is criminal violence a health issue? Should doctors embrace the role of crime-fighter?*

3. *Does 'school crime' occur at, around, or within schools?*

4. *Does exclusion assign school troublemakers to a life of crime or improve the learning opportunities for students?*

Further Reading

Leon Feinstein and Ricardo Sabates (2005) *Education and Youth Crime.* Centre for Research on the Wider Benefits of Learning. London: Institute of Education. www.learningbenefits.net

Nicola Gray, Judith Laing and Lesley Noakes (2002) *Criminal Justice, Mental Health and the Politics of Risk.* London: Cavendish.

Carol Hayden, Tom Williamson and Richard Webber (2006) 'Schools, Behaviour and Young Offenders' *British Journal of Criminology.* Advance access published 28 July 2006. doi:10.1093/bjc/az1053

Gerry Johnstone (1996) *Medical Concepts and Penal Policy.* London: Cavendish.

Crime and Unemployment

SUMMARY

- The relationship between unemployment and crime has been explained as a feature of short-term consumption cycles, potential victims, and profound discouragement
- The relationship between unemployment and crime may be explained by: secondary labour market participation, 'worklessness' in communities, the social 'embeddedness' of work and crime
- The belief that unemployment leads to crime may lead to more unemployed people in prison
- The crime wave that did not occur during the depression suggests that economic policy reduces crime when it is not seen as crime reduction strategy

The Italian film *Ladri di Biciclette* (1948), 'Bicycle Thieves', depicts the connection between unemployment and crime common to mainstream criminology and orthodox economic theory. Just when Antonio receives a job posting bills that allows his family to avoid destitution, his bicycle, essential for the new job, is stolen. He makes a desperate search through the streets of Rome, but cannot recover his property. Demoralised and disillusioned, he resorts to stealing someone else's bicycle.

But as obvious as this connection would seem to be, it is surprisingly difficult to demonstrate statistically. Looking back at the twentieth century, crime rates did not increase during the depression of the 1930s but did increase during the decades of prosperity following the Second World War. The relationship begins to emerge during the 1970s when crime rates and unemployment rates both increase. While this statistical picture has led some to the conclusion that there is in reality 'no relationship', to others it suggests that the relationship is more complicated than the simple prediction suggests. Unemployment does not lead to crime directly but contributes to the overall effect of economic conditions on crime rates.

This chapter reviews major themes in research on unemployment, crime, and imprisonment. We will review key conceptual themes and methodological disputes en route to exploring the wisdom of utilising economic policy for crime-reduction purposes. The first part reviews three explanations for links between unemployment and crime trends. The second part considers three theories about the social meaning of unemployment. The third part describes research concerning links between unemployment and imprisonment. The final part considers the issue of 'economic anti-crime policies' in the context of relief efforts during the depression of the 1930s.

Crime Trends and Economic Conditions

Criminologists have offered several interpretations of trends in crime rates and unemployment rates in the decades since the Second World War (the post-war period). Rival interpretations reflect conceptual as well as methodological controversies.

Business Cycles and Crime

In 1990, Simon Field produced a report dealing with unemployment and crime for the Home Office that proved controversial politically. Home Office Minister John Patten dismissed Field's findings as soon as they were published (Cook, 1997: 35).

What Field (1990) said is that levels of unemployment influenced crime rates but the effect was mediated by short-term fluctuations in consumption. He connected the analysis of post-war crime trends in England and Wales with economic theorising about the importance of distinguishing between short-term and long-term influences. Economic models tend to assume that variables responsible for economic trends in the short-term have little influence on the overall economy in the long-term. Field proposed that crime, like the economy generally, is subject to short-term influences, which are very different from long-term causes. While unemployment has little significance in explaining the overall level of crime in the long-term, it does produce significant effects on changes in crime rates in the short-term (Field, 1990: 3–7).

At the national level, the unemployment rate over time is coincident with business cycles. Changes in unemployment rates do not reflect rising and lowering levels of poverty; the rate rises and falls rapidly without corresponding changes in other social factors such as housing conditions, family, educational or demographic circumstances. Unemployment, Field (1990: 7) contends, adds nothing to the explanation of crime trends once the key factor, consumption, is taken into account. During the four decades after the Second World War in England and Wales, the pattern of consumption growth mirrored the upward trend in property crime. He observed this same relationship in figures for the USA, Japan, and France, and to a lesser extent in Sweden and (what was then) West Germany.

Field's (1990) reading of the figures for Britain convinced him that fluctuations in crime were not associated with levels of unemployment, with one interesting exception: crimes of violence against the person were found to be strongly correlated to changes in the level of beer consumption and to changes in the amount of unemployment. This finding, he reasoned, could be explained by the fact that the statistical category of violent crime includes offences ranging from pub brawls to domestic violence. Following Bonger (1916), he suggested that violent crime increases during periods of prosperity owing to the tendency for young men to gather in pubs, consume a lot of beer, and get into fights. The relationship between violent crime and unemployment is likely to be related to the frustration of unemployment, particularly long-term unemployment. During periods of recession, the frustration of material deprivation may precipitate domestic violence.

Subsequent research has extended Field's model to find a more significant role for unemployment. Hale (1999) looked at crime and the business cycle in England and Wales between 1948 and 1991, and, by altering the statistical procedures, discovered significant relationships between unemployment and crime. While unemployment does not affect crime over the long term, it does nevertheless play some role in short-term fluctuations in property crime. When unemployment increases year after year, burglary and robbery are also likely to increase (Hale, 1999: 694). Scorcu and Cellini (1998) analysed the economic determinants of crime rates in Italy over the period of 1951 to 1994 and found that Field's views of the inter-relationships between crime, unemployment and consumption 'can hold in the long-run analysis as well'. They determined the level of real per capita consumption to be the best single explanatory factor for the long-run trend in homicide and robbery rates while the unemployment rate worked better as an explanation for trends in theft.

Behaviour of Criminals and Victims

Five years before Field's report, David Cantor and Kenneth Land (1985) produced an analysis leading to a methodological and conceptual dispute criminologists have been contributing to ever since.[1] They proposed that unemployment affects not only the behaviour of potential criminals, but also the behaviour of potential victims, and set out to test their theory with a look at crime rate and unemployment fluctuations in the USA between 1946 and 1982.

Cantor and Land expected that rising unemployment would lead to both a *decrease* and an *increase* in criminal activity. The most immediate consequence would be a decrease owing to the 'opportunity effect' consistent with routine activities theory (Cohen and Felson, 1979). As a result of fewer people working, there would be fewer people in public places, and this reduction in the 'circulation of people and property' reduces the opportunity for crime. At the same time, unemployment would lead to an increase in crime due to the

---

[1]The Journal of Quantitative Criminology devoted a special issue in 2001 to methodological arguments arising in the wake of their analysis.

'motivational effect'; unemployed people would be more highly motivated to break the law because they have a reduced income and financial needs. As unemployed people are unlikely to feel the economic impact of loss of income immediately, this effect should be more gradual. Cantor and Land found, across all crime categories studied, a negative impact overall suggesting that the negative opportunity impacts outweighed the positive motivational impacts. But they stressed the importance of both 'positive motivational and negative opportunity impacts'. Attempts to measure the impact of unemployment on crime rates would need to account for these counter-acting causal structures.

Based on their analysis of unemployment and crime in the UK, Chris Hale and Dima Sabbagh (1991: 401) challenged the American researchers' methodology and the theory behind it. Hale and Sabbagh found the opportunity effect argument, 'the idea that the unemployed spend long hours at home and hence less opportunity for burglary', to be 'somewhat contentious', and found the empirical analysis to be 'statistically inadequate within the terms of reference they set for themselves' (Hale and Sabbagh, 1991: 413). Their own analysis of the situation in England and Wales for 1949–87 turned up significant statistical relationships for the majority of crime categories they studied. This suggested that unemployment did increase crime, although it was important to distinguish the unemployment effect from effects of criminal justice (likelihood of detection and severity of punishment). They added that unemployment has a separate effect on use of imprisonment (to be discussed below). Cantor and Land responded, defending both their methodology and conclusions (Cantor and Land, 1991; Cantor, Land and Russell, 1994).

Subsequent researchers have put the Cantor and Land model, or variations of it, to good effect. Beki, Zeelenberg, and van Montfort (1999) found evidence of the opportunity effect in their analysis of crime in the Netherlands for the period 1950–93. Their findings were consistent with the theory that a higher unemployment rate decreases the number and value of the goods stolen: unemployment has a significant negative effect on most crimes of theft. The Dutch researchers also suggest why such knowledge might be important in a policy context; building an accurate model of the relationships would be of use in forecasting criminal justice resources (Beki, Zeelenberg, and van Montfort, 1999: 415). Arvanites and Defina (2006) applied the model to American data for the period 1986–2000. Rates of street crimes increased during the 1980s before declining in the 1990s, and the economy, while in recession in the 1980s, had begun to rebound after 1992. They determined that their results supported the motivation hypothesis: an improving economy is associated with decreasing rates of property crime (burglary, larceny, and motor vehicle theft) as well as robbery (a violent crime with economic motivation). A stronger economy, they conclude, would bring about reductions in crime.

Cultural Meaning and Social Contexts

Steven Box went a long way toward unravelling the intricacies of unemployment and crime. Drawing on strain and anomie elements of sociological theory, he argued that research findings related to crime and unemployment could only be resolved by research taking into account the *'meaning* and *duration* of the unemployment'* (Box, 1987: 97).

Box theorised that only a portion of the unemployed during a recession would be likely to turn to property and violent crimes, based on their understanding of, and intensity of feelings about, their failure to remain employed. Those who believe themselves to be temporarily out of work due to wider economic forces are unlikely to cross the line into illegal work because they do not want to jeopardise what they expect will be a return to work. But those who view unemployment as a personal crisis are likely to turn to crime as the period of unemployment becomes longer and the sense of injustice, discontent, despair and hopelessness grows. 'What inequalities and unemployment *mean* becomes crucially important', and this subjective element is likely to vary by gender, age-cohort, and over time. So although many factors contribute to this subjective element, one in particular – the duration of unemployment – is expected to lead to criminal behaviour. 'The long-term unemployed, especially the young long-term unemployed who see no future before them, clearly have greater problems than those who merely slip on and off the unemployment register because of minor friction in the labour market' (Box, 1987: 40).

Subsequent studies of Box's theory produced mixed results. Orme (1994) looked for a relationship between rates of change in unemployment and recorded crime across police force areas in the UK during the period 1984 to 1992. To learn whether the amount of time out of work was associated with increased crime, she lagged the unemployment data by one and four quarters. Overall, there was not enough evidence to suggest a correlation between unemployment and recorded crime. Nor was she able to test Box's other argument about gender and age as police information about crime rates did not break them down in this way and the data did not include information for youth unemployment. Dorling (2005), who points to an extraordinary murder rate for the cohort of British men born in 1965 and after, does offer some support. He explains that these men would have left school during the recession of the early 1980s. The summer of 1981 was the first summer in 40 years that a man living in a poor area would have faced a scarcity of work and training. There is no 'natural' rate of murder, Dorling insists. For the murder rate to increase for a particular group of people, 'life in general has to be more difficult to live, people have to be made to feel more worthless' (Dorling, 2005: 190).

Box's argument about the meaning of unemployment, and particularly about how women might see unemployment differently from men, raises a question about whether the popular theory that unemployment leads to crime really only has to do with how men perceive work. 'If criminologists were to commence their theorising with female data', Naffine and Gale (1989: 154) have argued, 'it is unlikely that they would draw a connection between unemployment and crime'. They point out that in most studies, the relationship between gender, unemployment, and crime sinks to insignificance because the figures involved are overwhelmingly male. Researchers tend to see unemployment as a factor in crime as a feature of the way men see it; unemployment is thought to be such a calamity that it provokes criminal activity. Naffine and Gale (1989: 146), quoting Box and Hale (1985: 215), point out that women who find themselves without work in the public sphere do not resort to crime but are more likely to 'slip back into or take up the wife/mother social role'.

The Social Meaning of Work

Orthodox economic theory assumes that unemployment leads to crime as persons resort to acquiring by illegal means what they cannot afford to purchase. Several criminological theories question this assumption. These theories contend that it is not the financial aspect of unemployment but social and cultural aspects of work and worklessness that lead to crime.

Labour Markets

The focus on unemployment understates the importance of labour markets. Many dimensions of the labour market, such as the distribution of jobs by skill and location, affect crime rates. The theory of a dual or split labour market holds that there are two kinds of employment sectors. The primary labour market features stable employment, meaningful wages, and prospects for advancement. Workers in this sector tend to be better educated, to be older, and to be more motivated. The secondary labour market is characterised by lower wages and frequent periods of joblessness. Workers tend to be low-skilled, less educated, and younger (Fagan and Freeman, 1999). The work-related incentives to commit crime are not evenly distributed across society but occur in a labour market environment in which individuals choose legal work or crime as a function of risk, legal wages, and criminal returns. Further, these incentives occur at the group level. Those within the secondary labour market are more likely to see some advantage in criminal activity than those in the primary labour market. The poor, less educated, and young have more to gain from crime because they have less to gain from working in a legal job.

   The idea of becoming unemployed and turning to crime implies that the decision is an either/or, but many youths combine crime and work or shift between them readily. As Fagan and Freeman (1999: 260) point out, the attractions of illegal work are reflected in variables often unmeasured in econometric analyses of crime and work, especially tastes and preferences. For many young men, illegal activities serve as temporary or transitional work or supplement difficult low-wage or otherwise unsatisfactory work, a strategy that has been called 'doubling-up'. For others, legal work provides an alternative to riskier illegal work or perhaps offers opportunities for particular kinds of crimes. Essentially, labour market incentives influence the supply of young men to crime, and specifically the collapse of the job market for those with few skills during the 1980s and 1990s contributed to an increase in their criminal activity (Freeman, 1996: 30).

Freeman advocates a carrot-and-stick policy: the carrot, improvement in the labour market situation for youth with few skills, and the stick, increased spending for police and prisons. To reduce the level of crime over the long-term, more resources need to be devoted to improving job opportunities for young people, the poor, and other groups likely to turn to crime otherwise. One means of doing this would be to alter wage incentives for the low-skilled labour market by means of the minimum wage. Hansen and Machin (2002) evaluated crime patterns across England and Wales before and after introduction of the National Minimum Wage in 1999. This regulation provided pay increases for quite a large number of low-wage workers (£3.60 for workers 22 years of age or older and £3 for those between 18 and 21 years of age.) They found a significant relationship, revealing crime reductions in areas that had a larger number of low-wage workers, which led them to conclude that altering wage incentives can lead to measurable reductions in crime.

The Impact of Worklessness

Sociological theories emphasise how the behaviour of individuals in one area of the labour market influence the individual's decision to engage in crime. Chiricos (1987: 195) points out that studies of unemployment and crime involving comparison of areas of cities at the neighbourhood level (as opposed to time series analyses of national data) are more likely to turn up 'milieu effects'. High unemployment in a particular area of a city that creates a climate of despair or hopelessness has a criminogenic effect even for those who are not unemployed, such as teenagers and others not in the labour force.

William J. Wilson (1996) explains unemployment in the context of the 'new urban poverty' in the USA, a reference to residential areas in which the majority of adults are either unemployed, have dropped out of the job market, or have never been part of the labour force. Many problems of Black ghetto neighbourhoods – crime, poverty, family dissolution – are a consequence of the disappearance of work. In the 1950s, a substantial portion of the ghetto Black population was poor, and by the 1970s, this poverty had become increasingly concentrated. By the 1990s, levels of joblessness reached unprecedented levels, due to the spread of new technologies, increasing suburbanisation of jobs, and the growing internationalisation of economic activity. This had disastrous consequences. Wilson (2003: 1103) states: 'A neighbourhood in which people are poor, but employed, is very different from a neighbourhood in which people are poor and jobless'.

Being unemployed does not necessarily mean 'not working', being totally removed from all forms of work activity. Many people who are officially unemployed are involved in all kinds of work, including participating in informal or illegal economies that derive income. There is an important difference in the sense that work within informal and illegal economies is less regulated by expectations and standards that require discipline and punctuality. Participation in the formal economy provides a framework for daily behaviour because of the discipline and regularity it imposes. In the absence of a regular job, a person lacks not only a predictable source of income, but also a coherent pattern for daily life, that is, a system of concrete expectations and goals. Regular employment provides an anchor for social life; it establishes a place to be and time for being there. Persistent unemployment thwarts daily planning in social life, a necessary condition for full participation in industrial society (Wilson, 1999: 481–2).

The criminogenic aspect of unemployment then is 'worklessness' which makes it increasingly difficult to sustain neighbourhood institutions (McGahey, 1986). Parents in workless neighbourhoods have a much more difficult time controlling the behaviour of their teenage children as a result. People who reside in such neighbourhoods also find it more difficult to find secure work owing to the stigma associated with these areas and as a consequence of being isolated from conventional social institutions. Persons from workless neighbourhoods lack not only the 'hard skills' (literacy, numeracy, mechanical skills) but the 'soft skills' (grooming, conversation). The social skills acquired by residing in workless neighbourhoods – maintaining a tough demeanour, avoiding eye contact – are helpful for survival in the ghetto but hinder integration in mainstream society (Wilson, 1999: 487).

Social Embeddedness

John Hagan (1993) argues that the missing piece in understanding crime and unemployment is recognising 'the social relations in which economic life is embedded'. Drawing on work from Granovetter (1992), Hagan proposes that there is a social structure to the employment process; it involves socially embedded networks of contacts. Within this setting, jobs are not obtained through individual efforts or characteristics alone, but connections available within social frames. Initial job mobility is important because of its potential to widen these connections and facilitate upward job mobility. At the same time, difficulty in breaking into the labour force dampens employment prospects by limiting these contacts. The relationship between unemployment and crime does not depend on the assumption of need-based material motivation, but youth crime prior to employment (Hagan, 1993: 468–9).

Thornberry (1987: 883) argued that youths who live in impoverished neighbourhoods have difficulty finding employment because their families and friends are likely to have few job connections. This places them on a 'behavioural trajectory' likely to result in delinquency and crime. He explained the situation in sociological terms borrowed from Hirschi's social bond theory; initially weak bonds coincident with economic marginality lead to delinquent involvement, and more serious delinquent involvement further weakens these bonds by contributing to marginality with respect to the labour force. The combination of this process makes it extremely difficult to secure a place within the conventional labour force. Hagan's analysis of a cohort of boys born in 1950 in London led him to place delinquency *before* unemployment in the life course. The youths Hagan studied did not move from unemployment to crime, but instead, their adolescent ties involving gang activity made it increasingly difficult as adults to find employment. 'The analysis indicates that early embeddedness among delinquent friends and continuing delinquent behaviour leads to adult unemployment' (Hagan, 1993: 486).

Embeddedness explains a counter-intuitive finding related to youth employment and delinquency: a number of researchers have concluded that youth employment leads to delinquency (Ploeger, 1997; Cullen, Williams and Wright, 1997). A study from Finland, where a significant portion of grade 9 students work during the school year, found that working long hours led to delinquency; in this case, activities such as beating someone, buying stolen goods, vandalism at school, and drunken driving. Youth employment does not necessarily encourage delinquent behaviour, however; it depends on the kind of job. Traditionally adolescent jobs (babysitting and piece-rate hobby work) decreased the likelihood of heavy drinking while adult-like jobs (fast food restaurant, clerical and cleaning work) increased heavy drinking (Kouvonen and Kivivuori, 2001: 206). The primary advantage of traditional adolescent jobs may be the access they provide to social networks of adults in a position to offer stable and permanent employment, while youth employment in adult-like jobs places them in a social network where the adults are themselves unconnected to networks affording meaningful adult employment.

Unemployment and Imprisonment

In a sense, it does not matter whether criminologists and economists ever resolve the methodological issues involved in statistical models related to unemployment and crime. The belief that unemployment causes crime is likely to have more to do with policy than the 'facts' of the matter. As Box and Hale (1985: 209) observe:

> The relationship between unemployment and crime is nowhere near as simple or demonstrated as is commonly claimed ... . Nonetheless, it is clear that many people *believe* that unemployment causes crime, and this belief has real consequences, particularly when it affects decisions taken by state officials processing suspected and convicted persons.

Box and Hale are among a number of researchers to call attention to a relationship between unemployment and criminal justice decision-making within a larger economic context.

Punishment and Social Structure

Beginning in the 1970s, a series of empirical studies has appeared exploring the relationship between unemployment and imprisonment. Researchers in this genre typically cite *Punishment and Social Structure* by George Rusche and Otto Kirchheimer (1939), the first major work of the Frankfurt school of critical theory to appear in English.

In this historical study, Rusche and Kirchheimer aimed to show that the type of punishment in society (fines, deportation, prison) does not follow from the ostensible goal of suppressing crime but from specific economic conditions, chiefly the labour market. 'Every system of production', they (1939: 5) argued, 'tends to discover punishments which correspond to its productive relationships'. Essentially, they argued for an historically contingent connection between the kind of punishment in society and the state of the labour market, according to which the harshness of sanction is inversely proportional to the value of human beings, that is, the value of labour. 'Less eligibility', as they explained, became the leitmotif of prison administration (Rusche and Kirchheimer, 1939: 94).

Less eligibility refers to a principle established in the Poor Laws (1834) that the living situation of the able-bodied recipient of poor relief should not be made as 'eligible' or comfortable as the lowest paid labourer. Consistent with this logic, a rise in unemployment would lead to an increase in prison commitments because the policy of deterrence indicates that harsher or more intensive punishments are needed to counteract the increased temptation to commit crime. In an economic environment characterised by labour surplus and declining conditions for the working class, the conditions of confinement for prison workers had to be harsh enough to keep the working class from turning to crime. In support of this logic, Rusche offered George Bernard Shaw's comment: 'if the prison does not underbid the slum in human misery, the slum will empty and the prison will fill' (quoted in Feest, 1999: 105).

By 1990, the theoretical argument in *Punishment and Social Structure* had inspired at least 44 empirical studies (Chiricos and DeLone, 1992). More studies have appeared since then, leading to lively debates about just what Rusche and Kirchheimer would predict. Researchers have taken 'harsher punishment' to mean greater use of incarceration, longer sentences, or both. Generally, researchers have tried to explain changes in rates of imprisonment as a function of economic conditions, including unemployment. A major strategy is to divide the twentieth century into periods based on changes in the economy – and usually the economy of interest is the American economy – and equate these with fluctuations in imprisonment rates. Michalowski and

Carlson (1999), for instance, examine three production cycles in the USA from 1933 to 1979. They argue that while the 1930s and 1970s were periods of high structural unemployment, social welfare programmes targeted toward White men in the 1930s reduced what would otherwise have been a greater reliance on imprisonment.

The theoretical argument in *Punishment and Social Structure* does not specify a direct and positive relationship between imprisonment rates and unemployment rates. Melossi (2003: 250) points out that Rusche did not intend to explain the *size* of the prison population in a historical period, but rather the *conditions* of confinement that imprisonment as a form of punishment would take. In periods when the market is flooded with labour, the conditions of confinement deteriorate along with the general standard of living for the working class. In periods of labour scarcity, the conditions of confinement improve, and work becomes part of the disciplinary regimen. Melossi (2003: 255) also points out that the Rusche/Kirchheimer hypothesis does not really aim to explain imprisonment as a result of short-term economic fluctuations or business cycles. Changes in prison conditions respond to long cycles within capitalism, and as such, reflect much more of the sense of punishment within the surrounding culture.

What has made *Punishment and Social Structure* so popular within the sociology of punishment is the contention that punishment serves a purpose other than crime control. Dominant groups within market economies make use of legal sanctions whenever the interests of these elites are threatened, typically when living standards are decreased, or unemployment increased. In other words, imprisonment should be understood as a form of economic policy. Large surplus labour populations threaten market economies, and economic elites within these nations use imprisonment to manage the underclass when employment increases (Ruddell, 2005: 8–10).

Western and Beckett (1999) and Wacquant (2000) extend this logic to the growth of imprisonment in the USA in recent decades. Western and Beckett argue that the high rate of imprisonment lowers government figures for unemployment by concealing joblessness among able-bodied, working-age men. At the same time, it raises unemployment over the long-term by damaging employment possibilities of prisoners once released. Imprisonment deepens inequality because it affects disproportionately African-American men, who experience the highest imprisonment rates along with lowered labour market potential. They predict that sustaining low unemployment in future will depend on a continuing expansion of the prison system. Wacquant argues that the prison has replaced the ghetto as a means of containing African Americans. The decline of the manufacturing economy of the 1970s meant that America's industrial cities lost their ability to confine outcast Black men and the prison was needed to enclose the threat of deproletarianised actions of the Black working class. Increasing numbers were sent to prison, Wacquant proposes, owing to a combination of skills deficit, racial discrimination and competition from immigrants, and the refusal of Black men to submit to the indignity of substandard work – referred to by ghetto residents as 'slave jobs'.

Imprisonment and Economic Policy

Thinking about imprisonment as a form of economic policy invokes two conundrums of critical criminology: determinism and conspiracy. Rusche's and Kirchheimer's model has been criticised for overestimating the influence of economic conditions in determining punishment practice. David Garland (1990: 105–10) says that they produced a selective account of historical practices in keeping with their 'single-minded interpretation' of punishment and attitudes about crime and punishment. This suggests the need to grasp the internal dynamics of punishment policy, as well as the 'symbols and social messages' conveyed to the wider public. Why, Garland (1990: 109) asks, does support for punitive measures receive such widespread support among the working class (if such measures are about suppressing their interests)? Rusche and Kirchheimer do not explain this.

Studies conducted across national contexts support Garland's claim about the political aspect of punishment. Sutton (2000) looked at imprisonment rates in Australia, Canada, New Zealand, the UK and the USA from 1955 to 1985. He concluded that prison growth in these countries is driven by both crime rates and unemployment rates, but also by welfare spending and the relative political power of rightist political parties. Fluctuations in labour markets do shape levels of imprisonment: when opportunities for legitimate employment expand, prison growth slows. Or, to put it the other way around, prison populations increase during economic downturns, when social spending is constrained, and when conservative political parties control the police agenda. Von Hofer (2003) analysed imprisonment trends in Finland, Netherlands, and Sweden from 1950 to 2000. He found that fluctuations in imprisonment did not reflect those for crimes rates in these countries, but neither did they follow trends in economic development, unemployment or social marginalisation. Rates of prisoners were a function of criminal justice and social policies that encouraged or discouraged the use of incarceration, and increases in incarceration always occurred because no strong political opposition challenged the course of events.

The Rusche–Kirchheimer model has also been criticised for implying a conspiracy model of policymaking. Greenberg (1977: 650) has argued that Rusche's and Kirchheimer's proposal that judges in criminal courts adjust their sentencing practices chiefly or solely to accommodate the requirements of employers is 'far-fetched'. Perhaps the monarchs of the seventeenth century could inform judges of their need for galley slaves, but in the contemporary era, prime ministers and presidents exercise no such power. The greater likelihood of a prison term for unemployed lawbreakers, he suggests, results from decision-making processes in which judges are less willing to assign community penalties to unemployed, or that unemployment affects levels of community tolerance and exerts a kind of political pressure to which judges respond. Box and Hale (1982: 21), agreeing with Greenberg, find unsatisfying the 'conspiracy account' of unemployment and imprisonment 'in which the powerful deliberately attempt to fragment and...discipline the unemployed by increasing rates of ... imprisonment'.

The tendency to imprison unemployed lawbreakers operates as an unintended, even unconscious, aspect of every decision-making within the court environment, and not, as an overly enthusiastic reading of *Punishment and Social Structure* would lead one to surmise, as the conspiratorial strategy of industry leaders and their political operatives. Judges do not make sentencing decisions involving unemployed convicts within a mindset of the economic value of labour nor as a matter of political legitimacy, but see their work within an organisational context consistent with bourgeois ideology. Although they do not impose sentences with the economic value of labour or the political legitimacy of the State in mind, their decisions reproduce an ideology consistent with system maintenance. Judges are more likely to assign prison to unemployed defendants convicted of crimes in the belief that they represent greater risks to the community, attributing their joblessness to a character flaw that makes them less likely to succeed or even a greater risk to the community (Box and Hale 1982).

Hale (1984) describes the political environment that developed in Britain in the years after 1974. The Labour party of 1945–51 committed the government to full employment and improved living conditions for the working class. But following the payments crisis of 1965–6, the full employment policy was replaced by sterling devaluation and industrial rationalisation. These measures failed, leading to a growing fiscal crisis in the 1970s. There were increasing tensions in industrial relations culminating in the Miners' strike of 1974. The number of men unemployed doubled by 1976 and increased by a factor of five by 1984. In the 1979 election, the Conservative party made law and order a recurring them; Conservative rhetoric emphasised the activity of labour unions as a threat to public order and welfare dependency as symptomatic of moral decline and faltering personal responsibility. It is no coincidence, Hale (1984) insists, that 1974 marked the end of proportionate use of imprisonment and the beginning of a prison-building programme. More unemployed men went to prison, not because judges joined in a Thatcherite conspiracy, but because 'the climate developed in this period in Britain was one in which the prejudices of the judiciary were reinforced by a media campaign supportive of the Conservative Party's ideas on moral decay and overdependence on the state' (Hale, 1984: 343). Punishment, from this perspective, does reflect interests other than crime control, but these 'other interests' are political and not exclusively economic. (We will consider the impact of imprisonment on social welfare in Chapter 8.)

Crime and the Depression

Every discussion about unemployment, crime, and the appropriate policy response invokes, sooner or later, the issue of crime during the depression era. In Britain, the fear that wide-scale unemployment would lead to crime and social conflict was put forward by several commentators. Articles appeared in newspapers with titles such as 'The Deadly Dole: From Idleness to Crime'. But as early as 1940, when Mannheim published his study of crime in England and Wales, he concluded that no direct correlation had been found (Stevenson and Cook, 1994: 101–2). The fact that the economic slump did not correspond with a massive crime wave has generated evocative arguments about the potential for economic policy to affect crime.

One of most compelling explanations for the crime wave that did not occur has to do with the economic policies put in place as a response. In the USA, it was the 'New Deal' initiated after Franklin D. Roosevelt became president in 1933. Criminologists have seen in the New Deal not only an explanation for why crime did not increase despite massive unemployment and poverty, but a contemporary policy solution for crime in the USA (Wilson, 1996; Currie, 1998) and UK (Downes, 1997). Downes points to the criminogenic situation brought about by despair and pessimism experienced in connection with prolonged unemployment. Primary labour market work is the most effective means of circumventing this spiral of despair as 'nothing short ... of Roosevelt's New Deal is needed to halt, let alone reverse this trend' (Downes, 1997: 3; see also NACRO, 1995: 35). Understanding *why* the New Deal worked as a crime-reduction measure affords significant insight into the effectiveness of economic policies as anti-crime policies.

Crime rates in the United States increased during the late 1920s until 1933, one of the highest-crime years of the decade, then began to decline. This decrease might be explained, as Pandiani (1982) argues, by the operation of the Civilian Conservation Corps (CCC), a New Deal economic measure. The programme offered jobs working in forests and national parks to young, unemployed men from the cities. The programme provided, in addition to room, board, and clothing, a salary of $30 a month; the enrolees were required to allot all but $5 each month to their dependants. During its eight years, the CCC planted more than two million acres of trees, constructed 6837 dams, and built 118,000 miles of roads. At its peak in 1935, the CCC operated 2650 camps with a total enrolment of 500,000 men (Pandiani, 1982: 350). Pandiani (1982) suggests that the voluntary migration of thousands of men, in their crime-prone years, from the cities to work-camps in wilderness areas, where they existed under military discipline, probably circumvented the amount of criminal activity that would have occurred otherwise. The CCC, he contends, should be thought of as the 'Crime Control Corps'.

Roosevelt did not propose the CCC with crime reduction in mind. Although the Roosevelt Administration was concerned about crime, they believed in the federalisation of law enforcement as a solution and consciously built up the

Federal Bureau of Investigation (FBI) to lead a crusade against it. Roosevelt regarded the CCC, as he explained in his initial message to Congress, as a means of providing economic relief for unemployed men and their families. When he addressed the nation in 1936 on the third anniversary of the CCC, he made no reference to crime. Attempting to win support for the programme as a crime-reduction strategy would have undermined one of his chief aims for New Deal programmes: respite from fear. He did want to instil fear, but hope and confidence. Not until 1939, in a speech to the National Parole Conference, did Roosevelt realise he had come up with a successful crime prevention measure.

> When we instituted these activities we did not have in mind merely the narrow purpose of preventing crime. However, nobody who knows how demoralising the effects of enforced idleness may be, will be inclined to doubt that our effort to provide our needy unemployed citizens with the opportunity to earn by honest work at least the bare necessities of life. (Pandiani, 1982: 352).

The CCC succeeded as a crime-reduction measure, it would seem, because neither the general public, nor the enrolees themselves, thought about it in this way. Had Roosevelt told the American people he was engaged in staving off a crime wave, he would have stigmatised hundreds of thousands of men as 'potential criminals' and their dependants as 'problem families'. The return of hundreds of thousands of 'dangerous men' to the cities would have generated local politicians' concern about rising crime rates and public anxiety over outbreaks of criminality. Roosevelt had described the programme as a means of restoring dignity to idle workers and in this way reinforced the meaningfulness of their pursuits. Men planted trees, dammed rivers, and so on, in the belief that they were restoring vital natural resources as well as contributing to their families. Had they been told their hard work was primarily intended to keeping them out of the city and out of trouble, it would have demoralised their interest and undermined their willingness to shoulder improvements to the nation's infrastructure. They would have resented austere conditions at the camps as ahead-of-schedule imprisonment. Justifying the Civilian Conservation Corps as a crime-reduction measure would have been a disaster.

The lesson about crime and unemployment to be taken from the depression era seems to be that economic policies are successful as crime reduction measures when they are *not seen* as crime reduction measures. For this reason, policymakers should avoid justifying economic relief policies as crime-reduction strategies. This line of political argument makes the potential for criminality, rather than a state of need, the reason for government provision of social welfare. Raising the idea of criminal threat as a rationale for meeting people's needs not only maligns the intended recipients of government economic relief, but alienates the people who imagine themselves paying for it. Economic policies should be justified on the basis of hope, not fear.

Conclusion

Methodological and conceptual controversies make it difficult to draw firm conclusions about the relationship between crime and unemployment. The relationship between crime and unemployment is important in the context of overall economic conditions. And, drawing on historical experience, what can be said is that economic policies with the biggest potential to reduce crime are those that remain invisible as crime policies.

Questions for Discussion

1. *Does unemployment lead to crime? What is the best explanation for trends in crime and unemployment since the Second World War?*

2. *Should young people be encouraged to work while in school or not?*

3. *Does unemployment have the same effect on women as is does on men?*

4. *Is the fact that a majority of people in prison were unemployed prior to sentence proof that unemployment leads to imprisonment? What would it take to demonstrate that unemployment leads to imprisonment?*

5. *Should politicians concerned about reducing crime pursue economic policy? How should they go about it?*

Further Reading

Dee Cook (1997) *Poverty, Crime and Punishment*. London: Child Poverty Action Group.

Elliott Currie (1985) *Crime and Punishment in America*. New York: Henry Holt.

Raymond Paternoster and Shawn D. Bushway (2001) 'Theoretical and Empirical Work on the Relationship Between Unemployment and Crime', *Journal of Quantitative Criminology* 17: 391–407.

Ian Taylor (1990) *Crime in Context: A Critical Theory of Market Societies*. Cambridge: Polity Press.

Crime, Family and Youth Policy

SUMMARY

- Research concerning families and crime has been associated with contested policy terms such as 'problem families' and the 'cycle of deprivation'
- The relationship between families and crime has been explained along the lines of: developmental pathways, structural disadvantage, and the cycle of violence
- Youth policy is increasingly driven by concepts of early intervention and risk-focused prevention

Youth policy has always included a focus on delinquency prevention, but in recent years the aims of prevention have shifted. Traditionally, the goal has been to prevent delinquents from growing up into adult criminals. This has been replaced to an increasing extent by the goal of preventing young persons from engaging in delinquency. This newer goal has led to the search for more accurate means of identifying those children headed for trouble and finding the earliest possible points for intervention. And it has brought about a re-location of the centre of youth policy, from a legal institution, the youth court, to a social institution, the family.

Since the Second World War, the family has never been far away from discussions of youth, crime, and social policy. So long as prevention and early intervention remain key aspects of youth policy, it is likely to remain so. That said, formulating a consistent policy guide has proven difficult because of the tendency to see the family in very different ways. The family is seen as the principal site for the manufacture of social problems and as a roundabout where major social pressures converge. Family-centred crime policies tend to fuse images of families as both troubled and troublesome.

The first part of this chapter reviews recent interest in the family as a site for criminality prevention. The second part reviews three lines of criminological research on the relationship between families and crime. The third part deals with two themes important to contemporary policy discussions: early intervention and risk-focused prevention.

Family-Centred Crime Policy

Politicians have conceptualised the family's relationship to crime in different ways. Terms such as 'problem families', 'cycle of deprivation', and 'pro-family policies' have contributed to the social policy response.

Problem Families

During the 1940s, Bowlby (1944) popularised the view that family dynamics led to delinquency. He completed his first empirical study, 'Forty-Four Juvenile Thieves', while a fellow in psychiatry at the London Child Guidance Clinic. He found that delinquents were more likely than non-delinquents to have suffered the trauma of separation from their mothers during the first five years of life. Borrowing insights from Freud, he concluded that most of these delinquents could be characterised as displaying an 'affectionless character'. Prolonged separations of children from mothers explained both frequent delinquent activity as well as particular kinds of delinquent acts (Dixon, 2003).

Bowlby's perspective acquired significance in problem-families research. The 'problem families' concept originated in middle-class concern over the 'underclass', occasioned by the wartime evacuation of London children to rural locations. The *Our Towns* report of 1943, produced by the Women's Group on Public Welfare, said the evacuation had brought to light a *sub rosa* category of persons.

> Within this group are the 'problem families', always on the edge of pauperism and crime, riddled with mental and physical neglect, a menace to the community, of which the gravity is out of all proportion to their numbers. (Quoted in Macnicol, 1999: 70)

The problem families concept guided interventions carried out by a generation of public health authorities, social workers, and housing managers. Also, it attracted the interest of several groups who made use of the concept in advancing their own agendas. The Eugenics Society, Family Service Units, and local Medical Officers of Health sponsored a series of problem family investigations during the 1940s and 1950s (Macinol, 1999: 72).

A few investigators offered formal definitions, but most went ahead with their research as if the meaning of the term was obvious. For C.P. Blacker, writing on behalf of the Eugenics Society, problem families had to do with the failings of parents. 'Problem parents' did not grasp the benefit of education, lived in chaotic and dirty homes, and produced too many children. Other definitions zeroed in on the failings of mothers. Catherine Wright, Deputy Medical Officer of Health in Sheffield, contributed a series of reports beginning in 1955 that followed up 120 problem families. Her counterparts in Bristol, Liverpool, Southampton and other cities produced similar studies, collectively promoting the construct of the 'problem mother'. Problem mothers did not raise their children properly, the researchers said, because they suffered from a mental condition, were addicted to drink, or lacked maternal vigilance (Starkey, 2000).

Problem-families research can be said to have inspired theoretical and methodological innovations in criminology. In the USA, Robert Merton found in it a useful example of 'retreatism'. In 1957, he wrote that examples of retreatism had been uncovered among problem families in England (Welshman, 1999: 469). The problem-families concept also promoted the usefulness of lon-gitudinal studies to investigate inter-generational continuities in delinquency and other social problems. Longitudinal analysis involves identifying a sample of young persons (all born in a particular year, for instance) and collecting information about them (from interviews; school and other records) as they grow into adulthood.

By the late 1950s, however, the concept had become subject to criticism. *The Problem of the 'Problem Family'* (Timms and Philp, 1957) undertook a stock-taking exercise with respect to the literature and raised a number of concep-tual and policy-oriented shortcomings. Richard Titmuss provided an apt summation when he declared in the foreword of this book that the problem families theme had been pursued in a 'singularly uncritical manner' and served as a means of demeaning poor people.

The Cycle of Deprivation

During the 1970s, the family became the focus of a highly polarised policy debate. Sir Keith Joseph, Secretary of State for Social Services, proposed that many of the difficulties associated with social deprivation were 'home-made'. In referring to a 'cycle of deprivation', Joseph said that deprivation might be transmitted from one generation to the next through poor household manage-ment and broken homes.

Guided in part by problem-families research, Joseph talked about a category of poor families whose poverty was not caused by a lack of income, but inter-related difficulties of temperament, intelligence, income and health com-pounded across generations. While small in number, these families amplified the troubles of various groups including deprived children, deserted spouses, families of alcoholics and prisoners, and those who experienced family disso-lution. He established the Working Party on Transmitted Deprivation to pro-mote an understanding of the cycle. Between 1974 and 1982, the Working Party underwrote 19 research studies, 14 literature reviews and 4 feasibility projects (Welshman, 2005: 307).

Social policy analysts took little interest in Joseph's cycle of deprivation. Peter Townsend denounced it as 'a mixture of popular stereotypes and ill-developed, mostly contentious, scientific notions' (quoted in Welshman, 2005: 335). The theory of an inter-generational family cycle diverted attention from structural factors and tended to blame the victims. It confused structural and individual explanations of deprivation, and uncritical acceptance of it risked a return to the nineteenth-century view of poverty as the fault of the poor.

Joseph's efforts to promote marriage and family aroused the ire of some MPs who criticised the scapegoating of single parents. Critics of the pro-family project also sought to defend the 'Titmuss paradigm' – unconditional, non-judgemental welfare provision – against the insinuation that personal behaviour contributed to poverty and that social policy should be contingent on some element of personal responsibility (Deacon, 2000: 9). From this perspective, association of the idea of family factors in crime causation represented a politically motivated effort to undercut the welfare state. By the end of the 1970s, opposition to any explanation of poverty that strayed from a structural emphasis resulted in a moratorium on family as a topic of policy research. In the context of crime, research into the family became, like Mrs Thatcher's handbag, a symbol of rightist politics.

Family Support Policies

In 1993 or so, the idea of family-centred crime policy received new support from some unexpected sources. Tony Blair, then Shadow Home Secretary, insisted that Labour had to acknowledge the importance of family. Responding to John Major's 'back to basics' speech at the Conservative party conference, Blair insisted that there was a need for pro-family policies. 'I think the current debate about parenthood, families, and crime is important to people like me', he said, '... [because] it gives us the opportunity to restate some fundamental principles in a way that actually has some meaning for ordinary people in Britain today' (Blair, 1993b: 85). It was a matter of common sense that a child brought up in a stable family would have a better chance of success. But it made equal sense to understand that parents would have a better chance of succeeding in this task to the extent that they could count on a regular income, could reside in a decent house, and could put their children in a school offering a quality education (Blair, 1993: 85).

Utting (1993) took this argument a step further. The Conservatives' emphasis on broken homes as the source of delinquency led to misplaced priorities. The preoccupation with family structure, whether children live with one parent or two, offered an unsatisfactory approach to delinquency prevention. Broken homes are a symptom of larger issues that create conflict between parents. Rather than trying to recreate a family structure reminiscent of the 1950s, interventions should concentrate on reducing the many stress factors that inhibit parents' ability to extend the care they would otherwise wish to extend. Parenting is a 'direct channel' by which economic and socio-environmental factors, poverty and disadvantage, influence young people's behaviour and development (Utting, 1993: 19). Utting proposed measures to support families, improve parenting, and enhance school education. These included open-access family centres, home-visiting schemes, parental skills training, and other family support services. Pre-school education, to aid disadvantaged youths in schools, would also help (Utting, 1993: 20).

The Third Way programme advanced by the Labour party in these years gave particular attention to family life, crime, and deterioration of communities. In his statement of Third Way thinking on crime reduction, Giddens (2000: 4) put it simply: 'Changes in the family are related to antisocial behaviour and crime'. Not only do family dissolution and crime represent issues of public concern, they are linked together so that tackling one problem cannot be accomplished without taking on the others.

Following Blair's victory in 1997 and establishment of the Social Exclusion Unit, this strategy was put into place. The government supported a bundle of programmes in the area of Children, Families and Schools. These included Sure Start, Support for Parents, Literacy and Numeracy Strategies, Teenage Pregnancy Strategy, and Access to Childcare, among others (Young and Matthews, 2003: 10). The Third Way included a renewed interest in transmitted deprivation. The *Breaking the Cycle* (2004) report, produced by the Social Exclusion Unit, uses terminology such as 'intergenerational cycle of deprivation' and 'transmission' of disadvantage (Social Exclusion Unit, 2004).

The Criminology of Families

The criminological study of families and crime has tended to rely on a particular methodology. Many of the conclusions have been drawn from longitudinal research, the most extensive of which have been carried out in the UK and the USA.

Developmental Pathways

David Farrington has supervised the largest longitudinal study in Britain. The Cambridge Study of Delinquent Behaviour is a forty-year follow-up study of 411 males who attended primary school in south London during the 1950s. Information about the boys' development was obtained from parents during annual visits by social workers to the boys' homes during their middle childhood years. As the boys reached adulthood, and approached middle age, they were interviewed by researchers (Farrington and West, 1990).

The Cambridge study contributes to a larger body of work known as 'developmental pathways' analysis. Offending is seen as part of a syndrome that arises in childhood and tends to persist into adulthood. The chain of events leading from conduct problems, such as disruptive behaviour in school, to serious delinquency and a criminal career is described as a developmental trajectory or pathway. Developmental criminology seeks to identify the reasons behind turning points in criminal careers: 'activation' (the way criminal activities begin), 'aggravation' (escalation, increasing seriousness) and 'desistence' (decreasing frequency, cessation) (Loeber and LeBlanc, 1990; LeBlanc and Loeber, 1998).

The Cambridge research points to a number of criminogenic characteristics of families including the criminality of parents and large family size. 'Crime runs in families', Farrington (2004: 131–2) reports; some 6 per cent of the families accounted for half of all the convictions of family members in the cohort. The inter-generational transmission of crime is likely to be related to multiple risk factors at work in the most deprived neighbourhoods, or possibly that female lawbreakers tend to cohabit with male lawbreakers. 'Crime runs in large families' to the extent that boys who had four or more siblings by ten years of age doubled their chances of being convicted as a juvenile. This may be due to lack of parental attention given the relatively greater number of demands on parents' time, or frustration, irritation and conflict resulting from crowded conditions (Farrington, 2004: 135–6).

The Cambridge research also points to parenting methods and family disharmony. Of all the child-rearing methods under study, poor parental supervision remains the strongest predictor of childhood criminal behaviour. Other crime-producing methods include harsh and punitive discipline, erratic and inconsistent discipline, cold and rejecting parents, and parents' non-participation in children's activities (Farrington, 2004: 136–8). Children separated from a biological parent are more likely to run afoul of the law than children residing with both parents. In the Cambridge study, separations from a parent before ten years of age led to greater convictions and delinquency. Broken families may lead to crime because of enduring anxiety over the trauma of being detached from a parent, or the accumulation of stress (parental conflict, loss, reduced economic circumstances, step-parents with poor child-rearing practices) (Farrington, 2004: 140–1).

To some extent, Farrington's research revives earlier work by Bowlby. The terms 'broken homes' and 'problem families' have been replaced by 'disruption,' and the psychoanalytic interpretation is gone, but the import of the research remains the same. Juby and Farrington (2001) concluded that family disruption was an important factor in delinquency causation. It depended, however, on the cause of the disruption. Separations caused by parental conflict and family disharmony precipitated delinquent outcomes in a way that separations owing to death of a parent did not. They did find, as Bowlby suggested, that loss of a mother led to higher delinquency rates than loss of a father. This finding expressed the fact that it is not family disruption per se that leads to delinquency. Some kinds of broken homes are criminogenic, that is, those where the boy does not remain with his mother; some kinds of intact families are criminogenic, that is, those characterised by parental conflict.

Haas, Farrington and others (2004) explored these relationships in a study of 21,314 men in Switzerland. The biographical information they obtained, from a survey of 20-year-olds recruited for the Swiss army, showed that boys not living with their mothers were most likely to become persistent offenders.

Consistent with earlier results, the loss of a mother was more damaging than loss of a father. The Swiss study turned up an interesting finding in that the most traumatised boys (who had been institutionalised) appeared to have become less delinquent than those who were less traumatised but still subject to the same risk factors. The researchers suggest that more attention should be given to understanding 'resiliency', the ability of some children to thrive despite separation from parents and other adverse life circumstances.

Structural Disadvantage

For more than three decades beginning in 1939, Sheldon and Eleanor Glueck (1952) of the Harvard Law School carried out one of the most ambitious longitudinal studies of delinquency in America. They collated extensive information about the lives of 1000 boys from deprived backgrounds in Boston; 500 matched pairs of delinquents and non-delinquents. And they concluded that the most important difference between them was the family (Sampson and Laub, 1993: 42). Delinquents grew up in homes characterised by less effective household management, lower cultural atmosphere, lower standards of conduct, poorer parental supervision, and weak ties among family members. Delinquents came from less stable homes, homes in which they experienced broken relationships with one or both parents and endured one or more household changes. Delinquents grew up with parents who had low self-respect, had little ambition to improve the family's situation, and were indifferent or hostile to their children.

To solve such problems, the Gluecks recommended the combined resources of specialists in welfare, education and community-development. Delinquency prevention should focus on family life along with three other areas: traits and characteristics of delinquents, the school, and employment of leisure time. Intervening in other areas, with individualised psychiatric treatment and building of boys clubs, recreation centres, clinics and the like would be of limited value, they observe, without 'breaking the vicious cycle' leading to delinquency within families. As for rehabilitating the delinquent family, they explain that 'The problem is enormous in scope. It calls for the widespread cooperative endeavour of child-guidance clinics, school teachers, family welfare agencies, church and other communal resources' (Glueck and Glueck, 1952: 199).

In 1993, Robert Sampson and John Laub published their re-analysis of the Gluecks' data. The Gluecks followed up their initial data collection at two points in time – at 25 and 32 years of age – tracking down records in some 37 states. Sampson and Laub supplemented this with information about crimes from 32 to 45 years of age. They combined quantitative and qualitative data and took advantage of contemporary data analysis techniques unknown to the Gluecks when they conducted their study. Given the importance of family dynamics in the making of delinquents, Sampson and Laub (1993: 96–7) were troubled that so many sociological explanations of crime overlooked the family.

Sampson and Laub affirmed the conclusion the Gluecks had reached some forty years earlier, but with a different emphasis. The same 'family process variables' of supervision, attachment, and discipline re-emerged as the most powerful statistical predictors of delinquency (Sampson and Laub, 1993: 96). They also discovered the same structural disadvantages at work: weakened bonds to family, school and work and the disruption of social relations between individuals and institutions. Family relationships occur alongside other structural disadvantages. In this way, they emphasise the importance of a family-centred crime policy that avoids pathologising individuals and pursues ameliorating structural disadvantages (Haines, 1999: 268–9). Echoing the Gluecks conclusions, Sampson and Laub (1993: 3) 'believe that crime policy must be broader in scope and look to non-governmental institutions like families, schools, work settings, and neighbourhoods as the center piece of a crime reduction policy'.

In their recent work, however, Laub and Sampson (2003) attempt to balance structural disadvantage with human agency. They seek to distance their work from structuralist approaches in sociological criminology arguing that poverty and social class are 'all that matter'; they want to understand how individuals construct their own life course through the actions they take within the constraints of history and social circumstances. The structuralist view is inconsistent, Laub and Sampson contend, with what the subjects of longitudinal research say about themselves. In what is probably the 'longest longitudinal study' involving the same cohort, they interviewed 52 of the Glueck delinquents some five decades after the original project began. The men generally did not explain their criminal pasts with reference to downturns in the economy, poor schools, uncaring parents, or discrimination based on class or gender. Human agency emerged as an important theme in accounting for bad and good turns in the life course. One man, Sampson and Laub (2005: 38) report, when asked to reflect on why his life had turned out the way it did, put it this way: 'Not because of my mother and father. Because of me. I'm the one that made it shitty'.

The Cycle of Violence

Longitudinal research has also contributed the 'cycle of violence' as an explanation for crime. The cycle of violence suggests that today's abused and neglected children become tomorrow's habitual and violent criminals. People victimised in childhood grow up to victimise others in adulthood, frequently their own children.

Widom and Maxfield (2001) compared arrest records of 908 abused/neglected children processed through courts in an American city from 1967 to 1971 with 667 children with a similar social profile who were not abused/neglected. They found that those children who were abused or neglected were more likely to have been arrested as juveniles and adults, and that children who were physically abused (as opposed to neglected) were the most likely to have been arrested for a violent crime. Children who were abused or neglected also reported higher frequencies of mental health concerns (suicide attempts), educational problems (low IQ, reading difficulties), occupational difficulties (unemployment), and public health issues (prostitution, alcohol problems). Swanston et al. (2003) had similar results in their study of sexually abused children in Australia. They compared a sample of 38 children presented by Child Protection Units for treatment at Sydney hospitals for injuries related to sexual abuse with 68 children in similar life circumstances who had not been abused. Based on information obtained from the individuals and parents nine years after intake, they found a history of child sexual abuse to be associated with aggressiveness and criminal behaviour.

The cycle of violence retains its popularity as an explanation for family-induced criminality because it seems to be confirmed by the professional knowledge of those working on the front line. Police officers, social workers, and youth probation officers are familiar with the profile of the troubled individual who hails from a troubled family. Violent offenders tend to report that they were abused as children, also leading to the conclusion that children who are physically abused tend to become lawbreakers later in life. It may be that young people grow up to re-enact some version of the abuse they suffered. In this view, violent offenders are modelling behaviour they learned as children (Hill-Smith et al 2002). Others suggest a more psychological explanation rooted in mental trauma or deficient information processing. Through continuous exposure to violence, children grow up to misread social cues and ascribe hostile intentions where no threat was intended (Herrenkohl et al., 2003: 1190–1).

In Denmark, Christofferson and colleagues (2003) identified a cohort of 43,403 boys born in 1966. Using national criminal registers, they determined that when the cohort was between 15 and 27 years of age, 1936 of them had committed a violent offence. Comparing an extensive list of risk factors across this population and the cohort in general, they found that violent men came from families characterised by dissolution (parental break-up, placement outside the home), violence in the home and father's criminality, mother's alcohol abuse, and father's lack of vocation. Without education and vocational skills, the men could manage only remote chances of employment. This study is notable not only for the numbers involved, but for the lack of attention to the portion of young men in the cohort with disadvantaged family backgrounds and *without* a history of violent crime.

It is important to understand that most abused and neglected children do not grow up to be murderers and violent criminals. This has been referred to as the 'Robins paradox': antisocial behaviour in children is one of the best predictors of antisocial behaviour in adults, yet most antisocial children do not grow up to be antisocial adults (Robins, 1978). Looking backward, violent criminals will almost always be drawn from the pool of high-risk children, but looking forward from the pool of high-risk children, it is difficult to forecast who will become a criminal. The Robins paradox explains the popularity of the cycle of violence as an explanation for crime among police officers and social workers who will not have had the same contact with those persons abused as children but who did not turn to crime. It also has important implications for family and youth policy.

Social Policy, Youth and Crime

The principal message of family-centred criminology is that what goes wrong goes wrong early. In policy terms, this has meant early intervention and risk-focused prevention.

Early Intervention

The argument for early intervention is premised on the belief that criminal behaviour among adults is preceded by delinquent and antisocial behaviour in childhood, and that such behaviour originates in adverse circumstances during the first years of life. From this perspective, pruning young lives before they grow crooked is the most sensible means of reducing crime. Developmental prevention seeks to 'prevent the development of criminal potential in individuals' by targeting those factors identified in research of human development (Farrington, 2002: 657). And, in not only criminal justice, but also allied services. 'Early identification and intervention are the keys to reducing the personal costs to troubled children and their families as well as the financial costs to our health and social services systems' (Morrison, Macdonald, and LeBlanc, 2000: 477).

Many of the studies investigating family factors leading to criminal behaviour conclude with a call for early intervention. Preschool enrichment programmes coupled with family intervention have been found to have impressive results in reducing crime. The most successful programmes target at-risk children and begin interventions with children under four years of age. They involve both children (cognitive and emotional development) and parents (child care skills, discipline). Although successful programmes are small scale, high quality and consequently, high cost, they are less expensive than prisons (Donohue and Siegelman, 1998: 20). General parent education and more formal parent training have also been found to be effective techniques. Farrington and Welsh (2004), who reviewed 24 family-intervention programmes in Canada, the UK and the USA, suggest that most succeeded in reducing delinquency and, in some cases, their financial benefits exceeded costs.

But the wisdom of early intervention is not as simple or obvious as the early interveners imply. Harriett Wilson's (1980) study of parental supervision shows the importance of setting family intervention within a wider social policy framework. She explored the effect of varying levels of 'social handicap' across families in the West Midlands on delinquent behaviour of boys in these families, drawing on school and police records. The laxness of parental supervision did correspond with delinquency. But she went on to point out the 'very close association of lax parenting methods with severe social handicap' (Wilson, 1980: 233). Laxness resulted not from the attitude of parents, but from chronic stress, prolonged unemployment, physical or mental disabilities, and poverty in general. 'It is the position of the most disadvantaged groups in society, and not the individual, which needs improvement in the first place' (Wilson, 1980: 234).

Enthusiasm for early intervention on empirical grounds does not eliminate the ethical issues at stake. Targeting children with the potential to become criminal has side effects that, however unintentional, can be as criminogenic as some of the risk factors they are intended to eliminate. Early intervention programmes nurture and protect, but also label and stigmatise. Definitions such as 'pre-delinquent', 'potential delinquent', and 'at risk of delinquency' are extremely dangerous when applied to young children (Gatti, 1997: 115–16; Haines, 1999: 265). The potential for adverse affects due to labelling is less for universal than for targeted programmes. Universal programmes extend to all children in the country, whether or not risk factors are evident, and targeted programmes are aimed at specific populations. Even in the context of welfare provision and family support, terms such as 'at-risk populations' can become a means of marginalising the populations they are meant to include.

To the extent that poor parenting contributes to delinquency, training for parents with poor parenting skills will arguably bring about a reduction in delinquency and crime, but there are reservations over efforts to institutionalise the scheme, particularly the element of compulsion. Concern about problem families in the 1950s led to establishment of 'recuperative centres'. Located in rural areas removed from towns and cities where families resided, these centres aimed to teach housewifery and childcare. These programmes extended treatment to women in austere conditions, further strained family relationships, and stigmatised families in the communities to which they returned. Bowlby recognised the serious infringement of personal liberty and potential for abuse involved, but reluctantly agreed that until less obtrusive measures could be found, such centres might be the best solution (Starkey, 2000: 548–9).

Current government policy to turn around family dynamics – parenting orders – involves similar concerns about compulsion (Henricson, Coleman, and Roker, 2000). Arthur (2005) argues that parental responsibility laws enacted as part of the Crime and Disorder Act (1998) and Anti-Social Behaviour Act (2003) 'oversimplify the complex linkage between parenting and delinquency in a reductionist effort to blame parents for their children's wrongs'. This legislation introduced the parenting order enabling the court to require the parent of every convicted young offender to attend parenting programmes. The parenting order effectively requires a parent to attend counselling or guidance sessions once a week for a period of up to twelve weeks. Going about parent training in this way misses the point that many delinquents are from deprived families; government should assist families in guiding and nurturing the child through provision of resources and support services. Arthur (2005: 241) asks: 'How much better if parents attended these courses voluntarily, before the crisis?'

Finally, the logic of early intervention suggests that intervention is crucial, and, in the interest of minimising danger and saving money, the earlier the better. But pre-emptive measures directed at at-risk children can be *too early*. The conclusions from two studies in the USA suggest that legalising abortion has led to noticeable crime reduction. Using somewhat different methodologies, Donohue and Levitt (2001) and Berk et al. (2003) determined that the US Supreme Court's decision in 1973 to legalise abortion contributed to a significant drop in the violent crime rate during the 1990s. This finding can be attributed to a demographic effect, 'cohort reduction', meaning that fewer individuals came into their crime-prone years than would have otherwise. The 'more interesting' interpretation, as Donohue and Levitt (2001) put it, has it that extending the choice to delay or avoid pregnancy resulted in fewer children born into 'at-risk' circumstances. This sort of language suggests a eugenicist family policy of encouraging abortion as a means of reducing the cohort of at-risk children. To British ears, it is reminiscent of Keith Joseph's infamous Edgbaston speech in 1974 in which he warned of 'a high and rising portion of children being born to mothers least fitted to bring children into the world' (quoted in Welshman, 2005: 318).

Risk-Focused Prevention

In his presidential address to the American Society of Criminology in 1999, David Farrington (2000) outlined a model linking research knowledge and policymaking that has become a significant guide to delinquency prevention. He proposed the risk factor paradigm as the basis for the globalisation of criminological knowledge. In this model, an international network of researchers would catalogue factors responsible for crime and guide the design of policies to alleviate them. Risk factors could be identified, he said, through a wide-scale programme of cross-national longitudinal research as well as evaluation research incorporating experimental methods and cost–benefit analyses (Farrington, 1999: 2000). The conceptualisation of risk has had a major impact on youth policy as it has on social policy generally. 'Risk ... is replacing need as the core principle of social policy formation and welfare delivery' (Kemshall, 2002: 1).

The risk factor paradigm borrows its conceptualisation of risk from public health. The public health strategy for combating illnesses such as cancer and heart disease seeks to identify the risk factors (cigarette smoking, high-fat diet, sedentary lifestyle) within the population and reduce them with public health programmes (campaigns urging people to stop smoking, eat more fruits and vegetables, and take regular exercise). The delinquency prevention version of this strategy seeks to identify risk factors associated with youth crime and to mitigate them with programmes and policies (Farrington, 2000: 4). These programmes are organised along the lines of public health as well, using the language of primary, secondary, and tertiary prevention. 'Primary prevention' seeks to prevent the outbreak of a disease by cleaning up an environment in which it is likely to occur. 'Secondary prevention' seeks to reduce the vulnerability of individuals thought to be particularly 'at risk' to contracting the disease. 'Tertiary prevention' intervenes after the onset of the illness to minimise the extent and duration (Welsh, 2005).

The focus of risk-focused delinquency prevention has been secondary prevention. Intervention models such as Communities that Care (CtC) seek to match 'at risk' youths with bespoke prevention programming. This model originated in the USA with the work of David Hawkins and Richard Catalano in the 1980s. It calls on communities to assess their delinquency problem, specify risk factors, inventory resources for protection, and dispense them to those in need (Hawkins, 1999). CtC achieved national prominence after appearing in the Office of Juvenile Justice and Delinquency Prevention's *Comprehensive Strategy* (1993). This strategy, developed for mitigation of 'serious, violent and chronic juvenile offenders', outlined six risk factors: delinquent peer groups, poor school performance, high-crime neighbourhoods, weak family attachments, lack of consistent discipline, and physical or sexual abuse (OJJDP, 1993). In the UK, the Joseph Rowntree Foundation funded a prevention model based on CtC. This expanded by the year 2000 to include three demonstration projects and 30 locally based programmes in England, Wales, Scotland and Ireland (France and Crow, 2005).

The risk factor approach has tremendous appeal as a guide to policy given the ancient wisdom of an ounce of prevention being equal to a pound of cure. Risk-focused prevention proposes to interrupt the formation of youth crime in its early stages before habits form that are associated with a criminal career. The youth justice system essentially concerns itself with bringing about change after the fact while the prevention focus seeks to intervene before delinquent behaviour becomes a fact. Public officials, and the criminologists who advise them, point out that delinquency prevention is the most cost-effective response to crime. The commitment to 'riskfactorology' does, nevertheless, raise significant dilemmas (France, 2006).

Is it truly possible to identify a set of characteristics and circumstances that lead to criminality? Despite the appeal of the 'new science of prevention', the risk factor model offers much less certainty as a guide to policy than we would wish. There is a difference between significance in a statistical sense and in a theoretical sense. Shoplifting may represent the start of a criminal career or the culmination of a delinquent career. The expertise for identifying those children with conduct problems likely to lead to serious criminal behaviour as distinct from children who are merely being naughty simply does not exist (Armstrong, 2006: 270). Relying on risk factors as a guide to intervention leads to over-prediction and harmful consequences. There is also a conceptual problem in the modelling of pathways. As Hine, France and Armstrong (2006) suggest, being 'in' or 'out' of a pathway leading to crime is a false dichotomy. The 110 'at risk' youths they interviewed in England reported spending much of their everyday lives in pro-social pursuits with only occasional forays into criminal activity. The young people referenced a frequent avoidance of criminal opportunities presented to them. Categorising youth according to types of pathways invites concerns of stigmatising and self-fulfilling prophecy.

The reification of risk factors has brought about a significant realignment of priorities away from universal provision of social policy and toward targeted youth justice. Thinking about the aetiology of delinquency as a result of *earlier* life experiences leads toward conceptualising risk at the personal rather than community or social level. The advent of risk-focused prevention has led to a rationing of youth services consistent with 'birfurcation', the desire to distinguish persistent and serious offenders from occasional and mundane law-breaking (Bradford and Morgan, 2005: 284). Policymakers ostensibly concerned with youth crime have embraced a one-sided understanding of the model. While the research points to the role of protective factors, and as such is more appropriately labelled 'risk and protection-focused prevention', government ministers have themselves focused on risk (France and Utting, 2005: 80). Little effort has gone into conceptualising and promoting protective factors.

Government authorities have read developmental pathways and risk-factor research as a call for tracking and surveillance. In 2004, Hazel Blears, the UK Minister of State for Crime Reduction, Policing and Community Safety, said that the children of criminal offenders should be tracked from an early age to keep them from reverting to a life of crime as their parents did. 'We need to track the children who are most at risk', she said; 'We can predict the risk factors that will lead a child into offending behaviour' (quoted in Armstrong, 2006: 265). The desire for precise delinquency prediction has encouraged a technological solution in the form of risk assessment instruments. The Youth Justice Board uses a risk assessment device called *Asset* to catalogue information about risk factors contributing to criminal behaviour in young people. What could be read as a framework for expanding social policy has been read as a rationale for efficiency in criminal policy.

The most serious dilemma has to do with what Armstrong (2006) calls the 'cultural politics of risk', the overlap of risk factors with suspect communities. Not only is 'at risk' an ambiguous and patronising expression, it has become one of the most ubiquitous social markers of 'otherness'. 'Race', gender, and class become risk factors in themselves as groups become targeted as a matter of ethnic and gender identities. In France, for instance, an equivalent term is *les juenes des quartiers difficles*, or 'youth from difficult areas'. Although this term avoids specific reference to ethnic identity, the journalists and politicians who use it know it will be understood as referring to youths of North African heritage living in the suburbs of French cities.

Ajzenstadt (2005) offers an example of this from reactions to juvenile delinquency in Israel. During the 1950s and 1960s, media reporters, politicians and members of social work and medical professions aroused public concern about increasing levels of crime among Israeli youth. This occurred in the context of immigration. Following the founding of the State of Israel in 1948, the flow of immigration meant that about 90 per cent of Jewish residents were of Ashkenazi or European backgrounds and the remaining 10 per cent were 'Oriental' Jews from Asia and North Africa. What Ajzenstadt shows is how the professionals and the politicians tended to see the criminal behaviour of Ashkenazi youth as a natural, temporary phase of adolescence. As an ordinary and understandable part of growing up, this behaviour presented no special problem. But they tended to see the same behaviour among Oriental youth as a serious threat to the well-being and future development of the country. For these young people, delinquency signified deeper problems concerning rejection of essential Israeli values and the inability to assimilate into Israeli society.

Conclusion

The logic of contingent delinquency has led to interest in the relationship between families and crime. Researchers in this field have had some success in engaging the interest of policymakers, although family-centred crime policy remains ambiguous and contradictory. The emerging concerns with early intervention and risk-focused prevention, while enjoying support of first-rate criminological research, raise political, social, and moral dilemmas that should not be overlooked.

Questions for Discussion

1. *'Crime can be reduced by addressing the needs of families.' Does this statement reflect the concerns of the Conservatives, Labour, or the Liberal Democrats?*

2. *Which theory makes the most sense as a guide to policymaking in the area of families: developmental criminology, structural disadvantage, control, or the cycle of violence?*

3. *Can early intervention ever be too early? Should abortion be encouraged as a means of crime prevention?*

4. *Is there a meaningful difference between policies aimed at addressing 'at risk' communities or populations and those directed at 'at risk' individuals?*

Further Reading

Anna Coote, (ed.) (1993) *Families, Children and Crime*. London: Institute for Public Policy Research.

Norman Dennis (1993) *Rising Crime and the Dismembered Family*. London: Institute of Economic Affairs.

Alan France (2006) *Youth in Late Modernity*. Maidenhead: Open University Press.

Mooney, Jane (2003) 'It's the Family Stupid: Continuities and Reinterpretations of the Dysfunctional Family as the Cause of Crime in Three Political Periods', in Roger Matthews and Jock Young, eds., *The New Politics of Crime and Punishment*. Cullompton: Willan Publishing.

Police, Prisons and Social Welfare

SUMMARY

- Strategies to reduce urban crime, such as zero tolerance policing, may worsen problems of homelessness, mental illness, and poor health
- Mass imprisonment has brought about a considerable social welfare dilemma that has yet to be fully realised
- The resettlement needs of former prisoners include employment, housing, health services, and family concerns
- Persons released from prison, and persons released from local authority care, face similar challenges in overcoming marginalisation

Government strategies for tackling crime affect not only safety but social welfare as well. Measures undertaken as a means of fighting crime have repercussions for social policy in their wake. These side-effects might be called – to borrow a concept from economics – *externalities*. In economic theory, an externality refers to a cost arising from an economic activity that affects somebody other than the people engaged in the economic activity.

The idea here is that efforts to deal with crime spill over from issues of public safety into issues of social welfare. In Chapter 4, we explored unintended effects of social policy on crime: how housing policy affects the distribution of crime in cities. This chapter looks at the relationship the other way around. At issue here are the impacts on social policy of measures taken to reduce crime. Whether or not more policing and more prisons have decreased crime, they have brought about identifiable and substantial repercussions for social welfare.

This chapter explores the repercussions for social welfare of two crime reduction strategies: zero tolerance policing and mass imprisonment. The first half of the chapter deals with marginalised populations. During the 1990s, zero tolerance policing became a visible strategy for responding to marginalised populations according to the 'broken windows' theory of crime. The second half of the chapter explores the impact of mass imprisonment, and particularly the issues of resettlement on the part of offenders on release from prison.

Police, the Marginalised, and Crime

The sight of the most visible forms of marginalisation – begging and rough sleeping – in London during the 1980s prompted a series of responses in the 1990s. It was also during the 1990s that police were encouraged to 'do something' according to the theory that visible marginalisation was connected to violent crime.

Visible Marginalisation and Crime

Marginalisation from mainstream society can be understood along several dimensions; persons become marginalised politically, economically, and socially. Marginalisation becomes extreme when exclusions from the labour market and social networks overlap and reinforce each other to produce populations without some place to be and something to do. Such populations become visible in cities where the sight of begging, rough sleeping, and street drinking prompts a response from government (Juska, Johnstone and Pozzuto, 2004).

The relationship between extreme or visible marginalisation and crime has been theorised in more than one way. Criminologists have stressed that homeless persons are more likely to be the victims of crime rather than perpetrators (Barak and Bohm, 1989). Persons sleeping rough are victims of crimes against the person, often repeatedly; the level of victimisation exceeds that of the British population generally. Ballintyne's (1999) study of 120 rough-sleepers in Glasgow, Swansea and London revealed that 78 per cent had been victims of crime on at least one occasion during their most recent period of sleeping rough, and about the same portion say they fear further victimisation. Homeless persons do have a high level of contact with police, but this results in significant part from a lifestyle under public scrutiny rather their constituting a particular danger or threat to security.

Criminologists have also explored the ways in which extreme marginalisation induces persons to engage in criminal activity. McCarthy and Hagan (1991) point to homelessness as a situational factor affording greater likelihood for participation in crime. They collected information from interviews with 'street youth' in Toronto and Vancouver. While young persons admitted to criminal involvement before beginning life on the street, they reported greater criminal involvement after leaving home than before. A significantly greater number of adolescents chose to use hallucinogens and cocaine, steal, and engage in the sex trade once they became homeless. Crime became a recourse for those with a period of homelessness extending to a year or more. Similarly, Gaetz and O'Grady (2002), who studied street youth in Toronto as well, found that the overwhelming majority of street youth (nearly 90 per cent in their survey) desire paid employment, but few obtain it as a primary source of income (15 per cent). Crime, begging, squeegeeing,[1] and the sex trade are alternatives,

---

[1]'Squeegee merchants' position themselves at traffic lights, slosh water on the windscreens of waiting motorists, and seek payment for their 'services'.

generally to be avoided. Engaging in the sex trade, while a relatively high-income generating source is 'incredibly degrading' and has costly side-effects, including alcohol and drug abuse (Gaetz and O'Grady, 2002: 447).

Kennedy and Fitzpatrick (2001: 2008) emphasise begging as an alternative to crime. Many of the people they interviewed who had been living on the streets in Glasgow and Edinburgh chose begging over criminal means of making money because it was a lawful and 'honest' activity. Begging represents an attempt to stay out of trouble. Fitzpatrick and Jones (2005: 401) emphasise the links between begging, homelessness and drug misuse. They report that many homeless persons developed drug or alcohol habits early in life as a means of coping with traumatic experiences (leading to their homelessness), and engage in begging to feed an alcohol or heroin habit. They make the case that efforts to reduce income from begging, in the absence of support for tackling addiction, make it likely that those engaging in begging would turn to other means of fund-raising to feed their addictions, including prostitution and crime. Measures to eliminate street begging would be counter-productive in crime prevention terms and would be more destructive for those persons reduced to begging.

The criminological argument to have generated the most attention in recent years does not concern marginalised persons in the role of victims or criminals, but the contention that the visibility of marginalisation leads *other people* to commit crime. In 'Broken Windows' Wilson and Kelling (1982) argued that the sight of persons sleeping in doorways essentially signals that no one cares about 'what goes on here', inviting other forms of illegal activity. Social and physical disorder in city neighbourhoods can, if unchecked, lead to serious crime. Minor infractions and incivilities such as public intoxication, spray-painting graffiti, and buildings in disrepair can escalate into predatory crime because prospective criminals infer from these signs that residents are indifferent to what happens in their neighbourhoods. Signs of disorder trigger attributions in outsiders as well, influencing the calculus of prospective homebuyers, estate agents, and small-business owners and investors.

Essentially, Wilson and Kelling brought the idea of informal social control within a community into a new framework. They proposed that 'community policing' could be an important part of a city's attempts to regulate the behaviour of its members. Incivilities are not trivial; they intimidate residents. Fear of crime leads to a reluctance on the part of citizens to participate in public life, which leads in turn to surrendering common spaces to lawbreakers.

Zero Tolerance Policing

When in the 1990s, William J. Bratton, Commissioner of Police in New York City, claimed that his application of the broken windows theory had transformed the city from one of the most crime-ridden to one of the safer big cities in North America, the debate was on (Kelling and Bratton, 1998). Bratton (1997: 34) described New York as 'a city that had stopped caring for itself'. He made a number of changes to the way the NYPD went about serving the public, not least of which was a campaign against 'quality of life' crimes. Police began enforcing city ordinances aimed at reducing graffiti, littering, and public drinking. They used misdemeanour arrests to incapacitate those suspected of more serious crimes and persistent stop-and-search activities to reduce the number of handguns in circulation. The American experience coincided with comparable experiments in Australian, British and German cities.

In 1997, Bratton came to London to explain his New York success in 'a press conference disguised as a colloquium' (Berd and Helms, 2003: 1848). He trumpeted New York's falling crime rates: within three years, homicide declined by 51 per cent, violent crime fell by 38 per cent, and crime overall declined 37 per cent. Some criminologists have questioned the 'New York miracle'. Bowling (1999) is among those who argue that crime would likely have decreased anyway. While stop-and-search activities did reduce the lethality of drug and gang confrontations and decrease the number of homicides, rates of homicide were on the way down even before Bratton became commissioner. This was due to the decline of the crack cocaine epidemic. The crack form of cocaine generated significant violence, due to the intensity of its psychotropic effect and the extreme competition generated by its low price. The crime rate dropped with the decline of the 'crack wars' and the deaths of a generation of young men.

Other sceptics have argued the merits of a long-term social policy strategy against the short-term reductions gained by police crackdowns. Proactive policing strategies may succeed in bringing reported crimes down during a period of years, but deflect attention and resources from long-range efforts at working within communities and with other government agencies, such as health, education, and planning.

Sampson and Raudenbush (2001) have made this argument in reference to their research in Chicago neighbourhoods. The broken windows thesis contends that disorder causes crime. They insist that crime and disorder are both symptomatic of larger characteristics of the communities at issue: concentrated poverty. Crime and disorder share common roots in the structural characteristics of neighbourhoods, including neighbourhood cohesion and informal social control. Visible signs of disorder are relevant, as they influence migration, investment, and overall viability of a neighbourhood. Disorder can also trigger a cascade, motivating residents to move out and undermining residential stability, and thereby increasing the concentration of poverty of those left behind. Since residential instability and concentrated poverty erode collective efficacy, disorder leads to further disorder and crime. But relying on the police to deal with social welfare, Sampson and Radenbush insist, rather misses the point.

Kelling (2001) responds by declaring the debate to be more about word puzzles than policy differences. The description of 'broken windows' or 'community policing' he described became 'zero tolerance policing' in crossing the

Atlantic. He never used the term 'zero tolerance policing' and believes that it is contrary to his and Wilson's ideas.[2] Community policing had been understood in the 1980s as 'soft policing', providing services and seeking community approval, rather than aggressive or mean-spirited law enforcement. The reforms suggested by the critics of zero tolerance policing – multi-agency approaches, intermediary agencies such as 'park keepers', improved design of public spaces, extension of housing provision – are consistent with, if not suggested by, he and Wilson as advocates of broken-windows policing.

Police and Social Welfare

The intellectual dispute over zero tolerance policing raises a significant question about police and social welfare. Encouraging police to do something about street drinking, begging, and rough sleeping may reduce the level of fear and anxiety about crime within the middle classes. But what are the impacts of this policing activity on marginalised populations themselves?

Policing for fear-reduction can deepen the problems to be overcome by visibly marginalised persons in the city. Some measure of homclessness is invisible owing to the efforts of homeless persons to remain inconspicuous. Homeless people, as Wardhaugh (1996) explains, engage in a high degree of 'self-regulation'. They prefer to avoid contact, and possible conflict over use of space, with other passers-by. Based on her study in Manchester, she explains how street people move in and out of prime public spaces as inconspicuously as possible. They avoid Piccadilly Gardens during 'respectable' daylight hours and venture to the soup kitchen in late evening, after shoppers, tourists, and office workers have gone home. The criminalisation of homelessness has adverse effects on these populations. Von Mahs (2005: 945) determined from interviews with 28 homeless persons in Berlin that criminalisation of homelessness had adverse effects. Aggressive policing disrupts the ability of homeless persons to obtain a daily living. Essentially, it thwarts efforts to accumulate the social capital needed to exit the streets, contributing to longer periods of homelessness.

Police crackdowns on drug markets bring about collateral damage to public health. Maher and Dixon (1999) argue, based on three years of ethnographic investigation into Australia's heroin markets, that the threat of aggressive policing creates an environment within the milieu of intravenous drug users leading them to damage their own health and others. Drug users respond to police intervention by seeking secretive, injecting episodes involving multiple persons using the same injection equipment. Users who seek to avoid

---

[2]The term may have originated from late 1996 when the London Metropolitan Police implemented 'Operation Zero Tolerance' in the King's Cross area.

detection, and consume drugs before they are confiscated, are more reckless and frenzied in their drug-taking, coinciding with greater risk of needle sticks, blood spills and person-to-person blood contact. Police crackdowns bring in their wake increased rates of overdose and blood-borne virus transmission. The researchers call attention to the damage done by Sydney's effort to implement New-York-style policing (Dixon and Maher, 2005).

The police are typically the first, and sometimes the only, governmental point of contact for mentally ill persons. A study of 131 police officers in Sydney revealed that more than 10 per cent of police time is expended in dealing with persons with mental health conditions (Fry, Riordan and Geanellos, 2002: 277). The opportunity provided by police contact for putting mentally ill persons in contact with health and social services is not taken as often as it might be (James, 2000). Police often lack sufficient training to recognise symptoms of mental illness and may mistake mental illness as indications of alcohol or drug misuse, particularly where the mentally ill person had been consuming such commodities prior to arrest. Police officers may also be more likely to regard belligerence or refusal to accept treatment on the part of mentally ill persons as a threat to their safety and respond with methods of restraint or immobilisation that while appropriate for the majority of suspects serve to aggravate mental conditions (James, 2000; Lamb, Weinberger and Gross, 2004).

While there are, in principle, sufficient resources available at police stations in the UK for diversion of mentally ill persons, there is evidence that the system does not work as designed. The Police and Criminal Evidence Act (1984) provides for a police surgeon, or the forensic medical examiner (FME), to examine persons taken into police custody who appear to be suffering from a mental condition. But mentally ill persons are being returned to the community without the opportunity for psychiatric or social intervention being taken (James, 2000). Adverse impacts on mentally ill persons who come into police contact also accrue from role conflict between law enforcement and mental health practitioners. Neither the police, nor the mental health establishment, regard police officers as an agency within the mental health system. Police officers do not see mental health conditions as a police matter and may dismiss their interactions as a diversion of time and resources. It is unlikely that police officers will take on the role of advocating for mentally ill persons, particularly where there is a perception of unreasonable or uncooperative responses from social welfare agencies contacted. Police are well aware of criminal justice as the system that 'can't say no' and may be resigned to processing persons suspected of mental conditions for misdemeanour offences as a means of last resort (Lamb, Weinberger and Gross, 2004: 112).

Young (1991) reflects on his experience as a police sergeant to explain how traditional responses to domestic violence fail to resolve underlying social problems. He describes the 'traditional practice' for dealing with 'domestics' in Newcastle upon Tyne during the 1950s and 1960s. The practice involved transporting the male side of a domestic quarrel to a distant part of the city, or better yet across the river into the Gateshead Borough area, and then abandoning him to walk home and sober up. The practice continues and is more widespread. Von Mahs (2005: 945) describes 'deportations' on the part of police in Berlin. A deportation consists of taking homeless persons to remote areas outside the city where they are left to their own devices. He points out that such actions are taken with the idea that they are a positive alternative to arrest and its damaging consequences. But for persons who are intoxicated or mentally ill, such actions can be life-threatening.

Mass Imprisonment

David Garland (2001) has called attention to 'mass imprisonment', the profound build-up of prisons within the USA. For most of the twentieth century, the incarceration rate fluctuated around a stable average of 110 persons per 100,000 population. But in 1973, the proportion of Americans in prison began to increase and it has increased every year since then. By 2001, it had reached 450 per 100,000, a level unprecedented in American history. 'We do not currently know', Garland (2001a: 6) says, 'what "mass imprisonment" will mean for the society in which it develops, or for the groups who are most directly effected'. The build-up of the prison population portends a wide-scale and massive problem of social welfare as unprecedented numbers of prisoners return to their communities on release. The number of prisoners released in America each year is about 600,000, an average of 1600 per day (Petersilia, 2003: 3).

From Garland's (2001a) perspective, the policymakers responsible for the prison build-up are sleepwalking into a social welfare dilemma of disastrous proportion. Americans did not decide to get into the mass imprisonment situation, in the same way they pursued Roosevelt's New Deal and Reaganomics for instance. It emerged instead as an unforeseen (but foreseeable) outcome of a series of decisions, including determinate sentencing, the war on drugs, and tough-on-crime politics. Resettlement has been understood as an individual issue, and not for the problem it truly is: its social impact on communities and neighbourhoods. The alienation of whole elements of the population, normalisation of the prison experience, and migration of prison attitudes and problems to communities have emerged as unintended effects. These effects will be most profoundly felt among African Americans in city-centre neighbourhoods.

What this means for the UK has been a point of contention among those engaged in the sociology of punishment. Some insist that the USA is exceptional in its enthusiasm for imprisonment and this enthusiasm originates in a source other than the politics of crime control. For Wacquant (2001a), mass imprisonment has less to do with crime control than 'race' control. The large portion of African Americans reveals the true purpose of the prison; it is an extension of the historic strategy of oppression that began with the enslavement of Africans in the seventeenth and eighteenth centuries and continued with ghettoisation into forgotten corners of cities in the twentieth. The prison has replaced the ghetto as a place of confinement for African Americans; the ghetto functions as a 'social prison' and the prison operates as a 'judicial ghetto'. Imprisonment serves to warehouse the Black working class, significant portions of which are unemployed due to skills deficits, workplace discrimination, competition from immigrants, and due to their refusal to submit to the indignity of 'slave jobs' (work without adequate pay and benefits).

Others, including Garland, point to larger economic forces, political pressures, and cultural sensibilities responsible for increased use of imprisonment in the Western, post-industrial world. There are obvious differences in scale and intensity of imprisonment, making the USA exceptional in this sense. Compared to the average for European nations, the American imprisonment rate is some six times higher. That said, the UK and the USA follow comparable historical trajectories and can be understood in similar structural terms (Garland, 2005). The UK has one of the highest rates of incarceration in Western Europe with 109 persons in prison for every 100,000. In 2005, there were more than 75,000 people in prison in England and Wales, double the number of 42,000 in 1991. There appears to be an Americanisation taking place, not only in the UK, but other nations as well, including New Zealand (Pratt and Clark, 2005) and Germany (Suling, 2003).

'Populist punitiveness', a term coined by Bottoms (1995), has become a central theme in the standard account of Britain's flirtation with the American approach to prisons. It has become a shorthand expression for explaining mass imprisonment as a consequence of the politics of fear. Self-serving politicians, catering to the anxieties of the public and fed by media exaggerations of crime, commit themselves to more and longer prison terms as a matter of remaining in office and extending their domain. In the 1970s, Thatcher's Conservative Party had moulded crime into an election-winning political issue, and the Labour Party, borrowing a page from President Bill Clinton's New Democrat Party, decided that it would take crime seriously as well in order to win the next election. From that point forward, the major political parties in Britain have attempted to out-bid each other's proposals, leading to more prisons.

Matthews (2005) expresses some scepticism about this account. The notion of punitiveness suggests a disproportionate use of sanctions, an excessive overuse of imprisonment. He suggests that the sanctions that have emerged in recent years which are taken as evidence of this overuse are in fact largely symbolic, political rhetoric that never really led to changes in sentencing practices. Despite all the tough-on-crime speechmaking during the Thatcher years, the number of people sent to prison in 1990 was *less* than it was in 1980 (Matthews, 2005: 190). Mrs Thatcher realised that prison was 'an expensive way of making bad people worse'. At the same time, the number of non-punitive elements of punishment policy have increased, reflecting the different directions that populist movements can take. However 'new' Blair's Labour government may be, a growing number of official reports in recent years have emphasised that while prison is necessary for some lawbreakers, it serves to compound a history of social exclusion. To represent the Blair government as a continuation of the Conservative government fails to appreciate the diversity and ambiguity of government policy (Matthews, 2005: 190).

The point is, if the current trend toward increased incarceration continues in the UK, there will be an increasingly large ex-offender population. This has implications for the administration of social welfare as former prisoners experience difficulties in finding their way once released.

Resettlement of Former Prisoners

The criminal justice bureaucracy is organised to process people entering the system. While a great deal of thinking has gone into the legal procedures and resources required for processing those entering the system, far less goes into the processing of those exiting the system. What policies and practices exist for those released from prison tend to be piecemeal and uncoordinated. The responsibility for providing opportunities for successful reintegration is the core responsibility of no criminal justice agency in particular and the partial responsibility of many. Each year, those released from prison must become reintegrated into society, securing employment, finding housing, accessing healthcare. In 2002, the Social Exclusion Unit released *Reducing Re-Offending by Ex-Prisoners*, motivated by concern about recidivism, or the failure of prisoners who return to crime after release (Social Exclusion Unit, 2002). As the report makes clear, whether former prisoners resume their roles as parents, workers, taxpayers and citizens, or return to crime and drug use, largely comes down to the effectiveness of social policies.

Employment

The single most important factor in whether a released prisoner succeeds in society or returns to prison is employment, and education as it is related to employment (Nilsson, 2003). Overcoming this barrier is extremely difficult as most prisoners have never experienced steady or satisfactory employment; nearly three-quarters were unemployed prior to imprisonment. Nearly all left school at 16 years of age or younger and significant numbers regularly truanted or were excluded from school. Half of men in prison, and three-quarters of women, have no qualifications (Social Exclusion Unit, 2002: 19–20).

For many, the prospect of looking for a job begins with overcoming attitudes and expectations affected by past experiences with the labour market. Many will have entered prison with an irregular history of employment resulting in part from little education success. Gill (1997) interviewed 47 prisoners serving the last six months of their sentence within one of nine prisons. Very few had ever had a continuous job or a job they considered fulfilling. They viewed the prospect of a job generating interest and sufficient income as a good incentive for giving up offending. They expressed concerns about low wages and concerns about how to approach employers; they tended to see past refusals as a consequence of the employer's prejudice rather than their lack of qualifications or skills.

Research from America suggests the largest numbers of ex-prisoners reside in a limited number of small geographic areas. Lynch and Sabol (2001) found that of all those imprisoned in the State of Ohio, some 20 per cent had come from a single county, and most of these from the same area within the city of Cleveland. In other words, a large portion of returning prisoners return to the same neighbourhoods of city centres, neighbourhoods that offer limited possibilities for stable employment because they are relatively removed from geographical centres of job growth.

Cooke (2004) describes the impact of this situation for 17 formally incarcerated African-American men in Seattle. The men told her that spending time in prison had decreased the range of employment options. Even those with good educational credentials, in one case a baccalaureate degree, found themselves working in minimum wage situations far below their experience or skill level. Stories of ongoing unemployment were often connected to homelessness. Most of the men Cooke interviewed were homeless or living in temporary housing with family or friends. Without a permanent address, finding and keeping a job became difficult. Imprisonment also complicated the job search. Ex-offenders do not disclose their past convictions, even when the law requires them to do so. This exposes employers and other employees to unknown risks. Several told stories about finding work, only to be sacked once the background check had been completed.

More could be done to improve educational and vocational training programmes within prisons. Such programmes represent a key platform for success after release. A study of 200 prisoners in the north-west of England found that prison courses were the only experience in post-compulsory education one-third of them ever had (Burns, 1998: 177). However, vocational and work-training experiences in prison may not be enough to counteract the disadvantages prisoners face in the labour market. Success in finding a job after release is likely to be related to experience and skills acquired prior to imprisonment (Burns, 1998: 179). Cooke (2004: 158) found that those who had the most success after release were self-employed. This suggests that encouraging prisoners to consider starting their own businesses and seeking to develop entrepreneurial skills might be a means of overcoming some of the barriers encountered in searching for a job.

Also, Gill (1997) points out that while some emphasis has been placed on the difficulties former prisoners encounter in finding employment, not much has been done on the reasons why employers should hire them. Part of the policy response to post-prison employment should involve finding ways to overcome whatever barriers employers have, or believe they have, in hiring ex-offenders.

Housing

Next to finding a job, securing a permanent residence can be one of the most challenging aspects of resettlement. 'Housing', it has been said, 'is the linchpin that holds the reintegration process together' (quoted in Petersilia, 2003: 121). Something like a third of prisoners do not anticipate 'returning home' on release from prison because they did not reside in permanent accommodation prior to imprisonment. Another third lose their housing on imprisonment, owing to failure to communicate with landlords, and housing benefit rules that allow prisoners to retain their accommodation only for a limited period of time (Social Exclusion Unit, 2002: 95). Often, strained family relationships contribute to homelessness. Several of the men Cooke (2004) interviewed reported histories of violence with their partners, and were unable to return to their former homes. Many men said that after their imprisonment, their girlfriends had left home to reside with family members or found new romantic partners.

For many former prisoners, social housing is the most obvious option. Private landlords, reluctant to let to an individual without a work history and with a criminal record, often pass over applications from ex-prisoners, leaving few options other than social housing. Nevertheless, the availability of housing provided by local authority or housing association varies considerably by region and ex-prisoners can find it difficult to establish the 'local connection' necessary for allocation. Private landlords may be unwilling to accept housing benefit claimants given processing delays and are more than likely to require a deposit and a month's rent in advance, which is more than most ex-prisoners can afford. Further, some housing providers have exercised the power provided by the Housing Act (1996) to exclude those convicted of a criminal offence. The law appears to be moving, however, in the direction of being excluded from housing based on current behaviour, rather than a past criminal offence. The Homelessness Act (2002) ended blanket bans on certain groups, including those convicted of a criminal offence (Social Exclusion Unit, 2002: 98–9).

The exclusion of ex-prisoners from social housing derives from the debate about housing priorities. In the USA, prisoners returning to their families in subsidised public housing complexes are likely to find that they are no longer welcome. Federal laws passed with a mind to protect public housing residents from criminal victimisation by neighbours *require* public housing agencies to deny housing to persons with certain criminal convictions. Under the US Department of Housing and Urban Development's policy, public housing authorities may evict all members of a household for the criminal activities committed by one member, even when this member has head of household status. One possible solution to meeting the housing needs of ex-prisoners and protecting the integrity of public housing communities may be amending the tax code to provide incentives to private landlords for letting to ex-prisoners (Petersilia, 2003: 121–3).

Healthcare

In the aggregate, prisoners have greater problems of mental and physical health than British people generally. About three-quarters suffer from two or more mental disorders, and more than half engage in drug use or hazardous drinking prior to imprisonment. Although physical health problems are not as pronounced, long-standing illness or disability affects about half of men, which compares to about a third of men in the general population (Social Exclusion Unit, 2002: 20–1). There are anecdotal reports suggesting the prevalence of chronic diseases among prisoners. Asthma, diabetes, seizure disorders, and hypertension may be more common among prisoners than the population in general.

The prevalence of mental health conditions among prisoners reflects an intentional, and quite possibly mistaken, contraction of the mental health system. The de-institutionalisation of the mentally ill in the USA has come to be seen as the largest failed social experiment of the twentieth century (with the possible exception of prohibition). America's prisons and jails have replaced mental asylums as the primary provider of institutional care for the mentally ill. The nation's largest mental health facilities are found in the gaols of Los Angeles, New York, Chicago, and other cities (Freudenberg, 2001: 217, 220). Birmingham (1999) argues that the closure of psychiatric hospitals together with under-funded community care centres had brought about a similar problem in the UK. Mental health services, particularly those in cities, cannot cope with the demand. He cites a study published by the Office for National Statistics revealing that 7 per cent of sentenced males and 10 per cent of male remand prisoners suffer functional psychotic disorders. Generalised to the prison population on the whole, these percentages would mean more than 4500 men with serious psychotic disorders in prison (Birmingham, 1999: 379).

From a public health standpoint, prisons tend to concentrate persons with health conditions. This situation has some benefits; it offers an opportunity for screening and preventive medicine, and for some prisoners a prison stay might improve access to health care. At the same time, it represents a challenge. The return of prisoners to neighbourhoods essentially shifts healthcare from prison health services to community health services. Community health services, particularly in areas of treatment for drug users, have been criticised as disorganised and under-resourced.

What becomes of drug misusers on release from prison? Mitchell and McCarthy (2001) interviewed 27 men and women in two London prisons anticipating release who were identified as drug users and re-interviewed nine of them after release. While a third had passed through the detoxification service, this information was not retained in the prisoner's file nor utilised in resettlement planning. In effect, resources expended for treatment while in prison were lost on release. Although most of those interviewed anticipated seeking help after release from voluntary and statutory services (health, social services, housing), they were infrequently put into contact with these services outside and community services did not prioritise ex-prisoners. Supported housing appeared crucial to their success; lack of adequate housing was a problem for those who deteriorated or relapsed (Mitchell and McCarthy, 2001: 211).

Family Issues

It is easy to forget that persons who are in prison are missing from somewhere else. A significant portion of those in prison are parents, with children who look to them for support. In one survey of remand prisoners in three London prisons, about half said they had children less than 18 years of age and nearly two-thirds had lived with their children prior to imprisonment. Women were more likely to report they had children – 64 per cent compared to 43 per cent of men (Caddle and White, 1994: 4).

At the very least, the imprisonment of parents places a severe economic and emotional strain on what may already be a fragile family situation. Prisoners are less likely than the general population to be in stable relationships and more likely to have experienced family dissolution. About 81 per cent of prisoners are unmarried compared to 39 per cent of the general population (Social Exclusion Unit, 2002: 18). Many of those on whom others rely for nurture and support are themselves in need of support. The financial, educational, medical and mental health profiles of prisoners means that those who would be parents on release from prison have substantial economic and psychological needs.

A troubling ramification of parents in prison is the risk of passing on criminal behaviour to children. Murray and Farrington (2005) investigated whether imprisonment of parents might lead to anti-social behaviour and crime in children and contribute to the intergenerational transmission of crime. They compared boys in the Cambridge study (there were 23) who had been separated from a parent (mostly fathers) during their first ten years of life owing to imprisonment with those who had not been separated and whose parents had not been imprisoned; 70 per cent of these were identified as having anti-social personality disorders compared to 19 per cent of boys whose parents had not been imprisoned. They surmise that parental imprisonment increases the risk of anti-social outcomes for children because of separation, stigma, loss of family income, poor parenting, and modelling of parents' behaviour.

Aside from the possibility of crime, there are difficult issues related to broken family ties, not least of which concerns child support. A considerable portion of men imprisoned in America begin their term of incarceration with unpaid balances of child support. Automated matches of prison and child support databases in Massachusetts and Colorado for 2001 found that between 22 and 28 per cent of inmates under supervision were involved with the child support system. Incarceration does not end child support obligations, meaning that, once released, fathers begin life on the outside without a job and already in debt. In

Massachusetts, men had accrued an average debt of $5250 during their prison stay, and in Colorado, an average of $6402 (Griswold and Pearson, 2005: 359).

Under US law, former prisoners, like all non-custodial parents, face aggressive enforcement action for failure to pay child support. Employers are legally required to report new hires within 20 days, and the information is matched locally and nationally to identify child support obligations. Parents may have up to 65 per cent of take-home pay automatically garnished; arrears balances are routinely reported as delinquent on credit reports; they may have their licences revoked, both professional and driver's licences (Griswold and Pearson, 2005: 360). These policies may create a burden perceived as too great to bear, discouraging men from pursuing meaningful employment and driving them away from their families. Griswold and Pearson conclude that pressuring ex-prisoners to pay child support without changing their employment and earnings picture had little success; employment is the key to child support payment during release.

For women in prison, separation from children invokes considerable stress. The majority of women in prison are mothers – some 66 per cent according to a study of 567 women released from fourteen HM prisons and four HM Young Offender Institutions (Hamlyn and Lewis, 2000: x). Unlike fathers in prison, who may be able to count on a spouse or girlfriend to parent children in their absence, women suffer more anxiety about the type of care their children are receiving. Less than one quarter of those with children report that they are can depend on fathers to care for their children while they are in prison. Dodge and Pogrebin (2001) found that of the 300 women they interviewed, who had been released from state prison in the USA, most reported 'extreme difficulties' in regaining custody of their children. On release, the women must prove to child welfare workers that they have become responsible adults and negotiate the legal process involved in child welfare proceedings.

The Impact of Local Authority Care

It is a significant but under-theorised fact that those released from local authority care experience many of the same problems of resettlement as those released from prison. The numbers are not comparable. There are about 136 prisons in England and Wales, holding more than 71,000 people on any given day, and about 90,000 prisoners are released every year (Social Exclusion Unit, 2002: 23). There are, in contrast, about 50,000 youngsters who are 'looked after' by local authorities and some 8000 exit the system each year (Mendes and Moslehuddin, 2004: 333).

But while the magnitude of the problem differs, the profile of care leavers is eerily familiar. A survey of 2905 young people who had left local authority care across England and Wales revealed that a mere 11 per cent had secured full-time employment; about 52 per cent were unemployed, and 28 per cent were pursuing further education or training (Broad, 1999: 86–7). People who have been looked after possess much lower educational qualifications than their peers who have never been in care; they are likely to be unemployed, and when they find jobs are more likely to be in lower-level jobs (Cheung and Heath, 1994). There is a high correlation between local authority care and homelessness. The British Department of Health estimated in 2001 that 40 per cent of homeless young people in London and other large cities were graduates of local authority care. Care-leavers are more likely to suffer poor mental and physical health. A follow-up survey of care-leavers in Surrey found that the majority had long-term illnesses and one in six had a chronic mental disorder (Mendes and Moslehuddin, 2004: 333–4).

A similar portrait emerges from American studies where about 20,000 persons each year exit the child welfare system. They face serious problems, including lack of employment, minimal educational achievement, homelessness, and unmet medical needs. A 1990 study of 55 former foster care youths in the San Francisco Bay area revealed that between one year and 10 years after exiting the system, 38 per cent had not completed high school, 25 per cent were unemployed, 35 per cent were homeless or had moved frequently, and 13 per cent had been hospitalised for an emotional problem. A 1991 study of 810 former foster care youths in eight states reported that 2.5 to 4 years after leaving care, 46 per cent had not completed high school, 51 per cent were unemployed, 62 per cent had not held a job for at least one year, and 25 per cent had been homeless for at least one night (Fagnoni, 1999).

There is also a correlation between being raised by a local authority and being sent to prison. Carlen (1987) estimates that as many as half of the population in British young offender institutions had previously been in local authority care. She explored this connection in interviews with 39 convicted women, 22 of whom said they would never have become involved in criminal careers had it not been for their experience in the child welfare system. The care experience represents a significant source of criminalisation, particularly for women, as it sets up material, ideological, and psychological barriers for living on their own. Mendes and Moslehuddin (2004: 334) found that 38 per cent of young prisoners and 23 per cent of adult prisoners had experienced local authority care as children. For too many people, the entry into criminal justice followed an exit from the child welfare system.

At the very least, the failure of care-leavers to become integrated suggests that clearing up the spill-over into social welfare from criminal justice may be more problematic than government pronouncements about joined-up strategies suggest. It is difficult to see how better coordination of two failed systems leads to one successful system. From a larger perspective, it would seem that there is something about the brush with government control that disables rather then empowers. Whether the ostensible purpose of this control is care or custody, the people who graduate from it are scarcely better off than they were before, and too many are worse off.

Conclusion

Government strategies for dealing with crime include costs in the area of social welfare that are often overlooked. Some practices, such as zero tolerance policing and mass imprisonment, have enjoyed considerable political and popular support. But the full costs, which include charges to the social policy budget, have not been fully realised. Improvements will need to be made in employment, housing, health and family programmes. The externalities of crime policies need to be appreciated as a social problem, particularly in the sense of the resources required, but understood at the level of the individuals who experience the deficiencies in available services.

Questions for Discussion

1. *How does the concept of an externality differ from that of unintended effect?*

2. *To what extent can zero tolerance policing represent a solution to the problem of crime in cities?*

3. *Should former prisoners be entitled to social housing? Should they be made to pay child support arrears?*

4. *Why do people graduating from local authority care experience many of the same resettlement problems as those released from prison?*

Further Reading

Eric, Jensen, Jurg Gerber and Clayton Mosher (2004) 'Social Consequences of the War on Drugs: The Legacy of Failed Policy', *Criminal Justice Policy Review* 15: 100–21.

Liebling, Alison and Shadd Maruna (eds) (2005) *The Effects of Imprisonment.* Cullompton: Willan.

Justice Policy Centre (2005) *Understanding the Challenges of Prisoner Reentry.* Washington, DC: Urban Institute. www.urban.org

Mike Stephens (2000) *Crime and Social Policy: The Police and the Criminal Justice System.* Eastbourne: Gildredge Press.

PART THREE

Emergent Issues

The Criminalisation of Social Policy

SUMMARY

- The politics of crime prevention has led to the use of social policy as a criminal sanction
- There is a trend in North America and Europe toward greater reliance on crime policy (over social policy) in responding to crime
- When practised in criminal justice settings, social work tends to emphasise control over care
- Since the 'discovery' of child abuse, child welfare has tended to prioritise child protection over family services

---

There are good reasons, as we have seen in previous chapters, for believing that social policy leads to reductions in crime. But making crime reduction a goal of social policy does present some unavoidable questions. Crawford (1998: 121) asks: Where does, or should, one end and the other begin? Is it appropriate to justify social policy by reference to its (potential) crime prevention qualities?

Crawford is speaking here about social crime prevention, but the questions he identifies have significance for the relationship between criminology and social policy generally. The trouble is that when the goal of crime reduction is stirred into the rationale for social policy, it tends to become the sole or most important justification. 'Criminalisation of social policy' refers to the situation in which social welfare issues become redefined as crime problems. When goals of providing affordable homes, improving health, and providing incomes through employment become secondary to crime reduction in social policy, criminalisation of social policy has occurred.

This chapter explores several dimensions of this process. The first half deals with the relationship between crime and social welfare within a larger political background. It explores the politics surrounding social crime prevention and the use of social policy as a criminal sanction. It also explores the trend within welfare states – the UK, North America and Western Europe – for increasing reliance on crime policy. The second half of the chapter focuses on the personal social services. The personal social services occupy a unique place, both in relation to social policy and criminal justice, which has allowed for some confusion about the primary purpose. The area of child welfare provides a stark example of what can happen when doing good becomes secondary to catching evil-doers.

The Politics of Crime Prevention

The politics of crime prevention can lead to a confusing blend of goals. Efforts to implement social crime prevention have been undermined by traditional crime policy and the link between crime and social conditions has led to the use of social policy as a criminal sanction.

Social Crime Prevention

Social crime prevention has become a major plank in national crime prevention strategies pursued in Europe and elsewhere. Beginning with Sweden in 1974, the governments of European nations have created national crime prevention councils and provided funds for social development programmes. Social crime prevention proposes that the most effective way to prevent crime is to invest in social development programmes that strengthen individuals, families and communities. Social crime prevention programmes seek to address the factors associated with delinquency, including violence in the home, poverty, inadequate housing, school failure, and unemployment (Canadian Crime Prevention Council, 1996: 3).

There is, as Gilling (1994) puts it, a certain 'definitional elasticity' to social crime prevention. This informational and conceptual ambiguity opens the door to multiple and contradictory political interests, and at the end of the day, makes it vulnerable to co-optation by conventional crime control agendas. This can be seen in community safety models that attempt to coordinate social programmes with criminal justice methods. As envisioned in the Morgan Report of 1991, 'community safety' represented a response that differed from crime policies in its attention to social welfare concerns. But as implemented by the Labour government after 1997, the community safety strategy came to encompass a mixed bag of local partnerships, zero-tolerance policing, and open street CCTV. It failed to influence crime control in the direction of welfarism, he concludes, because it was implemented within a political framework of neo-liberalism (Gilling, 2001).

Sutton and Cherney (2003) found this loss of focus to have occurred in an Australian crime prevention project. The State of Victoria implemented its Good Neighbour Programme in 1988 that sought to blend crime prevention and social policy objectives along the lines of the French Bonnemaison model. This initiative led to several related schemes during the 1990s, including Safer Communities and Safer Communities and Shires. Community safety not only included crime prevention, but public health issues such as injury prevention and anti-smoking initiatives. The community safety model led to the development of positive working relationships between state and local agencies, and had success in building crime prevention and public health considerations into the activities of business and government. But, at the same time, the focus on community safety meant the goals of the programme were far from clear: zero-tolerance police initiatives occurred under the same umbrella as social crime prevention.

Dixon (2006) provides an example from South Africa. In his review of crime prevention in South Africa from the end of apartheid in 1992, he found that what began with a commitment to economic growth and social development became subordinated to security concerns and the need for an immediate response to crime. Crime became *the* social problem and tackling it an essential pre-condition for development. Dixon concludes that safety and security comprise legitimate goals for social policy; preventing crime, like providing health care, family support, or income support is 'doing' social policy. But the harms associated with criminal victimisation should not be given automatic priority over other harms because they are itemised within criminal law (Dixon, 2006: 185–6). He refers to the criminalisation of social policy as an instance of 'cosmetic crime prevention':

> To see and respond to deep-rooted social problems only when, where and to the extent that they manifest themselves as crime problems is ... to treat the symptoms as worse than the disease, and then to offer only the most cosmetic crime prevention remedies. (Dixon, 2004: 176)

Social Policy as a Criminal Sanction

Linking crime reduction with social policy is meant to operate in one direction, that is, the extension of social welfare benefits to pre-empt criminal behaviour. Graham and Bennett (1995) insist that crime prevention should not be seen as a justification for the provision of welfare as this would lead to the provision of social benefits only to the extent that they led to a reduction in crime. Programmes in areas of housing, education, and employment found to be ineffective as a means of crime reduction would be discontinued according to this logic even if they succeeded in providing better housing, extending educational opportunity, and so on. In their view, the relationship should only be seen the other way around. The withdrawal of social benefits from those accustomed to them could result in elevated levels of crime as people could be forced into criminal behaviour as a means of subsistence. Even when a particular benefits programme fails to achieve the desired result as a matter of social policy, it should still be continued because of its potential for crime reduction. Policymakers should regard crime reduction as the sole or leading justification for social policy *only when* contemplating a withdrawal of social benefits (Graham and Bennett, 1995: 12).

But crime prevention is arguably a political business and engaging the political process means that the direction can be reversed. During the Blair years, crime has been seen as the basis for which social benefits may be *denied* rather than *extended*. Frank Field MP, the Labour government's first Minister for Welfare Reform, championed the idea of leveraging welfare benefits as a means of kerbing incivility and crime. He has developed the logic, implicit in criminal justice legislation such as the Crime and Disorder Act (1998) and Youth Justice and Criminal Evidence Act (1999), that provision of welfare services should be conditional on adhering to minimum standards of civility. The Conservatives have taken up aspects of this argument, insisting that local authorities should have the power to withhold housing benefit from people for persistent anti-social behaviour, and Blair has made 'respect' and tackling 'yob culture' the central theme of his third term (Rodger, 2006).

McKeever (2004) questions the attempt to leverage social benefits as a means of promoting proper behaviour. She writes about the use of social security as a criminal sanction. The Child Support, Pensions and Social Security Act of 2000 provided that social security benefits can be withheld from convicted offenders who breach the terms of their community sentences. This measure was intended to deter those on community sanction (as well as suitably punish) those who breach and emphasise the conditionality of benefits. McKeever argues that withdrawal of benefits achieves short-term gains at the expense of creating long-term problems. The withdrawal of benefits clearly poses problems for offenders that contribute to the cycle of re-offending, creating a bigger problem for both criminal justice and social security policies than the one it solves.

Rodger (2006) argues that while social policy has an important role to play in tackling incivility and criminality, the aims of social policy are significantly different from those of criminal justice. Social policy cannot change along the lines suggested by Field and remain social policy. The criminal justice system should concentrate on matters concerning violation of criminal law, and social welfare should centre on elevating social capital. Hope (2001) sees the other side of the coin. He argues for the successful application of social policy to crime prevention. Defending the idea behind community safety, he insists that such strategies are necessary to counteract the view that crime-specific approaches are sufficient. Crime policy alone cannot resolve the 'root causes' of crime.

Crime Policy in Welfare States

Comparing the crime policy situation of the 2000s with that of the 1970s, there appears to have been a marked change in governments' approach to crime. This trend might be described as 'the punitive turn', a turning away from social policy and toward crime policy (Pratt et al., 2005). It has occurred in the UK and the USA, and in France, the Netherlands, and the Nordic countries, although possibly for different reasons.

Crime Policy in the UK and USA

Britain appears to be following a course in its response to crime drawn by map-makers in America. Garland (2001b) describes the 'culture of control' that emerged during the final three decades of the twentieth century. He situates crime policy in a 'broad social field' that includes not only criminal justice institutions, but policies and practices concerned with social welfare. The decline of rehabilitation as a goal of criminal justice does not reflect a shift away from welfarism as an ideal so much as a reorganisation of control within the capitalist welfare state. Each system, social welfare and criminal justice, continues to reinforce and engage the other, though along different lines than before. Welfare policies are co-joined, coordinated, and mutually reinforcing with punishment. In Garland's (2005: 173) words: 'Penal policy – like welfare policy – is a set of laws, practices and representations designed by high-status social groups for the management of control of low-status groups who are regarded as problematic'.

Wacquant (2001b) sees the punitive turn in crime policy as symptomatic of the welfare state. Borrowing a metaphor from Pierre Bourdieu, the welfare state has a single body with two hands, the 'left hand' representing education, public health, social security, and housing, and the 'right hand' being the police, courts, and prisons. To understand their movements, even why they appear to differ, we need to understand the mind that controls them both (Wacquant, 2001b: 402). He points to a worldwide diffusion of 'made-in-the-USA' ideologies coincident with neo-liberalism and free market economics. He insists, however, that what has occurred in Europe does not merely replicate the American model: the right hand has *superseded* the left hand in the USA and has *supplemented* the left hand in Western Europe. In France, the government has simultaneously increased social and criminal intervention. It has expanded work contracts for unemployed youth and health coverage while dispatching riot police to 'sensitive neighbourhoods', substituted judges for social workers as decision-makers for run-away youth, instituting anti-begging ordinances in cities, deported foreigners sentenced to prison, and enhanced legal procedures for tackling urban violence. And the French government, unlike the American government, has opted to institutionalise this stance through police and courts rather than prisons (Wacquant, 2001b: 407).

Beckett and Western (2001) agree, at least in principle, with the proposition that the welfare state is interested in regulating and normalising behaviour and relies on mechanisms of care and control to achieve this. But, they see the punitive turn as a feature of the type of welfare state. A welfare state can be characterised as 'inclusive' or 'exclusive' depending on its response to social marginality. Inclusive regimes understand crime as a result of social conditions; they offer generous welfare benefits and curative anti-crime policies. Beckett and Western found evidence of this in a comparison of state spending; states with less generous welfare programmes feature higher incarceration rates and those states with more generous programmes imprison a smaller portion of their residents. Or, in their words, 'governments that provide more generous welfare benefits have lower incarceration rates' (Beckett and Western, 2001: 44–5). They do not see these developments so much as a blend of care and control attributable to changes in political economy as the result of a political process resulting in the preference for control over care. The idea here is that social marginality creates the need for government intervention and government can respond by *either* locking people up or extending welfare benefits.

Comparing the UK with the USA leads to worthwhile insights into the ethos of crime control in Britain. But it is important not to conceive of the punitive turn as an Anglo–American project. What is happening in Britain and America is also happening, albeit to a lesser extent, in the leading welfare states of Europe.

Crime Policy in Europe

For years the welfare states of Western Europe have been held up as models of a rational and humane response to crime. The Netherlands, Sweden, Denmark, and other countries have been seen as proof that social policy makes the best crime policy. European welfare states have sustained low levels of crime by government commitment to spending on social benefits rather than prisons.

Downes (1982, 1988) showcased the Dutch example of decarceration in the Netherlands after the Second World War, a time of rising crime rates when prison populations in England and Wales increased. In Europe, the Netherlands took the lead in reducing prison populations and the incarceration rate fell from 100 prisoners per 100,000 just after the Second World War to approximately 20 in 1975. This was a feature, Downes explained, of a Dutch culture of tolerance that he defined as 'a long tradition of relative leniency towards, and acceptance of, deviants, minority groups, and religious dissent, and which a respectable hearing to such views which elsewhere would be dismissed as extreme or eccentric' (Downes, 1988: 69).

The past few years have seen changes in this scenario. The model welfare states have displayed a disturbing enthusiasm for conventional crime policies of policing and imprisoning. In the Netherlands, Pakes (2005) reports, use of imprisonment has increased dramatically. The rate of imprisonment reached a low point in the 1970s at about 25 imprisoned per 100,000; by 2005 that rate was about 85 per 100,000 (Pakes, 2005: 146). The police and prosecution service has been expanded and continues to grow. Pakes argues that while tolerance continues to inform policy areas such as euthanasia and prostitution, it no longer informs matters of criminal policy generally. Changes in criminal policy reflect the influence of international concern with drugs and organised crime and the racialisation of crime, specifically concern about crime among immigrants from Morroco. Before he was assassinated in May 2002, populist political leader Pim Fortuyn had struck a chord with some portion of the Dutch population by calling the Muslim culture of recent immigrants as backward and anti-Dutch. He placed asylum-seekers, overrepresentation of Moroccans in criminal justice, and lack of integration of Muslims on the political agenda.

Estrada (2004), who examined the situation in Sweden, offers a complementary understanding. Crime, he argues, is a problem placed on the political agenda by conservatives when social democratic governments are in power. The emergence of youth crime as a political issue between 1970 and 1999 cannot be explained by actual trends in youth crime in these years. Rather, the conservatives became the first to exploit the problem of 'rising crime' and in so doing, moved the conservative position from the margins to the centre of Swedish political discourse about crime. At first the Liberals, and then the Social Democrats, adapted their position in response.

Other commentators on the European situation suggest that this political account is incomplete, if not inaccurate. Tham (2001) argues how the 'Swedish model' used to mean full employment policy secured by government intervention into the economy, but it has come to refer to drug policy aimed at securing a 'drug-free society'. Sweden's anti-drug policies do not reflect a surge in crime, but neither do they represent the capture of government by rightist political parties. The change appears to derive from a genuine commitment on the part of the left. The Social Democratic Party in the 1990s favoured increasing punitiveness and control. When the Minister of Justice announced in 1994 that there was no difference between the Social Democrats and the non-socialist parties on the matter of crime control, he seemed to be signalling that the interest was not a temporary change but a permanent change.

Balvig (2004) describes the existential origins of the renaissance of punishment in Denmark. Beginning in 2002, Danish crime policy began to change with the perception that the prison system was 'all sold out'. In 2003, for the first time in several decades, the majority in parliament decided to expand prison capacity by adding cells and committed to building a new prison in 2008. Further, plans were made to increase the size of the police service (Balvig, 2004: 169). Balvig explains this with reference to the 'second existential revolution', the way ordinary people relate to themselves and their surroundings. The first revolution, the foundation of the welfare state, expressed a belief in reducing crime by means of tackling poverty, lack of housing and so on. The second revolution sees crime in a free world and risk of crime against the need for protection. It derives in part from a crisis in the welfare state. The basic assumption (of the first revolution) that welfare would result in less crime was not confirmed: in Denmark registered crime was higher at the end of the twentieth century than it was at the end of the Second World War. This realisation led to reflection on the causes and background of crime: 'How can we explain crime, if it is not caused by poverty, bad living conditions, lack of education etc?' (Balvig, 2004: 182).

Saarinen (2003) adds support for Balvig's thesis from a curious source: sales of crime fiction. In Sweden, the best-selling novels during the past ten years or so have been detective fiction.[1] Henning Mankell's stories featuring the

---

[1]Scandinavian crime fiction offers a blend of the murder story with 'serious' literature, featuring melancholy characters and complicated plots reminiscent of P.D. James.

Swedish police detective Wallander have proved astonishingly popular. Mankell has sold more than 15 million books world-wide. Saarinen thinks the popularity of such literary fare reflects Scandinavians' anxieties about 'the surplus of evil' in welfare states, the inability of social policy to bring an end to intentional victimisation. The stories speak to worries politicians do not voice, chiefly the presence of criminal motivation in a society where every-body has nice clothing, healthy food, and a comfortable home.

Care, Control and Social Work

The area of social policy experiencing the most frequent attempts to link it with crime policy is the personal social services. This reflects the particular characteristics of social services as a medium of social policy as well as the historic overlap of social services with criminal justice.

The Logic of Social Services

The personal social services seek to assist populations with acute needs, including older people, physically and mentally disabled, children and dys-functional families. This area of government intervention was not included in the founding vision of the welfare state. While social work has since been inte-grated into welfare state provision (during the 1960s), it differs from other social policy areas in several respects.

Like other areas of social policy, social services espouses universalistic princi-ples. Social work philosophy invokes principles of social justice and love of humanity as its guiding ethos. In reality, the clients or users of social services come from a particular social category – the poor. And, unlike other social policy areas, the demand for social services does not arise from the potential recipients themselves, at least not in any straightforward sense. The pressures that lead to calls for social work come from anxieties of politicians and the pub-lic about child abuse or disturbances caused by aggressive, mentally ill persons (Hill, 2000: 178). The majority of clients do not contact social service agencies willingly but are sent by courts or other welfare agencies. Miller (1998) notes the extent to which the routine record-keeping of staff in social work settings antic-ipates escalation of staff–client disagreements into formal disputes. A significant aspect of the 'protection' function carried out by social workers is to protect themselves from legal, political, and professional challenges.

Kemshall and associates (1997) argue that *risk* has emerged as the central organising principle across the personal social services as well as the proba-tion service. Risk assessment, risk management, and the monitoring of risk have become the mantra of managers and practitioners in social service set-tings. Rather than seeking to meet needs and working to achieve fairer distribution of goods, modern society concerns itself with the distribution of hazards, dangers, and risks. Kemshall and associates argue that this modern formulation relates to the loss of faith in clinical and scientific knowledge as the basis for social services. Social services delivery has been reorganised to reflect three dimensions of risk: the desire for more accurate prediction of risk, the allocation of blame for failure to anticipate risk, and pursuit of multi-agency decision-making or openness of decision-making as a means of deflecting blame.

Svensson (2003) describes the practice of social work as the exercise of 'caring power'. Caring power is exercised in the spirit of doing what is best for a person in need or distress. The helper defines what is best and promises help provided the person follows the helper's advice. In this way, the helper dictates the conditions and the person seeking help must acquiesce. 'This caring power carries both help and control in the same actions', Svensson (2003: 85) says, 'and is the main characteristic of social work in all times and places'. In this way, she argues that the absence of resistance or outright conflict between social workers and their clients does not indicate a relationship without power. Since caring power is exercised with kindness, it requires amenable clients. When clients express agreement, power can be exercised in a way that avoids exposing its exercise. Social workers will always strive for maintaining the appearance of agreement, in order to avoid revealing the structure of caring power on which social work techniques are based.

Joined-up Services

In the UK, the argument for joined-up services sees the benefits of overlapping social work and criminal justice objectives. The argument for a multi-agency team approach to youth crime reflects this idea of police, social services, probation, education, and health services working within a single and coherent legal framework. The Crime and Disorder Act (1998) sought to change the operation of youth courts and the way in which the police, probation service, and child welfare organisations dealt with young lawbreakers. The act created youth offending teams (YOTs) under the supervision of the Youth Justice Board of England and Wales. Comprised of staff seconded from police, probation service, social service, and health organisations, these multi-agency panels are meant to respond to the criticism that the youth court focused on the bureaucratic processing of cases and did not do enough to divert youth away from criminal activities. The Youth Justice and Criminal Evidence Act (1999) introduced a method of referring young people convicted for the first time to Youth Offenders Panels (YOPs), established by YOTs. The panels conduct inquiries into the causes of anti-social behaviour within referrals, and draw up contracts with young lawbreakers and their parents, suited to the particulars of the situation (Burnett and Appleton, 2004).

The merging of social welfare and criminal justice within a single institutional framework involves conflicting ideologies. Blagg and others (1988) observed some years ago that achieving multi-agency cooperation in crime reduction schemes is difficult. Inter-agency relationships display inequities of power among the agencies to be enjoined, and failure to think this through can result in dominance of the 'police view'. Further, where multi-agency cooperation is taken as a strategy for crime prevention it should be clear what contribution agencies, other than the police, should be able to make. There is a tendency to focus on achievable goals, such as short-term crime reduction, rather than larger goals around expanding economic opportunities, improving housing, and promoting education.

King (1991) argues that the ideology of social welfare draws on knowledge without clear historical provenance. Are the statements social workers make about what is good and bad for children derived from common sense, medicine, science, politics, or religion? The statements the police make in this area are more likely to derive from law, a self-referential system built up over centuries, with its own aims and inherent logic. Social welfare practitioners have in recent years turned to science and the testing of empirical evidence by social-science techniques as a means of building up a base of 'child welfare science'. The problem for child welfare science is that it must operate in a legal arena, and social work statements derived from social science about what is best for a child will be subservient to legal requirements. 'Hybrid institutions', such as institutionalised social worker/police partnerships, are likely to be colonised by legal institutions. In putting themselves in joint enterprises with police, social workers risk losing their identity and finding themselves reconstituted as legal actors (King, 1991).

Penna (2005) discusses the social meaning of information-sharing among agencies under the Children Act (2004). Ostensibly, use of information retrieval and tracking systems is a beneficial, if not indispensable, part of inter-agency working. Computer technologies are utilised for benevolent case management and represent a major step forward in liberating children from abuse, deprivation and insecurity. Such systems also become the basis for social surveillance and social regulation. Welfare projects, Penna argues, are embedded in political projects, projects that are concerned with managing what is politically defined as 'desirable social development'. Welfare policies represent technologies of governance, used to normalise visions of the good society.

Forensic Social Work

Forensic social work refers to field of practice in social work broadly defined as that related to legal issues and litigation, both civil and criminal. This field is emerging in Australia, and re-emerging in the UK and USA, where it is already well-defined (Green, Thorpe and Traupmann, 2005: 142).

Roberts and Brownell (1999) review the history of social work in criminal justice, demonstrating how social workers have engaged in forensic social work since the early 1900s. They define 'forensic social work' as 'policies, practices and social work roles with juvenile and adult offenders and victims of crime'

(Roberts and Brownell, 1999: 143). Drawing on American examples, they describe how social workers led the movement for separate youth courts, beginning at Chicago in 1899, and during the 1920s established women's bureaus within municipal police departments. Social work involvement with wayward youth continued along with public concern about delinquency and expanded during the 1960s along with the federalisation of delinquency prevention efforts. Victims' rights legislation during the 1980s led to social workers being employed in programmes providing services to victims of crime, including victims of domestic violence, sexual assault and other violent crime. Roberts and Brownell insist that social workers should have a role within criminal justice settings in advocating for the social service needs of crime victims and offenders.

Historically, criminal justice has tended to have a bigger impact on social work than the other way around. The history of the probation service yields a prime example. The Probation Service began as a social work practice in the 1880s; the first probation officers, known originally as 'police court missionaries', were dispatched by private charity organisations. In 1938, they came into the direct employ of the Home Office and during the next few decades created a professional identity for themselves that differed from social work. New duties under the Criminal Justice Act (1972) further estranged probation officers from their social work genealogy. Probation officers became responsible for carrying out community service orders, which formally aligned probation officers with the day-to-day working of criminal courts rather than social service agencies. By 2000, the transformation into a 'punishing service' (Goodman, 2003) was complete: a policy document defined the National Probation Service for England and Wales as 'a law enforcement agency delivering community punishments ...' (Home Office, 2000).

The Disciplinary State and Child Welfare

Child welfare comprises a central aspect of social services involving families. The 'discovery' of child abuse transformed the relationship between social workers and families. It has led to the neglect of children in favour of a focus on targeting abusers for legal action.

The Disciplinary State

While members of the social work, education, and medical professions explain their motives with reference to benevolent concern for the least powerful members of families – women and children – the overall effect is discipline. Or so Donzelot (1980) and the architects of the social discipline perspective have argued. As they see it, the social services represent a disciplining mechanism intended to provide a more continuous and effective form of authority. A system of disciplinary technologies across the fields of health, education, and raising children became the most important feature of public policy in modern society. These technologies find their raison d'être in policing, understood not in the limited sense of criminal law enforcement, but in all methods for developing the strength of the nation. 'The aim of policing', Donzelot (1980: 7) explains, quoting an eighteenth-century source, 'is to make everything that composes the state serve to strengthen and increase its power, and likewise to serve the public welfare'. He notes how the emergence of 'children's rights' led, paradoxically, to a tightening of the state's control over private relationships. When the child came to be seen as a small citizen, the preservation of children became the basis on which the state advanced its control over poor families.

Social policy scholars working within the broad outlines of the social discipline paradigm regard the modern child welfare system as an extension of the disciplinary state. Jones and Novak (1999) contend that the care extended by social service authorities in Britain involves a substantial amount of control. To obtain assistance, clients must reveal details of personal, emotional, and financial life to a stranger, who expects 'cooperation' – changes in attitudes, behaviours, and values – in return for the assistance. Cash seldom changes hands. The assistance is more likely to be friendly, personal advice, backed by extensive power to remove children from family. 'The price of social work "help" is all too often state supervision' (Jones and Novak, 1999: 84).

Ericsson (2000) describes how Norwegian child welfare since the Second World War has liberated the less powerful, children and women, from patriarchal rule within the family and enclosed the family within the social regulation enforced by the state. She cites Anders Bratholm, a well-known child advocate during the 1970s, who argued that social workers' supervision of families within homes should be 'just as natural' as the control exercised by factory inspectors regarding health and safety in workplaces. Critics of the social discipline perspective suggest that such accounts render family policy much more coherent, even conspiratorial, than it actually is. There are political conflicts surrounding child welfare policy and these conflicts are reproduced in the administration of social services to families.

At a minimum, the contribution of the social discipline perspective is to point out that there are reasons, other than benevolence, for provision of benefits. Ginsburg (1992: 10) points out that nation states turn to social policy in efforts to engineer national solidarity. While the political language of welfare programmes appeals to human rights and universal values, the programmes themselves contribute to nationalism. The National Health Service, he observes, evokes a sense of British national pride. Or, to take an extreme example, Hitler saw family policy as a means of securing mass loyalty. National Socialist economic policy kept wages down but pursued a family policy including a child benefits scheme and family concession within income tax reform. To ensure *der innere Sieg*, 'the inner victory', Hitler felt it necessary to bolster ideological propaganda with tangible aid to families (Voegeli, 2003: 142).

The 'Discovery' of Child Abuse

The 'discovery' of child abuse transformed child welfare. In Britain, political and popular concern with child abuse, beginning in the 1960s, led to a redefinition of social services away from support, consistent with social policy objectives, and toward protection, consistent with crime policy.

Child abuse reporting became a priority for social welfare agencies in 1972. In May of that year, a Study Group on Child Abuse convened at Tunbridge Wells, financed in part by the DHSS. Sir Keith Joseph, Secretary of State for Social Services in the Health Administration, and others from the DHSS attended. Several days after the conference, the death of Maria Colwell made newspaper headlines. Not only did newspaper editors give extensive coverage to the story, but they also took an active role in campaigning for policy. *The Sunday Times* printed a series entitled 'The Battered Baby Scandal' featuring a picture of Maria Colwell and text asserting that more than seven hundred children died each year in this way (Parton, 1979: 441). These events followed identification of 'the battered child syndrome' by Dr Henry Kempe in 1962. Kempe's work led to the discovery of abuse as a major social problem in American society. National magazines published a series of sensational articles about 'beaten babies' and all three of the major television networks incorporated the issue within their medical drama series, which were enormously popular at that time. By 1966, every state legislature across the USA had enacted statutes to kerb parents' abuse of children (Pfohl, 1977: 310).

When applied to children, the term 'at risk' used to mean a child at risk of entering government care, but following the child abuse scare of the 1960s it came to mean children at risk from parents (and who needed to be rescued by social workers). The present system took shape during the 1970s with the formalisation of DHSS policy. In 1976, the DHSS released a circular stressing, for the first time, the importance of including a senior police officer in all area review committees and case conferences. This circular signalled the beginning of a trend in which the venerable principles of client confidentiality and due process would be suspended in the 'best interests of the child'. Conceptualisation of the problem shifted away from the narrowly defined battered baby syndrome to the more all-inclusive notion of 'child abuse', and was seen as symptomatic of much more fundamental problems in British society. By 1979, the problem of child abuse had been given the utmost priority within social service departments so that whatever else might be cut back, the non-accidental injury case always takes precedence (Parton, 1979: 443–5). As a result, social workers became channelled into an 'authoritative, intrusive, and insistent' role in relation to families; 'a style of intervention in families which regards the parents with watchful suspicion and sees protection and rescue of children from bad families as a primary objective' (Parton, 1981: 406–7).

The need for balance became clear in the wake of the Cleveland affair, which took place in 1987 in a large local authority area in the north-east of England.

Over a period of several weeks, social workers removed 121 children from their homes based on the assertions of two paediatricians concerning physical signs of abuse. Some of the children remained in local authority care for five months and more. The Dartington Social Research Unit, summarising a series of research projects commissioned in the wake of the Cleveland affair, found that most child protection referrals did not involve serious physical or sexual child abuse. Rather, they consisted of children believed to be at risk of harm due to parents' substance abuse, conflict between parents, poor parenting skills, and poverty-induced stress. Because social work practice with families had become focused on child protection, social workers responded as if they were serious cases of abuse. The child protection approach had two adverse effects. First, it resulted in responses that many parents perceived as stigmatising and officious. Second, it was rare for such families, once their children were found not to be at risk, to receive supportive resources (Corby, 2003: 196).

Social Workers and Police Officers

Social work with families embodies a contradiction in the state's concern with child protection over family services. 'Child protection' is characterised by a primary concern with protecting children from abuse by parents seen as morally flawed and legally culpable. The social work processes within this orientation are built around statutory and investigatory concerns in which the relationship between social workers and parents becomes adversarial. 'Family services' is characterised by a tendency to understand acts, regarded as harmful to children, in the contexts of psychological or social dynamics of families. Social worker activities in this outlook emphasise further assessment and the provision of therapeutic services. The relationship between social workers and parents is understood as a partnership (Spratt, 2001: 407).

Although the 1989 Children Act sought to address this dual role, there remains a real difficulty in pulling off this balancing act. Enacting carefully worded legislation and issuing new guidelines for social work with families does not address the essential problem of attempting to combine the social welfare function with the police function. Lord Justice Butler-Sloss, who chaired the Cleveland Inquiry, zeroed in on the ambiguity of the social worker's interview with the alleged victim of child abuse. Is the interview for investigation, assessment, or therapy? 'It doesn't matter in a way what you call it', Butler-Sloss (1993: 56) concluded, 'so long as you know why you are doing it'.

Blurring of the roles has been regarded as a positive development. The overall thrust of government policy, from the 1980s, has sought to improve coordination of statutory agencies in targeting and responding to 'dangerous families' where abuse in likely to occur. Since then, social workers and police officers have been encouraged to 'work together' as part of an inter-professional matrix mobilised to protect children. In 2001, the Chief Inspector of the Social Services Inspectorate proclaimed that 'traditional demarcation lines must be a thing of the past' (Garrett,

2004: 78–9). But there are 'dangers of collusion and merger'. In his address to the British Association of Social Workers the year after Cleveland, Terry Thomas wondered who was learning from whom in social work/police collaborations.

> It is not enough to say that we have 'educated' the police over the years through child abuse case conferences and other forums without at least being open to the idea that the police may have also been 'educating' us during the same period'. (Quoted in Garrett, 2004: 80)

Social work partnerships with police amounted to social policing, which, as Thomas pointed out, is only one step removed from *real* policing.

Research into social work/police collaborations suggests that social policing is an apt description. Scourfield and Welsh (2003), in an ethnographic study, explored the management of risk within a childcare social work team in northern England. They found much routine practice to reflect overt control. Not that the team did not offer help or support for clients at all, but that the team members clearly made use of their legal authority. 'Being clear about concerns' has achieved, according to Scourfield and Welsh, the status of a social work intervention. Social workers explained that the intervention depended on the parental response. Parents must acknowledge there has been a difficulty or problem and accept social service intervention as the means of 'moving forward', to avoid moving down the road toward legal proceedings. This orientation reflects the extent to which social workers see themselves as advocates for the best interests of the children, which in the case of young children will be decided by social workers themselves. 'Social workers tend to be very clear that their responsibilities are to children *rather than* adults' (Scourfield and Welsh, 2003: 415).

Garrett's (2004) research raises important questions about the logic of social workers and police working together. He interviewed social workers and police officers working conjointly in three child protection units. Social workers reported some positive impact on police, such as making police officers self-conscious about using racist language, but also reported the difficulty of maintaining their professional identity. One social worker interviewed reported that she no longer considered herself a social worker: 'I'm not really a social worker; I'm not a police officer … I'm in this "child protection unit thing" now'. She also emphasised her role in providing the police with 'clean evidence' for use in criminal proceedings against parents. 'As far as I'm concerned *I'm servicing the police*. I'm trying to get a child to tell me what happened so there's a weight for my police colleagues to go and confront a guy with', she explained. 'Quite clearly, I'm offering my skills to the police as a means of investigation' (Garrett, 2004: 89).

Conclusion

Criminalisation of social policy appears to be a recent event. Social policies have been directed, or perhaps *mis*directed, at crime reduction in the wake of recent political developments such as the child abuse panic of the 1970s and 1980s. But it may also be that this process occurs for reasons more central to the structure of the capitalist welfare state itself. Instances of the criminalisation of social policy can be found earlier in the twentieth century, suggesting that it is a more significant problem for the welfare state.

Questions for Discussion

1. *Is it appropriate to justify social policy with reference to its potential crime reduction qualities?*

2. *Why are the socialist welfare states in Europe adopting a 'tough on crime' stance?*

3. *Are the personal social services about care or control?*

4. *What is the proper mission of social workers in the area of child welfare? Does it overlap with the police?*

Further Reading

Katherine Beckett (1997) *Making Crime Pay: Law and Order in Contemporary American Politics*. Oxford: Oxford University Press.

Tony Fitzpatrick (2001) 'New Agendas for Social Policy and Criminology: Globalization, Urbanism and the Emerging Post-Social Security State', *Social Policy and Administration* 35: 212–29.

David Garland (1985) *Punishment and Welfare*. Aldershot: Gower.

John Pratt et al. (2005) *The New Punitiveness: Trends, Theories, Perspectives*. Cullompton: Willan.

The Pursuit of Social Justice   10

SUMMARY

- Theories of social justice tend to be constructed around concepts of rights, need, or membership
- Hayek was sceptical of social justice because he felt that it could not be successfully joined up with a market economy
- Rawls offers an influential theory of social justice grounded in political liberalism
- Useful insights about social justice and policymaking include the middle region, responsible commitment, and the principle of neutrality

Social justice is an evocative phrase. It envisions a future not only with less crime, but greater equality, broader citizenship, and more extensive public services (Cook, 2006: 1). In UK policy speak, the language of social justice has broad appeal. It has been attached to government activities ranging across the social policy spectrum to criminal justice and beyond. The Scottish Museums Council (2000), for instance, issued its report *Museums and Social Justice*, concerning the role of museums in reducing social exclusion.

Can social justice offer a coherent map for pursuing the terrain of criminology and social policy? In this chapter, we explore the extent to which social justice theorising furnishes a practical morality suitable for formulating a meaningful policy response. To do this, we will go beyond criminology in the sense that much of the discussion will involve thinkers not regarded as criminologists. Rather than reviewing empirical research as in earlier chapters, the discussion here will engage arguments more familiar to philosophy, or perhaps history, than social science. We will contemplate what criminology might learn from thinkers who see themselves as something other than social scientists.

This chapter is divided into four parts. The first part reviews three vocabularies of social justice emerging in the nineteenth century. The next two parts present the foremost sceptic of social justice, F.A. Hayek, and the most influential theoretician of social justice, John Rawls. The final part reviews several suggestions for policy change inspired by social justice.

Vocabularies of Social Justice

Thinking about social justice is a distinctively modern activity. Social philosophers and political reformers introduced the phrase 'social justice' in the nineteenth century (Miller, 1999). The concepts they introduced – rights, need, and membership – continue to supply the conceptual fuselage for contemporary philosophies of social justice.

The Vocabulary of Rights

The rights-based tradition of social justice thinking derives from political liberalism. Liberals have sought to build notions of social justice from ideas contained in the founding political doctrines of modern civil societies, primarily by extending notions of rights and equality from the political context into a market context.

The classic statement of political liberalism outlines a system of political rights ensuring equality of opportunity but not equality of outcome. Each individual is to have an equal right to own property, but the amount of property is thought to depend on personal capacities and efforts. John Stuart Mill introduced the phrase social justice into the English language, according to the *Oxford English Dictionary*, with his book *Utilitarianism* (1861). Despite occasional references to communism as a higher form of society than capitalism, he persisted in the liberal view of justice. He defended unequal outcomes, based on free competition within the market, but did not look at the capitalist society of his time uncritically. He suggested that the inheritance system should be modified, that women should be given equal opportunities with men, and that workers should form their own cooperatives rather than working for capitalists (Miller, 1978: 11).

Marshall (1950) pursued a comprehensive set of rights within his theory of citizenship. He described these rights as those enjoyed by the members of a civilised society:

1. *Civil rights* are those necessary for the exercise of political freedom: free speech, the right to own property and enter contracts.
2. *Political rights* concern the right to participate, including the right to vote and to stand for election to political office.
3. *Social rights* have to do with entitlements to economic security and welfare; principally, education and social services.

Marshall, who tended to see the post-war welfare state as the culmination of Western civilisation, saw these rights as emanating from British history as much as logic. Civil rights emerged in the eighteenth century, followed by political rights in the nineteenth and social rights in the twentieth (Roche, 1987: 382).

Rights-based formulations see the nation-state at the centre of the social justice universe. As Miller (1999) explains, the realisation of social justice requires 'a bounded society' in which distribution can be elaborated for its members in relation to one another. The nation-state represents this bounded society in most social justice theorising as it supplies the institutional structure to be modified for fairer distribution of benefits and duties. It also represents the agent of redistribution, the entity capable of initiating and directing the institutional changes needed to bring about social justice (Miller, 1999: 4–6). Social rights become realisable, or legally enforceable, in the context of a national government.

But in recent years it has become possible to talk of 'European social rights', the expansion of rights beyond the national community. Conant (2006) observes that social rights have expanded along with international structures such as the European Court of Justice and European Court of Human Rights. Social rights involve entitlements to social insurance schemes that protect against risks, social assistance benefits to needy persons, and social investment programmes that promote the future, such as education. These judicial forums have expanded social rights by making them legally enforceable. The powers of supranational courts and the ease of access to them have expanded the entitlement to social protection. Conant points out the usefulness of supranational courts in requiring EU member states to extend benefits, to migrants for example, that they have been reluctant to provide.

The Vocabulary of Need

The early socialists framed their critique of capitalism around the concept of need. They sought to build up a 'scientific' understanding of basic human needs in order to place social justice on an objective footing. If needs could be established as objective, then the argument for meeting needs by means of social justice would be a straightforward proposition.

Marx described a long list of human needs: 'to eat, drink, buy books, go to the theatre, go dancing, go drinking, think, love, theorise, sing, paint, fence, etc.' (quoted in Fraser, 1998: 149). These needs did not arise from an inner, fixed nature, but were defined by their social relationships, relationships that depended on the economic structure of society and the class divisions it produced. 'Natural needs', he said, are the needs that must be met in all societies for humanity to continue. In capitalism, natural needs are reduced to 'egoistic needs'; people are not recognised as human beings, as ends in themselves, but simply as a means to fulfilment of the needs of others. Or, in other words, egoistic needs are distinguished as the needs of individuals separated from the needs of the community (Fraser, 1998).

Social justice would prevail when individuals received what they needed on the basis of their humanity and not on the basis of what they extracted from the economy as a matter of class position. Natural needs could be met by welfare schemes within capitalist societies, but the optimal social arrangements, to be experienced under socialism, were those that corresponded with the scientific elaboration of human nature. Marx pursued a 'scientific' analysis of human nature because he wanted to establish the justification for meeting people's needs on a claim of justice rather than charity. Charity needs the support of religious thought, and for Marx, religious systems are embedded in bourgeois morality. This morality perpetuates the status quo in terms of a market, which is to say, unequal, distribution of goods (Robertson, 1998).

Marcuse's (1964) understanding of need draws on this distinction. He identifies the proliferation of false needs under capitalism, brought about by mass consumerism. In the process of manufacturing false needs, capitalism creates a new kind of person, one with willing compliance as an insatiable consumer. 'False needs' are those consumer goods and experiences made 'necessary' by advertising and culture in general. While such needs offer happiness, they also promote toil, misery and injustice. 'True needs' are the only vital ones – nourishment, clothing and lodging. These are true needs because they are a prerequisite for the realisation of all other needs, although, Marcuse (1964: 5–6) says, in the last analysis, the difference between true and false needs can only be settled by individuals themselves.

Robertson (1998) points out that protection from future harm constitutes one of the newest needs, something not considered a need prior to development of the welfare state. Much of the current safety regulations, seat belt and child restraint laws, workplace safety, and public health efforts (for example, to protect individuals from effects of passive smoking) address aspects of protection from future harm. Boutellier (2004) describes modern society as a 'safety utopia' in which people want to be free from the restraints imposed by traditional moral codes yet desire to pursue this freedom in safe surroundings. This has put a premium on health and safety standards supported by science and technology.

The Vocabulary of Membership

There is a forgotten social justice nineteenth-century discourse of membership. This vocabulary is at least as old as that of need, but has been overlooked because it originated in a religious context and social justice advocates tend to see themselves as secular thinkers. Luigi Taparelli, a Jesuit priest, invented the term *social justice* around 1840 in his book on natural law (Behr, 2005). He wrote in a context of dramatic social and political change leading up to Italian unification. He sought a middle ground between laissez-faire liberals and socialists. Specifically, he sought to carve out a place for the Catholic church in poor relief against the incursions of the market and nation-state.

Taparelli proposed that social justice does not occur in the context of a relationship between individual and state, but rather in relation of the state to a system of secondary societies. Taparelli referred to the national state as *protarchie*, primary, and smaller societies within it as *deutarchie*, or secondary. As Behr (2005) explains, Taparelli has in mind the guilds and charitable associations that had been abolished as revolutionary regimes (in France and Italy) came to power. Taparelli proposed 'subsidiarity' as the principle for national government and smaller associations. The word comes from the Latin *subsidia*, meaning 'help', a reference to auxiliary troops within the Roman legions that 'sat below', ready to assist in battle. According to this principle, the supreme authority of the national government should allow the smaller associations to handle matters of domestic and immediate importance. This would free the national government to attend to foreign policy, for instance, while allowing the secondary associations in society to respond to domestic needs. This doctrine also prevents the hypostatic concept of absorption of individuals into the state (as would occur in Italy under fascism).

Catholic social doctrine found its way into Britain's political landscape in the form of the Distributivist and Guild Socialism movements of the interwar years. These groups rejected legislative proposals of the Fabians because they smacked of statism and because they believed smaller associations, rather than the national government, represented a more realistic means of achieving redistribution of property (particularly land) than trade unions or legislative proposals. Instead of national trade unions and marketing centres, such as Covent Garden, they favoured regional distribution schemes, smallholdings, and workers' cooperatives. They encouraged workers to form guilds on a voluntary basis. In one of their earliest campaigns, the Distributivists supported small London bus companies driven out by the monopolistic London General Bus Company. They purchased a number of buses, painted them red, green and blue, and adorned them with sayings taken from William Morris (Wilson, 1984: 294).

The idea of smaller societies responding to the needs of members alongside national societies providing for citizens has been most often approached with reference to 'community'. Clear and Cadora (2003) describe 'community justice' as a bridge between criminal justice and social justice. Community justice aims to increase the capacity of places hardest-hit by criminal behaviour; it is pursued with the goal of improving the criminal-justice response, but also with restoring relationships, repairing damage to the community, and building a more neighbourhood life. Links between community and social justice are also made in some visions of 'restorative justice'. Victim–offender mediation programmes[1] have been initiated in France and England with reference to restoring community life as well as the lives of individual victims and perpetrators (Crawford, 2000b). Mika and Zehr (2003: 148) explain that restorative justice regards crime as a form of conflict that is social and relational. Because the sources of conflict extend to the community and beyond the relationship between individual offenders and the national government, restorative justice should pursue social justice issues.

---

[1]Originating in Canada in 1974, these programmes seek to arrange face-to-face meetings between victims and offenders, facilitated by a community volunteer, primarily to work out restitution to the victim.

Hayek's Challenge

In Britain, Friedrich von Hayek's reputation is tied closely with Thatcherism. While he has tended (for that reason) to be seen as a right-wing ideologue, he did manage to raise useful questions about the relationship between government, market, and social welfare (Gamble, 1996). In *The Mirage of Social Justice*, Hayek (1976) contended that the attempt to combine the individualism of a market economy with the collectivism of social justice was an inherently contradictory and self-defeating task.

Meaningless in Market Economy

Hayek regarded social justice talk as a misguided excursion into anthropomorphism. Advocates imagine that society can be virtuous in the same way a person can. It makes no sense, he argues, to talk about society, an abstract entity, as being just or unjust.

Hayek derived his view of social justice from the understanding of society maintained by the Austrian School of economics. This tradition sees spontaneous orders in society, forms of organisation that are the result of human action but not of human design. Language, law and the market are orders of this type; they arise as the unplanned consequence of decisions by many individuals. Once established, they allow human interaction to proceed in an efficient way. Hayek's word for a spontaneous order is 'catallaxy', which refers to an order based on repeated exchanges and mutual adjustment by agents of their interests and plans. In such an order, calls for re-distribution of economic statuses are 'empty and meaningless' because no one person or entity distributes such statuses in the first instance. Success is 'partly dependent on accident' (Hayek, 1978: 68–9). Success or failure depends on ability, knowledge and skill, but also serendipity and unforeseen events. No one can insulate their position from the decisions of others, even those in remote corners of the globe. The only way to carry out the distribution required in social justice is to create a 'command economy' in which people are told what to do so that laws can be written to guide what they are told.

Shklar (1990) argues, against Hayek, that the idea of social justice is not founded on the mistake that no one entity is responsible for pursuing greater equality. Rather, it is founded on the belief that we can intervene, should we choose to do so, in a democratic context. Social policy need not take the form of comprehensive economic planning, but can be modest efforts to promote access to safety-net benefits such as health services, housing, and unemployment insurance. How the market allocates rewards is beyond human control, but how government responds to that allocation is not. Or to put it another way, Hayek is right in saying that economic rewards accrue partly from accident. And precisely because some part of wealth is accidental, it follows that economic fortunes are not entirely deserved. People who acquire some part of their wealth by accident should not be reluctant to assist those who have acquired some part of their poverty by accident.

Threat to Personal Autonomy

Hayek recognised the value of a 'safety net' in a market economy, a threshold below which no one should be allowed to fall. But he worried that political control of the economy, implied by even the mildest measures of state intervention, would endanger human freedom (Gamble, 1996).

Each gain in social justice, Hayek argued, results in a loss of personal autonomy. Social justice involves the expansion of rights, but because positive rights are not the same thing as negative rights, this leads to a net loss in freedom. 'Positive rights' invoke an inferior kind of justice or a mirage in the sense that they bring about less freedom. 'Negative rights' describe a condition in which people are free to do whatever they wish, so long as such acts are not specifically prohibited. Such rights also limit the extent to which government can interfere in personal pursuits. A social position determined by positive rights makes freedom subject to the will of government. People able to do only what government enables or allows them to are not free. In making the requirements of social justice universal, political leaders seek to reduce the entire population to dependence on a single centralised bureaucracy. The resulting configuration will not deliver benevolence, but the conception of benevolence contained in the minds of a small group of mandarins in government (Minogue, 1998: 258).

Hayek clearly had in mind the totally administered society that was Stalin's Soviet Union. Once conceding the desirability of a welfare state, the argument for negative rights loses much of its force. There is, Plant (1998) argues, a greater link between freedom and ability than Hayek admits. To exercise the freedom to engage in any activity, people must have the ability to do so. The invention of aeroplanes gave people the freedom to fly. Making air travel possible for more people, by means of government subsidy to airports, means that more people have the freedom to fly (Plant, 1998: 271). Greater social justice extends the benefits of political freedom to more people.

The Pretence of Knowledge

Hayek does not argue that catallaxies are perfect, in the sense that no individual can be made better off without someone else becoming worse off. Rather, he argues that government has no source of knowledge for redistribution. We simply do not know as much about society as we would like, and to act on the belief that we possess the knowledge to shape society entirely to our liking is likely to bring about injustice (Hayek, 1989). No government authority could know enough because the data required for a fairer redistribution are simply unavailable. Social goods are not commensurable. How is one person's medical need for relief of pain to be weighed against another's need to escape from the pressure of living in crowded quarters?

Johnson (1997) replies that if the standard of success for an effort to reduce social inequality is perfect equality, then all efforts will inevitably fail. Socialist revolutionaries have oversold what can be achieved, either as a result of mistaken philosophies of history or their own political ambitions. But the impossibility of attaining a perfect society should not prevent us from aspiring to achieve a more just society than the one we now have. If crime reduction efforts were to be judged against the standard of a crime-free society, then they will inevitably fail. Maintaining a society without crime remains an elusive goal, but few would argue that, because of this, no effort should be made to reduce the amount of criminal victimisation in the present (Johnson, 1997: 607).

Rawls and Beyond

American philosopher John Rawls has devoted his entire professional life to the question of how persons with different values, who begin life with diverse abilities, and who wish to pursue their own hopes, can live together in a political society considered just. His proposals have found their way into political discourse about social policy (Horton, 2002). Where social justice is concerned, Rawls is to Blairism what Hayek was to Thatcherism.

A Theory of Justice

In *A Theory of Justice,* Rawls (1971) offered an influential statement of social justice grounded in political liberalism. He does not express controversial or novel ideas, but instead systematised ideas that had been expressed by social and political movements during the previous decades. Rawls' vision of social justice is an attempt to balance the benefits of a market-based economy with the assurances of a welfare state. Individuals should be allowed to pursue personal wants and desires but not at the expense of denying others' basic needs. Government should pursue the collective well-being of all citizens but cannot in the process override individual liberties under the rule of law.

Rawls (1971: 83, 250) expressed his theory in two principles:

1. Each person is to have an equal right to the most extensive basic liberty compatible with similar liberty for others (the principle of equal opportunity).
2. Social and economic inequalities are to be arranged so that they are (1) to the greatest benefit of the least advantaged (the difference principle) and (2) attached to offices and positions open to all members of society under conditions of fair opportunity (the principle of fair equality of opportunity).

Rawls further specifies that these principles are to be applied in lexical order, meaning that equal liberty has the first priority, followed by the demand for fair equality of opportunity. Where the principle of fair equality of opportunity has been met, 'All primary social goods – liberty and opportunity, income and wealth, and the bases of self-respect – are to be distributed equally unless an unequal distribution of these goods is the advantage of the least favoured' (Rawls, 1971: 303). This results in a 'just basic structure' in which individuals have the right to own property, to political liberty and the kind of rights afforded by due process of law. In this way, Rawls believes he has avoided Cook's (2006) dilemma of how to administer criminal justice in a socially unjust society. A society established on Rawls' principles will deliver justice to criminals because it has been founded on a basic structure that is fair.

To defend his theory, Rawls makes use of a tactic known to philosophers as 'conjectural history'. The strategy is to construct an argument about what could or might have happened in light of knowledge of human nature and the workings of society (Campbell, 2001: 65). Beginning with a hypothetical device he calls 'the original position', Rawls tries to show that his principles of justice would be adopted by rational individuals operating under a 'veil of ignorance' about their abilities and place in society. The original position is Rawls' Garden of Eden, complete with Adams and Eves who must decide the rules that will govern future generations. In proposing the veil of ignorance he adds a reincarnation element: these Adams and Eves know that they will live in the society that they set in motion but do not know whether they will live in it as a shopkeeper, footballer, or disabled person. He concludes that those in the original position, operating on the basis of such limited knowledge, would choose the principles he proposes for ordering society.

In 1992, when John Smith MP established a commission to think through a national reform agenda for the Labour Party, the members adopted a set of principles much like those in the original position. The Commission on Social Justice (1994) produced a series of reports dealing with improving social and economic conditions in Britain culminating in *Social Justice: Strategies for National Renewal*. The Commission's initial report, *The Justice Gap* (1993), made specific reference to Rawls. They formulated four principles of social justice:

1. The foundation of a free society is the equal worth of all citizens.
2. Everyone is entitled, as a right of citizenship, to be able to meet their basic needs.
3. The right to self-respect and personal autonomy demands the widest possible spread of opportunities.
4. Not all inequalities are unjust, but unjust inequalities should be reduced and where possible eliminated. (Commission on Social Justice, 1993)

Both Tony Blair and Gordon Brown, Chancellor of the Exchequer, have made use of this language (whether taken from a page in *A Theory of Justice* or *Social Justice: Strategies for National Renewal*) in justifying their policies. Blair's statement of the Third Way defined social justice as establishing 'the moral worth of the individual' (Buckler and Dolowitz, 2000: 306) and Brown has explained that 'wealth and incomes inequalities … can be justified only if they are in the interests of the least fortunate' (Horton, 2002: 154).

Except, perhaps, where crime is concerned. Crime figures in the Commission's conception of social justice in the context of opportunities and not basic needs. Basic needs are the need for money, shelter, food, education and health. Opportunities and life-chances consist of lifelong learning, work, good health, financial independence, and a safe environment. To pursue life chances, persons must experience personal safety at home, work, and in the community. The Commission observed that those least able to protect themselves from crime are the most likely to experience it. People residing in the poorest housing estates are at the greatest risk of burglary. Poor people are also more likely to be killed or injured in road accidents (Commission on Social Justice, 1993: 40–1). Blair's formulation seems to reverse this. 'Tough on crime, tough on the causes of crime' appears to put safety in the category of basic need, ahead of enlarging opportunities and life-chances.

Wiles and Pease (2001) outline several problems with implementing this formula. The statement seems contradictory. If the government invested sufficiently in crime prevention (tough on the causes of crime), there would be less reason to rely on more prisons and police for dealing with criminals (tough on crime), as presumably there would be fewer of them. The problem can be resolved, perhaps, by being tough on the causes now and becoming tough on the criminals later on. But the gist of the contradiction stems from what appears to be an acknowledgement that if government had delivered social justice, we would not need to be dispensing retributive justice now. Wiles and Pease argue that both senses of toughness are limited to offenders, or those thought likely to become offenders, rather than those for whom victimisation is a calculable hazard. They take up the Commission's point about the poorest sections in society being least able to defend themselves. Using social justice as a guide to crime policy would mean taking into account the uneven distribution of crime in society. Greater emphasis on preventing repeat crimes directed at the same victims would be the most elegant application of Rawls' difference principle (Wiles and Pease, 2001: 237).

Liberalism and Multiculturalism

Critics of *A Theory of Justice* have zeroed in on Rawls' endorsement of the individualist tradition within political liberalism. We experience injustice as a consequence of membership in social groups based on gender, 'race', immigrant status, etc. and to achieve social justice it is necessary to define it in a way that specifically acknowledges differences between social groups as political communities. Those seeking change in social policy toward economic restructuring oriented to meeting need require differentiating needs of social groups and of fostering respect for these needs. Or as Hudson (2006) phrases it, the notion of justice needs to move beyond 'white man's justice'. Kymlicka and Young have offered important adaptations of Rawls to reflect the multicultural reality of North American and European democracies.

Kymlicka (1989, 1995) suggests that members of minority communities should be afforded 'group rights' that allow them to protect their cultures from destruction. He accepts the idea of impartiality as a starting point and agrees that justice should be elaborated by political institutions within an impartial state. But for this elaboration to be truly impartial, the starting point must take into account the specific interests of minority cultures. Group rights have to do with regulating membership, limiting non-members' rights to residence within their geographic space, and perpetuating culturally significant activities. Kymlicka has in mind the aboriginal peoples of Canada.

Young's (1990) solution seeks a 'politics of difference' that allows oppressed groups to insert their perspectives directly into the institutional contexts that interpret and administer justice. She calls on democracies to set up procedures to ensure special representation for oppressed groups. The politics of difference advocates creation of participatory structures in which social differences can be recognised, affirmed and brought to bear on public policy. Oppressed groups would retain the right to generate their own policy proposals and to have them considered by policymakers. In her model, justice can only occur in an ongoing democratic context; oppressed groups would retain veto power over public policies on issues that affect them directly, such as women and abortion. For Young, justice is not blind as Rawls supposes; a theory of social justice should not rely on an assumption of undifferentiated humanity but on the assumption that group differences matter and that groups are the basis on which individuals experience oppression.

These solutions have been more influential than Rawls' own attempt to outline an alternative to traditional liberalism. In *Political Liberalism* (1993), he backs away from his claim to offering 'the true principles of justice' in favour of proposing 'some principles we can all live with'. He outlines a strategy for establishing political rights on a universal basis while leaving enough room for exercise of cultural differences. What Rawls fails to understand, Parekh (2000: 312) says, is that political deliberation is contextual and culturally embedded. Drawing on the Rushdie Affair, Parekh explains why Rawls' American-style multiculturalism cannot be imported to Britain. Reactions to the *fatwa* issued against Rushdie[2] exposed profoundly different understandings of liberal political values among Muslims and non-Muslims. Attempting to set up a single medium for political discussion fails to appreciate the depth of national diversity within modern democracies.

Social Justice, Social Policy and Crime

Theories of social justice raise important questions about policymaking frameworks for pursuing goals of social welfare and crime reduction. Simone Weil, Raymond Aron, and Michael Polanyi offer thought-provoking commentary on this project.

---

[2]British author Salman Rushdie was forced into hiding following publication of *The Satanic Verses* (1988) and a call for his execution by the Iranian cleric Ayatollah Rullah Khomeini.

The Middle Region

Weil's thoughts on social justice can be gleaned from an unfinished book written several months before her death in 1943. Weil, who was living in London, had been asked by the Free French to think about the prospects for national renewal. She urged the French people to recover their spiritual roots.

There are, Weil (1990) suggests, two regions of social justice: a middle region and an upper region. Each has its own language, its own institutions. The middle region concerns the question: 'Why has someone else got more than I have?' The answer is expressed in words such as 'right', 'democracy', and 'person'. Weil did not regard rights-based doctrines as expressing the highest ideals of justice because they resemble commercial speech. The notion of rights suggests a sharing-out, an exchange, a measured quantity as specified in the law of a capitalist economy. Asserting one's rights occurred in a tone of contention, and with force always in the background, or else the assertion will be laughed at. Ordinary institutions – of law, courts and police – she writes, are capable of delivering justice of this sort, rights and freedoms of citizens in a democracy. The upper region references the existential dimensions of pain and suffering: 'Why am I being hurt?' Responding to this question requires the language not of rights, but obligation. Words such as 'justice', 'good', and 'love' comprise the vocabulary of social justice in its superlative form. Obligations derive from what we owe one another as human beings; they are not contained in the law of the land, but in the 'oldest written texts', in codes of conduct defined by religion. Political institutions for delivering this kind of justice 'must be invented', Weil (1990: 288) writes, 'for they are unknown, and it is impossible to doubt that they are indispensable'.

Weil feared that we have become stuck in the middle region. The rights imagined in 1789 by founders of the French state did not recognise the higher region, but in aiming to propound universal doctrines, introduced 'a confusion of language and ideas which is largely responsible for the present political and social confusion' (Weil, 1952: 4). Weil subtitled her book *Prelude to a Declaration of Duties towards Mankind*, a twist on the Declaration of the Rights of Man. The afflicted, she wrote, cry out from hurt, but they have no coherent language. They are unable to identify the source, why and by whom it is being done to them. The 'category of men' who speak of rights have a monopoly of language, and when acting in the form of political parties seeking to gain or maintain power, hear only noise. How deeply or permanently we are stuck is debateable. From her vantage point in history, Weil did not experience the *Trente Glorieuses*, 'thirty glorious years' of economic expansion and reduction of poverty in France after the war, nor the declarations of internationalisation organisations in the area of human rights. But her belief that progress was an illusion of Western culture merits reflection. As does her insight into the realisation of social justice in modern society: when limited to the language of rights, the government's celebration of social welfare culminates in criminal justice.

Mishra's (1998) critique of 'social rights' is consistent with Weil's. Conceptualising social rights as analogous to political rights creates more than one problem. This situation pits social rights against economic and property rights, which are fundamental to capitalism, and that means that social rights will take second priority. Further problems ensue from limiting social welfare to an individual-centred activity and expressing commitment to social welfare in terms of receipt of a minimum. Mishra admonishes us to think of community standards rather than individual rights and pursue what this means in a context in which nation-states appear to be declining in their influence.

Responsible Commitment

Aron wrote editorials for *Le Figaro*, lectured in sociology at the Sorbonne, and worked for a time in the Ministry of Information. His understanding of what it means to be an intellectual, and the role of intellectuals in society, offers insight into making social justice happen at the policy level.

Unlike French intellectuals, who took it as their primary mission to denounce injustice on any occasion, he chose to follow the position of a committed observer. The 'committed observer' seeks to understand social affairs as scholar and critic by taking into account: 'What would you do if you were a Cabinet minister?' The point of this question is to bring 'ideological poetry back into realistic prose', to find in airy sentiments a course of action. In his memoirs, Aron recalls a conversation with a fellow journalist who had criticised the government in an editorial. Aron asked: 'What would you do in its place'? He answered, more or less: 'That's not my problem; it has to find what to do, I have to criticise' (Aron, 1990: 42). Aron argues that expressing indignation about the present state of things is not good enough. Criticism of government should be accompanied by a discipline of thought which does not fail to consider alternatives. The responsible critic should state the alternative, and the justification for it, even when such alternatives are not applicable in the short term.

Aron would advise thinking about social justice not only in terms of values but as a matter of historical possibilities. This means avoiding declarations of social justice rendering it universal and abstract in favour of specific proposals that are particular and contextual. In *The Opium of the Intellectuals*, Aron (1955) criticised the idea of an 'eternal left' that is the same across nations, historical periods, inspired by the same values, committed to the same aspirations. The left has sometimes been anti-state, sometimes bureaucratic. Some leftist arguments are nationalistic, some elevate the autonomous individual. There is, following Aron's line of argument, no social justice pro forma. Social justice should be pursued in specific policy contexts, formulated in definable and realisable terms. To demonstrate responsible commitment in this area is to think about political agents; to analyse their decisions, their goals, their means, and their mental universe (Aron, 1990: 53).

To oversimplify, there is a difference between responsible commitment to social justice and irresponsible grandstanding. There is no doubt that previous societies have been unjust when measured by current representations of justice. It remains to be found what a just society would be and whether it is definable and realisable. Modern societies seem more unjust to us today than pre-modern societies seemed to their inhabitants, Aron argues, because modern democratic societies invoke ideals that are to a large extent unrealisable and, through the speeches of political leaders, aspire to complete mastery of our fate (Aron, 1990: 86).

The Principle of Neutrality

Michael Polanyi wrote about economics after his emigration from Hitler's Germany to Manchester in the 1930s. He had been a professor at the University of Berlin, carrying out research at the Kaiser Wilhelm Institute for Physical and Electrical Chemistry.

Polanyi (1998) recognised that capitalism did produce social repercussions, such as ill-health brought about by industry and moral frustration of workers brought about by commercial cycles and economic crises. The biggest problem is recurrent economic crises, commercial cycles, and consequent deflation and unemployment, and because of this, government had a duty to act in promotion of social welfare. Generally, he argued that the government's response should be 'negative rather than prescriptive'. This consists of restricting a range of commercial activities by outlawing what he called 'unsocial transactions', the social costs of unregulated capitalist markets. What Polanyi seems to have in mind here is a strategy in which the state seeks to regulate an activity without seeking to take over or run it. The role of government intervention in these situations is to safeguard a certain value put in jeopardy as a result of a market system that would otherwise determine this activity. Consumer and environmental protection provide two examples.

At the same time, Polanyi (1998: 183) argues that government has the duty to act positively in areas such as education, health and social amenities insufficiently supplied by commercial sources. He rejected the idea that economic problems can be successfully merged with social problems to enable a universal policy that both 'makes money' and eliminates 'unsocial transactions', or, in other words, that an economic system could avoid any need for mindful government action. Private individualism did not provide a sufficient principle on which to establish economic justice. He insisted that the capitalistic system could be made to conform to any standard of social justice on which society agrees; there is no reason why profit-making should lead to economic injustice. 'A free society' Polanyi (1998: xviii) wrote, 'is not an Open Society, but one fully dedicated to a distinctive set of beliefs'.

He argued for intervention consistent with the 'principle of neutrality' (Manucci, 2005). Modern societies are too complex to be managed by a single formula. Managing modernity requires a definite series of areas of policy concern each of which operates according to particular rules. In such a system, government actors can be made accountable with reference to their decisions and the impact of their decisions within the given area of interest. Only in such a delineation can public opinion 'scrutinise and guide' the functions of government. Unemployment represents an economic problem, not a political problem, meaning that policies should be adopted with the aim of improving the economic situation of displaced workers. The maintenance of full employment, Polanyi argued in *Full Employment and Free Trade* (1945), requires nothing more than maintaining a sufficient supply of money in circulation. He worried that the politicisation of unemployment would be used by fascists and extremist political parties to gain power as had occurred in Germany and Russia (Manucci, 2005).

Extending this principle to crime and social policy would mean that crime represents an unsocial transaction. Criminal victimisation, like poverty, is the price some people pay for other people's progress. But the solution, according to the principle of neutrality, would involve separate political responses. Steps taken to counteract crime should be understood within the framework of crime policies and not attempt to advance a social policy agenda. Similarly, steps taken to reduce poverty should not be taken with the idea of crime reduction. Each of these functions represent separate 'departments' of government, and decisions on the part of each department should be analysed in terms of whether they contribute to that department's remit.

Conclusion

Criminology can benefit from 'accidental criminologists', social thinkers who would not describe themselves as criminologists but who have thought deeply about issues with which criminology is concerned. Policymaking in the area of crime and social policy is a prime example. Social justice has the potential to offer a coherent guide to the pursuit of this area if for no other reason than it reminds us of what is at stake. The pursuit of improved social welfare and reduced crime involves challenges, dilemmas, and obstacles, the most important of which are matters of *justice*. Criminology and social policy is embedded within larger moral priorities, ideals, and principles.

Questions for Discussion

1. *Is social justice an important theme because it offers the dream of a better world or a substantive guide to policy?*

2. *Has Rawls answered Hayek's concerns about social justice?*

3. *Can Rawls' theory of social justice accommodate a multi-cultural British society?*

4. *Who makes the best point about social justice: Weil, Aron or Polanyi?*

Further Reading

David Boucher and Paul Kelly (eds) (1998) *Social Justice from Hume to Walzer*. London: Routledge.

Dee Cook (2006) *Criminal and Social Justice*. London: Sage.

Barbara Hudson (1993) *Penal Policy and Social Justice*. Basingstoke: Macmillan.

Howard Zehr (1990) *Changing Lenses: A New Focus for Crime and Justice*. Scottsdale, PA: Herald Press.

References

Abbott, Pamela and Emma Williamson (1999) 'Women, Health and Domestic Violence', *Journal of Gender Studies* 8: 83–102.

Ainsworth, Janet (1991) 'Re-Imaging Childhood and Reconstructing the Legal Order: The Case for Abolishing the Juvenile Court', *North Carolina Law Review* 69: 1083–132.

Ajzenstadt, Mimi (2005) 'Reactions to Juvenile Delinquency in Israel, 1950–1970: A Social Narrative', *Journal of Policy History* 17: 404–24.

Alexander, Claire (2004) 'Imagining the Asian Gang: Ethnicity, Masculinity, and Youth after "the Riots"', *Critical Social Policy* 24(4): 526–49.

Allot, Rory, Roger Paxton and Rob Leonard (1999) 'Drug Education: A Review of the British Government Policy and Evidence of Effectiveness', *Health Education Research* 14: 491–505.

Ananiadou, Katerina and Peter Smith (2002) 'Legal Requirements and Nationally Circulated Materials Against School Bullying in European Countries', *Criminal Justice* 2: 471–91.

Andershed, Henrik, Margaret Kerr and Håkan Stattin (2001) 'Bullying in School and Violence on the Streets: Are the Same People Involved?', *Journal of Scandinavian Studies in Criminology and Crime Prevention* 2: 31–49.

Andrew, Edward (1986) 'Simone Weil on the Injustice of Rights-Based Doctrines', *Review of Politics* 48: 60–91.

Angel-Ajani, Asale (2001) 'Italy's Racial Cauldron: Immigration, Criminalization, and the Cultural Politics of Race', *Cultural Dynamics* 12: 331–52.

Armstrong, Derrick (2004) 'A Risky Business? Research, Policy and Governmentality and Youth Offending', *Youth Justice* 4: 100–16.

Armstrong, Derrick (2006) 'Becoming Criminal: The Cultural Politics of Risk', *International Journal of Inclusive Education* 10: 265–78.

Aron, Raymond (1990) *Memoirs: Fifty Years of Political Reflection*. London: Holmes and Meier.

Arthur, Raymond (2005) 'Punishing Parents for the Crimes of their Children', *The Howard Journal* 44: 233–53.

Arvanites, Thomas and Robert Defina (2006) 'Business Cycles and Street Crime', *Criminology* 44: 139–64.

Bagguley, Paul and Kirk Mann (1992) 'Idle Thieving Bastards? Scholarly Representations of the "Underclass"', *Work, Employment and Society* 6: 113–26.

Baldwin, John and Anthony Bottoms (1976) *The Urban Criminal*. London: Tavistock.

Ball, Caroline and Jo Conolly (2000) 'Educationally Disaffected Young Offenders: Youth Court and Agency Responses to Truancy and School Exclusion', *British Journal of Criminology* 40: 594–616.

Ballintyne, Scott (1999) *Unsafe Streets: Street Homelessness and Crime*. London: Institute for Public Policy Research.

Balvig, Flemming (2004) 'When Law and Order Returned to Denmark', *Journal of Scandinavian Studies in Criminology and Crime Prevention* 5: 167–87.

Barak, Gregg and Robert Bohm (1989) 'The Crimes of the Homeless or the Crime of Homelessness? On the Dialectics of Criminalisation, Decriminalisation and Victimisation', *Contemporary Crises* 13: 275–86.

Barke, Michael and Guy Turbull (1992) *Meadowell: The Biography of an 'Estate with Problems'*. Aldershot: Avebury.

Baumeister, R.F., L. Smart and J.M. Boden (1996) 'Relation of Threatened Egoism to Violence and Aggression: The Dark Side of High Self-Esteem', *Psychological Review* 103: 5–33.

Beckett, Katherine and Bruce Western (2001) 'Governing Social Marginality: Welfare, Incarceration, and the Transformation of State Policy', *Punishment and Society* 3: 43–59.

Behr, Thomas (2005) 'Luigi Taparelli and Social Justice: Rediscovering the Origins of a "Hollowed" Concept', *Social Justice in Context* 1: 3–16.

Beki, Cem, Kees Zeelenberg and Kees van Monfort (1999) 'An Analysis of the Crime Rate in the Netherlands 1950–93', *British Journal of Criminology* 39: 401–15.

Berd, Belina and Helms, Gesa (2003) 'Zero Tolerance for the Industrial Past and Other Threats: Policing and Urban Entrepreneurialism in Britain and Germany', *Urban Studies* 40: 1845–67.

Berk, Richard, Susan Sorenson, Douglas Wiebe and Dawn Upchurch (2003) 'The Legalisation of Abortion and Subsequent Youth Homicide: A Time Series Analysis', *Analyses of Social Issues and Public Policy* 3: 45–64.

Bernburg, Jon (2002) 'Anomie, Social Change and Crime: A Theoretical Examination of Institutional-anomie Theory', *British Journal of Sociology* 42.

Berridge, Virginia (2003) 'Post-war Smoking Policy in the UK and the Redefinition of Public Health,' *Twentieth Century British History* 14: 61–82.

Birmingham, Luke (1999) 'Between Prison and the Community: The "Revolving Door Psychiatric Patient" of the Nineties', *British Journal of Psychiatry* 174: 378–9.

Blagg, Harry, Geoffrey Pearson, Alice Simpson, David Smith and Paul Stubbs (1988) 'Inter-Agency Coordination: Rhetoric and Reality' in Tim Hope and Margaret Shaw (eds) *Communities and Crime Reduction*. London: HMSO.

Blair, Tony (1993a) 'Why Crime is a Socialist Issue', *New Statesman and Society*, 29 January: 27–8.

Blair, Tony (1993b) 'Sharing Responsibility for Crime' in Anna Coote (ed.) *Families, Children and Crime*. London: Institute for Public Policy Research.

Blandy, Sarah (2004–5) 'Gated Communities as a Response to Crime and Disorder: Effectiveness and Implications'. Centre for Criminal Justice Studies Working Papers, University of Leeds.

Blythe, Eric (2001) 'The Impact of the First Term of the New Labour Government on Social Work in Britain: The Interface Between Education Policy and Social Work', *British Journal of Social Work* 31: 563–77.

Bondeson, Ulla (2005) 'Levels of Punitiveness in Scandinavia: Description and Explanation' in John Pratt, David Brown, Mark Brown, Simon Hallsworth, and Wayne Morrison (eds) *The New Punitiveness: Theories, Trends, Perspectives.* Cullompton: Willan Publishing.

Bonger, Wilhelm (1916) *Criminality and Economic Conditions*. London: Heinemann.

Bonnemaison, Gilbert (1992) 'Crime Prevention: The Universal Challenge', in Sandra McKillop and Julia Vernon (eds) *National Overview of Crime Prevention*. Canberra: Australian Institute of Criminology.

Bottoms, Anthony (1995) 'The Philosophy and Politics of Punishment and Sentencing', in Chris Clarkson and Rod Morgan (eds) *The Politics of Sentencing Reform*. Oxford: Clarendon.

Bottoms, Anthony, Rob Mawby and Polii Xanthos (1989) 'A Tale of Two Estates', in David Downes (ed.) *Crime and the City*. Basingstoke: Macmillan.

Bottoms, Anthony and Paul Wiles (1986) 'Housing Tenure and Residential Community Crime Careers in Britain', *Crime and Justice* 8: 101–62.

Bottoms, Anthony and Paul Wiles (2002) 'Environmental Criminology', in Mike Maguire, Rod Morgan and Robert Reiner (ed.) *The Oxford Handbook of Criminology*. Oxford: Oxford University Press.

Bottoms, Anthony and Polii Xanthos (1981) 'Housing Policy and Crime in the British Public Sector', in P. Brantingham and P. Brantingham (eds) *Environmental Criminology*. London: Sage.

Boutellier, Hans (2001) 'The Convergence of Social Policy and Criminal Justice', *European Journal on Criminal Policy and Research* 9: 361–80.

Boutellier, Hans (2004) *The Safety Utopia: Contemporary Discontent and Desire as to Crime and Punishment*. Dordrecht: Kluwer.

Bowlby, John (1944) 'Forty-Four Juvenile Thieves: Their Characters and Home Life', *International Journal of Psycho-Analysis* 25: 107–28.

Bowling, Benjamin (1999) 'The Rise and Fall of New York Murder: Zero Tolerance or Crack's Decline?', *British Journal of Criminology* 39: 531–54.

Box, Steven (1987) *Recession, Crime and Punishment*. Basingstoke: Macmillan.

Box, Steven and Chris Hale (1982) 'Economic Crisis and the Rising Prisoner Population in England and Wales', *Crime and Social Justice* 17: 20–34.

Box, Steven and Chris Hale (1985) 'Unemployment, Imprisonment and Prison Overcrowding', *Contemporary Crises* 9: 209–28.

Bradford, Steve and Rod Morgan (2005) 'Transformed Youth Justice?', *Public Money and Management* 283–90.

Braithwaite, John (1993) 'Beyond Positivism: Learning From Contextual Integrated Strategies', *Journal of Research in Crime and Delinquency* 30: 383–99.

Brake, Mike (1983) 'Under Heavy Manners: A Consideration of Racism, Black Youth Culture, and Crime in Britain', *Crime and Social Justice* 20: 1–15.

Bratton, William (1997) 'Crime is Down in New York City: Blame the Police', in N. Dennis (ed.) *Zero Tolerance: Policing a Free Society*. London: Institute of Economic Affairs.

Broad, Bob (1999) 'Young People Leaving Care: Moving Towards "Joined Up" Solutions?', *Children and Society* 13: 81–93.

Brown, Alison (2004) 'Anti-social Behaviour, Crime Control and Social Control', *Howard Journal of Criminal Justice* 43: 203–11.

Buckler, Steve and David Dolowitz (2000) 'Theorising the Third Way: New Labour and Social Justice', *Journal of Political Ideologies* 5: 301–20.

Burnett, Ros and Catherine Appleton (2004) 'Joined-up Services to Tackle Youth Crime', *British Journal of Criminology* 44: 34–54.

Burney, Elizabeth (1999) *Crime and Banishment: Nuisance and Exclusion in Social Housing.* Winchester: Waterside Press.

Burns, G. (1998) 'A Perspective on Policy and Practice in the Re-Integration of Offenders', *European Journal on Criminal Policy and Research* 6: 171–83.

Butler-Sloss, Elisabeth (1993) 'From Cleveland to Orkney', in Stewart Asquith (ed.) *Protecting Children: From Cleveland to Orkney.* Edinburgh: HSMO.

Caddle, Diane and Sheila White (1994) *The Welfare Needs of Unconvicted Prisoners.* Research and Planning Unit, No. 81. London: Home Office.

Campbell, Beatrix (1993) *Goliath: Britain's Dangerous Places.* London: Methuen.

Campbell, Jacquelyn (2002) 'Health Consequences of Intimate Partner Violence', *The Lancet* 359, 13 April: 1331–6.

Campbell, Tom (2001) *Justice* (2nd edn). London: Macmillan.

Canadian Crime Prevention Council (1996) *Safety and Savings: Crime Prevention Through Social Development.* Ottawa: NCPC

Cantor, David and Kenneth Land (1985) 'Unemployment and Crime Rates in Post World War II United States: A Theoretical and Empirical Analysis', *American Sociological Review* 50: 317–25.

Cantor, David and Kenneth Land (1991) 'Exploring Possible Temporal Relationships of Unemployment and Crime: A Comment on Hale and Sabbagh', *Journal of Research in Crime and Delinquency* 28: 418–25.

Cantor, David, Kenneth Land and Stephen Russell (1994) 'Unemployment and Crime Rate Fluctuations in the Post-World War II United States', in John Hagan and Ruth Peterson (eds) *Crime and Inequality.* Stanford: Stanford University Press.

Cao, Liqun, Jian Cao and Jihong Zhao (2004) 'Family, Welfare and Delinquency', *Journal of Criminal Justice* 32: 565–76.

Carlen, Pat (1987) 'Out of Care, Into Custody: Dimensions and Deconstructions of the State's Regulation of Twenty-Two Young Working Class Women', in Pat Carlen and Anne Worrall (eds) *Gender, Crime and Justice.* Milton Keynes: Open University Press.

Cavender, Gray (2004) 'Media and Crime Policy: A Reconsideration of David Garland's The Culture of Control', *Punishment and Society* 6: 335–48.

Cheung, Sin Yi and Anthony Heath (1994) 'After Care: The Education and Occupation of Adults Who Have Been in Care', *Oxford Review of Education* 29: 361–74.

Chiricos, Theodore (1987) 'Rates of Crime and Unemployment: An Analysis of Aggregate Research Evidence', *Social Problems* 34: 187–212.

Chiricos, Theodore and Miriam DeLone (1992) 'Labour Surplus and Punishment: A Review and Assessment of Theory and Evidence', *Social Problems* 39: 421–36.

Christie, Nils (1981) *Limits to Pain.* Oxford: Martin Roberston.

Christoffersen, Mogens; Brian Francis and Keith Soothill (2003) 'An Upbringing to Violence? Identifying the Likelihood of Violent Crime Among the 1966 Birth Cohort in Denmark', *Journal of Forensic Psychiatry and Psychology* 14: 367–81.

Chunn, Dorothy and Shelley Gavigan (2004) 'Welfare Law, Welfare Fraud, and the Moral Regulation of the "Never Deserving" Poor', *Social and Legal Studies* 13: 219–43.

Clarke, Ronald (2000) 'Situational Prevention, Criminology and Social Values', in Andrew von Hirsch, David Garland and Alison Wakefield (eds) *Ethical and Social Perspectives on Situational Crime Prevention.* Oxford: Hart Publishing.

Clarke, Ronald (2004) 'Technology, Criminology and Crime Science', *European Journal on Criminal Policy and Research* 10: 55–63.

Clarke, Ronald and Patricia Mayhew (1980) *Designing Out Crime*. London: HMSO.

Clear, Todd and Eric Cadora (2003) *Community Justice*. Belmont, CA: Wadsworth.

Cloward, Richard and Lloyd Ohlin (1960) *Delinquency and Opportunity*. New York: Free Press.

Cohen, Laurence and Marcus Felson (1979) 'Social Change and Crime Rate Trends: A Routine Activities Approach', *American Sociological Review* 44: 588–608.

Coleman, Alice (1990) *Utopia on Trial: Vision and Reality in Planned Housing* (2nd edn). London: Hilary Shipman.

Coles, Bob, Jude England and Julie Rugg (2000) 'Spaced Out? Young People on Social Housing Estates: Social Exclusion and Multi-Agency Work', *Journal of Youth Studies* 3: 21–33.

Commission on Social Justice (1993) *The Justice Gap*. London: Institute for Public Policy Research.

Commission on Social Justice (1994) *Social Justice: Strategies for National Renewal*. London: Vintage.

Conant, Lisa (2006) 'Individuals, Courts and the Development of European Social Rights', *Comparative Political Studies* 39: 76–100.

Cook, Dee (1987) 'Women on Welfare: In Crime or Injustice?', pp. 28–42 in Pat Carlen and Ann Worrall (eds) *Gender, Crime and Justice*. Milton Keynes: Open University Press.

Cook, Dee (1989) *Rich Law, Poor Law: Different Responses to Tax and Supplementary Benefit Fraud*. Milton Keynes: Open University Press.

Cook, Dee (1997) *Poverty, Crime and Punishment*. London: Child Poverty Action Group.

Cook, Dee (2006) *Criminal and Social Justice*. London: Sage.

Cooke, Cheryl (2004) 'Joblessness and Homelessness as Precursors of Health Problems in Formerly Incarcerated African American Men', *Journal of Nursing Scholarship* 2: 155–60.

Cottee, Simon (2005) 'Sir Leon's Shadow', *Theoretical Criminology* 9: 203–25.

Cozens, Paul, David Hillier and Gwyn Prescott (2002) 'Criminogenic Associations and Characteristic British Housing Designs', *International Planning Studies* 7: 119–36.

Crawford, Adam (1998) *Crime Prevention and Community Safety*. Harlow: Longman.

Crawford, Adam (2000a) 'Why British Criminologists Lose Their Critical Faculties upon Crossing the Channel: Some Thoughts on Comparative Criminology from an Empirical Investigation in France and England', *Social Work in Europe* 7: 22–30.

Crawford, Adam (2000b) 'Contrasts in Victim–Offender Mediation and Appeals to Community in France and England', in David Nelken (ed.) *Contrasting Criminal Justice: Getting from Here to There*. Ashgate: Dartmouth.

Crocker, A.G. and S. Hodgins (1997) 'The Criminality of Institutionalised Mentally Retarded Persons: Evidence from a Birth Cohort Followed to Age 30', *Criminal Justice and Behaviour* 24: 432–54.

Cullen, Francis (1983) *Rethinking Crime and Deviance*. Totowa, NJ: Rowman and Allanheld.

Cullen, Francis (1994) 'Social Support as an Organising Concept for Criminology', *Justice Quarterly* 11: 427–59.

Cullen, Francis, N. Williams and John P. Wright (1997) 'Work Conditions and Juvenile Delinquency: Is Youth Employment Criminogenic?', *Criminal Justice Policy Review* 8: 119–43.

Cullen, Francis, John P. Wright and Mitchell Chamlin (1999) 'Social Support and Social Reform: A Progressive Crime Control Agenda', *Crime and Delinquency* 45: 188–207.

Currie, Elliott (1998) *Crime and Punishment in America*. New York: Henry Holt.

Dahrendorf, Ralf (1987) 'The Erosion of Citizenship and its Consequences for Us All', *New Statesman and Society*, 12 June, 13–.

Damer, Seán (1974) 'Wine Alley: The Sociology of a Dreadful Enclose', *Sociological Review* 27: 221–48.

Deacon, Alan (2000) 'Learning From the US? The Influence of American Ideas Upon 'New Labour' Thinking on Welfare Reform', *Policy and Politics* 28: 5–18.

DeFronzo, James (1983) 'Economic Assistance to Impoverished Americans', *Criminology* 21: 119–36.

DeFronzo, James (1996) 'Welfare and Burglary' *Crime and Delinquency,* 42: 223–30.

DeFronzo, James (1997) 'Welfare and Homicide', *Journal of Research in Crime and Delinquency* 34: 395–406.

DeKeseredy, Walter and Martin Schwartz (2002) 'Theorising Public Housing: Woman Abuse as a Function of Economic Exclusion and Male Peer Support', *Women's Health and Urban Life* 1: 26–45.

DeKeseredy, Walter; Martin Schwartz, Shahid Alvi and Andreas Thomaszeski (2003a) 'Crime Victimisation, Alcohol Consumption, and Drug Use in Canadian Public Housing', *Journal of Criminal Justice* 31: 383–96.

DeKeseredy, Walter; Martin Schwartz, Shahid Alvi and Andreas Thomaszeski (2003b) 'Perceived Collective Efficacy and Women's Victimisation in Public Housing', *Criminal Justice* 3: 5–27.

Dixon, Angela (2003–4) '"At All Costs Let Us Avoid Any Risk of Allowing Our Hearts to be Broken Again": A Review of John Bowlby's Forty-Four Juvenile Thieves', *Clinical Child Psychology and Psychiatry* 8: 278–89.

Dixon, Bill (2004) 'Cosmetic Crime Prevention', pp. 163–92 in Bill Dixon and Elrena van der Spay (eds) *Justice Gained? Crime and Crime Control in South Africa's Transition*. Cape Town: UCT Press.

Dixon, Bill (2006) 'Development, Crime Prevention and Social Policy in Post Apartheid South Africa', *Critical Social Policy* 26: 169–91.

Dixon, David and Lisa Maher (2005) 'Policing, Crime and Public Health: Lessons for Australia from the "New York Miracle"', *Criminal Justice* 5: 115–43.

Dodge, Mary and Mark Pogrebin (2001) 'Collateral Costs of Imprisonment for Women: Complications of Reintegration', *The Prison Journal* 81: 42–54.

Donnellan, M. Brent, Kali Trzesniewski, Richard Robins, Terrie Moffitt and Avshalom Caspi (2005) 'Low Self-Esteem Is Related to Aggression. Antisocial Behaviour, and Delinquency', *Psychological Science* 16: 328–35.

Donohue, John and Steven Levitt (2001) 'The Impact of Legalised Abortion on Crime', *Quarterly Journal of Economics* 65: 379–420.

Donohue, John and Peter Siegelman (1998) 'Allocating Resources Among Prisons and Social Programmes in the Battle Against Crime', *Journal of Legal Studies* 27: 1–43.

Donzelot, Jacques (1980) *The Policing of Families*. Hutchinson: London.

Dorling, Danny (2005) 'Prime Suspect: Murder in Britain', in Paddy Hillyard, Christina Pantazis, Steve Tombs and Danny Dorling (eds) *Beyond Criminology: Taking Harm Seriously*. London: Pluto Press.

Downes, David (1982) 'The Origins and Consequences of Dutch Penal Policy Since 1945: A Preliminary Analysis', *British Journal of Criminology* 22: 325–57.

Downes, David (1988) *Contrasts in Tolerance: Post War Penal Policy in Netherlands and England and Wales*. Oxford: Oxford University Press.

Downes, David (1997) 'What the Next Government Should do About Crime', *Howard Journal of Criminal Justice* 36: 1–13.

Downes, David (1998) 'Back to the Future: The Predictive Value of Social Theories of Delinquency', in Simon Holdaway and Paul Rock (eds) *Thinking About Criminology*. London: UCL Press.

Downes, David and Rod Morgan (2002) 'The Skeletons in the Cupboard: The Politics of Law and Order at the Turn of the Millennium', in Mike Maguire, Rod Morgan and Robert Reiner (eds) *The Oxford Handbooks of Criminology*. Oxford: Oxford University Press.

du Plessis, Irma (2004) 'Living in "Jan Bom": Making and Imagining Lives after Apartheid in a Council Housing Scheme in Johannesburg', *Current Sociology* 52: 879–908.

Durham, Martin (2001) 'The Conservative Party, New Labour and the Politics of the Family', *Parliamentary Affairs* 54: 459–74.

Elston, Mary Ann, Jonathan Gabe, David Denney, Raymond Lee and Maria O'Beirne (2002) 'Violence Against Doctors? A Medical(ised) Problem? The Case of National Health Service Practitioners', *Sociology of Health and Illness* 24: 575–98.

Engbersen, Godfried and Joanne Van der Leun (2001) 'The Social Construction of Illegality and Criminality', *European Journal on Criminal Policy and Research* 9: 51–70.

Ericsson, Kjersti (2000) 'Social Control and Emancipation Ambiguities in Child Welfare', *Journal of Scandinavian Studies in Criminology and Crime Prevention* 1: 16–26.

Estrada, Felipe (2004) 'The Transformation of the Politics of Crime in High Crime Societies', *European Journal of Criminology* 1: 419–43.

Evans, Kate, Penny Fraser and Sandra Walklate (1996) 'Whom Can You Trust? The Politics of "Grassing" on an Inner City Housing Estate', *Sociological Review* 44: 361–80.

Ewin, Jeanette (2002) *Fine Wines and Fish Oil: The Life of Hugh Macdonald Sinclair*. Oxford: Oxford University Press.

Fagan, Jeffrey and Richard Freeman (1999) 'Crime and Work', *Crime and Justice* 25: 225–90.

Fagoni, Cynthia (1999) *Challenges in Helping Youths Live Independently*. Washington, DC: US General Accounting Office.

Fairchild, Halford (1994) 'Frantz Fanon's *The Wretched of the Earth* in Contemporary Perspective' *Journal of Black Studies* 25: 191–9.

Farrington, David (1994) 'Human Development and Criminal Careers', in Mike Maguire, Rod Morgan and Robert Reiner (ed.) *The Oxford Handbook of Criminology*. Oxford: Clarendon Press.

Farrington, David (1999) 'A Criminological Research Agenda for the Next Millennium', *International Journal of Offender Therapy and Comparative* Criminology 43: 154–67.

Farrington, David (2000) 'Explaining and Preventing Crime: The Globalization of Knowledge', *Criminology* 38: 1–24.

Farrington, David (2002) 'Developmental Criminology and Risk-Focused Prevention', in Mike Maguire, Rod Morgan and Robert Reiner (eds) *The Oxford Handbook of Criminology* (3rd edition). Oxford: Clarendon Press.

Farrington, David (2003) 'British Randomised Experiments on Crime and Justice', *Annals of the American Academy of Political and Social Science* 589: 150–67.

Farrington, David (2004) 'Families and Crime' in James Q. Wilson and Joan Petersilia (eds) *Crime: Public Policies for Crime Control*. Oakland: Institute for Contemporary Studies.

Farrington, David and Anthony Petrosino (2001) 'The Campbell Collaboration Crime and Justice Group', *Annals of the American Academy of Political and Social Science* 578: 35–49.

Farrington, David and Brandon Welsh (1999) 'Delinquency Prevention Using Family-based Interventions', *Children and Society* 13: 287–303.

Farrington, David and Donald West (1990) 'The Cambridge Study in Delinquent Development: A Long-term Follow-up of 411 London Males', in Hans Kerner and Gunther Kaiser (eds) *Criminality: Personality, Behavior and Life History*. Berlin: Springer-Verlag.

Featherstone, Richard and Mattieu Deflem (2003) 'Anomie and Strain: Context and Consequences of Merton's Two Theories', *Sociological Inquiry* 73: 471–89.

Feest, Johannes (1999) 'Imprisonment and Prisoners' Work: Normalization or Less Eligibility?', *Punishment and Society* 1: 99–107.

Feinstein, Leon and Ricardo Sabates (2005) *Education and Youth Crime*. Centre for Research on the Wider Benefits of Learning. London: Institute of Education.

Felson, Marcus (1987) 'Routine Activities and Crime Prevention in the Developing Metropolis', *Criminology* 25: 911–31.

Felson, Marcus (2002) *Crime and Everyday Life* (3rd edn). Thousand Oaks, CA: Sage.

Field, Frank (1989) *Losing Out: The Emergence of Britain's Underclass*. Oxford: Blackwell.

Field, Simon (1990) *Trends in Crime and their Interpretation: A Study of Recorded Crime in Post-war England and Wales*. Home Office Research Study No. 199. London: HMSO.

Fitzpatrick, Michael (2001) *The Tyranny of Health: Doctors and the Regulation of Lifestyle*. London: Routledge.

Fitzpatrick, Suzanne and Anwen Jones (2005) 'Pursuing Social Justice or Social Cohesion?: Coercion in Street Homelessness Policies in England', *Journal of Social Policy* 34: 389–406.

Flint, John (2002) 'Social Housing Agencies and the Governance of Anti-Social Behaviour', *Housing Studies* 17: 619–37.

Fontaine, Philippe (2002) 'Blood, Politics, and Social Science: Richard Titmuss and the Institute of Economic Affairs, 1957–1973', *Isis* 93: 401–34.

Foster, Janet (2000) 'Social Exclusion, Crime and Drugs', *Drugs: Education, Prevention and Policy* 7: 317–30.

Foucault, Michel (1975) *The Birth of the Clinic*. New York: Random House.

France, Alan and Iain Crow (2005) 'Using the "Risk Factor Paradigm" in Prevention: Lessons from the Evaluation of Communities that Care', *Children and Society* 19: 172–84.

France, Alan and David Utting (2005) 'The Paradigm of "Risk and Protection Focused Prevention" and Its Impact on Services for Children and Families', *Children and Society* 19: 77–90.

Fraser, Ian (1998) *Hegel and Marx: The Concept of Need*. Edinburgh: Edinburgh University Press.

Freeman, Richard B. (1996) 'Why do so Many Young African American Men Commit Crimes and What Might we do About it?', *Journal of Economic Perspectives* 10: 25–42.

Freudenberg, Nicholas (2001) 'Jails, Prisons and the Health of Urban Populations: A Review of the Impact of the Correctional System on Community Health', *Journal of Urban Health* 78: 214–35.

Fry, A.J., D.P. O'Riordan and R. Geanellos (2002) 'Social Control Agents or Front-Line Carers for People With Mental Health Problems: Police and Mental Health Services in Sydney, Australia', *Health and Social Care in the Community* 10: 277–86.

Furniss, Clare (2000) 'Bullying in Schools: It's Not a Crime – Is it?', *Education and the Law* 12: 9–29.

Gaetz, Stephen and Bill O'Grady (2005) 'Making Money: Exploring the Economy of Young Homeless Workers', *Work, Employment and Society* 16: 433–56.

Galster, George, Kathryn Pettit, Anna Santiago and Peter Tatian (2002), 'The Impact of Supportive Housing on Neighbourhood Crime Rates,' *Journal of Urban Affairs* 24: 289–315.

Gamble, Andrew (1996) 'Hayek and the Left', *Political Quarterly* 67: 46–53.

Garland, David (1988) 'British Criminology Before 1935', *British Journal of Criminology* 28: 131–47.

Garland, David (1990) *Punishment and Modern Society*. Oxford: Oxford University Press.

Garland, David (1992) 'Criminological Research and Its Relation to Power', *British Journal of Criminology* 32: 403–22.

Garland, David (2000) 'The Culture of High-Crime Societies: Some Preconditions of Recent "Law and Order" Policies', *British Journal of Criminology* 40: 347–75.

Garland, David (2001a) 'The Meaning of Mass Imprisonment', *Punishment and Society* 3: 5–7.

Garland, David (2001b) *The Culture of Control*. Oxford: Oxford University Press.

Garland, David (2002) 'Of Crimes and Criminals: The Development of Criminology in Britain', in Mike Maguire, Rod Morgan and Robert Reiner (eds) *The Oxford Handbook of Criminology*. Oxford: Oxford University Press.

Garland, David (2005) 'Beyond the Culture of Control', in Matt Matravers (ed.) *Managing Modernity: Politics and the Culture of Control*. London: Routledge.

Garland, David and Richard Sparks (2000) 'Criminology, Social Theory, and the Challenge of Our Times', *British Journal of Criminology* 40: 189–204.

Garrett, Paul (2004) 'Talking Child Protection: The Police and Social Workers "Working Together"' *Journal of Social Work* 4: 77–97.

Gatti, U. (1998) 'Ethical Issues When Early Intervention is Used to Prevent Crime', *European Journal on Criminal Policy and Research* 6: 113–32.

Gesch, C. Bernard, Sean Hammond, Sarah Hampson, Anita Eves and Martin Crowder (2002) 'Influence of Supplementary Vitamins, Minerals and Essential Fatty Acids on the Antisocial Behaviour of Young Adult Prisoners', *British Journal of Psychiatry* 181: 22–8.

Giddens, Anthony (2000) *The Third Way and its Critics*. Cambridge: Polity Press.

Gill, Martin (1997) 'Employing Ex-Offenders: A Risk or an Opportunity?', *The Howard Journal* 36: 337–51.

Gill, Owen (1977) *Luke Street: Housing Policy, Conflict and the Creation of a Delinquent Area*. London: Macmillan.

Gilling, Daniel (1994) 'Multi-Agency Crime Prevention in Britain: The Problem of Combining Situational and Social Strategies', *Crime Prevention Studies* 3: 231–48.

Gilling, Daniel (2001) 'Community Safety and Social Policy', *European Journal on Criminal Policy and Research* 9: 381–400.

Ginsburg, Norman (1992) *Divisions of Welfare*. London: Sage.

Glueck, Sheldon and Eleanor Glueck (1952) *Delinquents in the Making*. New York: Harper and Row.

Goodey, Jo (1995) 'Fear of Crime: Children and Gendered Socialization' In R. Emerson Dobash, Russell Dobash and Lesley Noakes (ed.) *Gender and Crime*. Cardiff: University of Wales Press.

Goodey, Jo (2001) 'The Criminalisation of British Asian Youth: Research from Bradford and Sheffield', *Journal of Youth Studies* 4: 429–50.

Goodman, Anthony (2003) 'Probation into the Millennium: The Punishing Service?', in Roger Matthews and Jock Young (eds) *The New Politics of Crime and Punishment*. Cullompton: Willan Publishing.

Goodwin, Shirley (2004) 'Health and Crime', in *Hillingdon Annual Public Health Report*. Middlesex: Hillingdon Primary Care Trust.

Gottfredson, Denise, Stephanie Gerstenblith, David Soule and Shannon Womer (2004) 'Do After School Programmes Reduce Delinquency?', *Prevention Science* 5: 253–66.

Gottfredson, Michael and Travis Hirschi (1990) *A General Theory of Crime*. Stanford: Stanford University Press.

Gottfredson, Michael and Travis Hirschi (2002) 'National Crime Control Policies', in John Laub (ed.) *The Craft of Criminology*. London: Transaction.

Graef, Roger (2004) 'Hope, not Fear, is the Key', in John Grieve and Roger Howard (eds) *Communities, Social Exclusion and Crime*. London: Smith Institute.

Graham, John and Trevor Bennett (1995) *Crime Prevention Strategies in Europe and North America*. Helsinki: European Institute for Crime Prevention and Control.

Graham, John and Benjamin Bowling (1995) *Young People and Crime*, Home Office Research Study No. 145. London: HMSO.

Granovetter, Mark (1992) 'The Sociological and Economic Approaches to Labour Market Analysis: A Social Structural View', in Mark Granovetter and R. Swedberg (eds) *The Sociology of Economic Life*. Boulder, CO: Westview.

Green, Gail, Joanne Thorpe and Myrean Traupmann (2005) 'The Sprawling Thicket: Knowledge and Specialisation in Forensic Social Work', *Australian Social Work* 58: 142–53.

Green, Geoff, Jan Gilbertson and Michael Grimsley (2002) 'Fear of Crime and Health in Residential Tower Blocks', *European Journal of Public Health* 12: 10–15.

Green, Lawrence and Marshall Kreuter (1990) 'Health Promotion as a Public Health Strategy for the 1990s', *Annual Review of Public Health* 11: 319–34.

Greenberg, David (1977) 'The Dynamics of Oscillatory Punishment Processes', *Journal of Criminal Law and Criminology* 68: 643–51.

Griswold, Esther and Jessica Pearson (2005) 'Turning Offenders into Responsible Parents and Child Support Payers', *Family Court Review* 43: 358–71.

Groves, W. Byron and Robert Sampson (1987) 'Traditional Contributions to Radical Criminology', *Journal of Research in Crime and Delinquency* 24: 181–214.

Haas, Henriette, David Farrington; Martin Killias and Ghazala Sattar (2004) 'The Impact of Different Family Configurations on Delinquency', *British Journal of Criminology* 44: 520–32.

Hagan, John (1993) 'The Social Embeddedness of Crime and Unemployment', *Criminology* 31: 465–491.

Haggerty, Kevin (2004) 'Displaced Expertise: Three Constraints on the Policy Relevance of Criminological Thought', *Theoretical Criminology* 8: 211–31.

Haines, Kevin (1999) 'Crime is a Social Problem', *European Journal on Criminal Policy and Research* 7: 263–75.

Hale, Chris (1984) 'Economy, Punishment and Imprisonment', *Contemporary Crises* 13: 327–50.

Hale, Chris (1998) 'Crime and the Business Cycle in Post-War Britain Revisited', *British Journal of Criminology* 38: 681–98.

Hale, Chris (1999) 'The Labour Market and Post-war Crime Trends in England and Wales', in Pat Carlen and Rod Morgan (eds) *Crime Unlimited? Questions for the Twenty-first Century*. Basingstoke: Palgrave.

Hale, Chris and Dima Sabbagh (1991) 'Testing the Relationship Between Unemployment and Crime: A Methodological Comment and Empirical Analysis from England and Wales', *Journal of Research in Crime and Delinquency* 28: 400–17.

Halsey, A.H. (2004) *A History of Sociology in Britain*. Oxford: Oxford University Press.

Hamlyn, Becky and Darren Lewis (2000) *Women Prisoners: A Survey of Their Work and Training Experiences in Custody and on Release*, Home Office Research Study No. 208. London: HMSO.

Hannon, Lance and DeFronzo, James (1998) 'The Truly Disadvantaged, Public Assistance and Crime', *Social Problems* 45: 383–92.

Hansen, Kirstine (2000) 'Time to Educate the Criminals?', *Centrepiece* (LSE Centre for Economic Performance) 5: 6–11.

Hansen, Kirstine (2003) 'Education and the Crime-Age Profile', *British Journal of Criminology* 43: 141–68.

Hansen, Kirstine and Stephen Machin (2002) 'Spatial Crime Patterns and the Introduction of the UK Minimum Wage', *Oxford Bulletin of Economics and Statistics* 64: 677–97

Harris, Neville (2002) 'The Legislative Response to Indiscipline in Schools in England and Wales', *Education and the Law* 14: 57–76.

Harris, Suzy (2003) 'Inter-agency Practice and Professional Collaboration: The Case of Drug Education and Prevention', *Journal of Education Policy* 18: 303–14.

Harrison, Malcolm (2001) *Housing, Social Policy and Difference*. Bristol: The Policy Press.

Hasian, Marouf (2000) 'Power, Medical Knowledge, and the Rhetorical Invention of "Typhoid Mary"', *Journal of Medical Humanities* 21: 123–39.

Hawkins, David (1999) 'Preventing Crime and Violence through Communities that Care', *European Journal on Criminal Policy and Research* 7: 443–58.

Hayek, F.A. (1976) *The Mirage of Social Justice*. Chicago: University of Chicago.

Hayward, Keith and Majid Yar (2006) 'The "Chav" Phenomenon: Consumption, Media and the Construction of the New Underclass', *Crime, Media, Culture* 2: 9–28.

Henricson, Clem; John Coleman and Debi Roker (2000) 'Parenting in the Youth Justice Context', *The Howard Journal* 39: 325–38.

Hermsen, Joke (1999) 'The Impersonal and the Other: On Simone Weil (1907–43)', *European Journal of Women's Studies* 6: 183–200.

Herr, Kathryn and Gary Anderson (2003) 'Violent Youth or Violent Schools? A Critical Incident Analysis of Symbolic Violence?', *International Journal of Leadership in Education* 6: 415–33.

Herrenkohl, Todd, Bu Huang, Emiko Tajima and Stephen Whitney (2003) 'Examining the Link Between Child Abuse and Youth Violence: An Analysis of Mediating Mechanisms', *Journal of Interpersonal Violence* 18: 1189–208.

Hill, Michael (1988) *Understanding Social Policy* (3rd edn). Oxford: Blackwell.

Hill, Michael (2000) *Understanding Social Policy* (6th edn). London: Blackwell.

Hill-Smith, Andrew, Pippa Hugo, Patricia Highes, Peter Fonagy and David Hartman (2002) 'Adolescent murderers: Abuse and Adversity in Childhood', *Journal of Adolescence* 25: 221–30.

Hine, Jean, Alan France and Derrick Armstrong (2006) 'Risk and Resilience in Children who are Offending, Excluded from School, or have Behaviour Problems', Briefing Paper. Pathways into and Out of Crime: International Symposium, Leicester, April.

Hirsch, Arnold (1983) *Making the Second Ghetto: Race and Housing in Chicago*. Chicago: University of Chicago.

Hirschi, Travis (1969) *Causes of Delinquency*. Berkeley: University of California Press.

Hirschi, Travis and Michael Gottfredson (2000) 'In Defence of Self-Control', *Theoretical Criminology* 4: 55–69.

Hodgson, Philip and David Webb (2005) 'Young People, Crime and School Exclusion: A Case of Some Surprises', *Howard Journal of Criminal Justice* 44: 12–28.

Holloway, Steven and Thomas McNulty (2003) 'Contingent Urban Geographies of Violent Crime: Racial Segregation and the Impact of Public Housing in Atlanta', *Urban Geography* 24: 187–211.

Holzman, Harry (1996) 'Criminological Research on Public Housing: Toward a Better Understanding of People, Places and Spaces', *Crime and Delinquency* 42: 361–78.

Home Office (2000) *National Strategy for the Probation Service for England and Wales*. London: Home Office.

Hood, Roger (2002) 'Criminology and Penal Policy: The Vital Role of Empirical Research', in Anthony Bottoms and Michael Tonry (eds), *Ideology, Crime and Criminal Justice*. Cullompton: Willan Publishing.

Hood, Roger (2004) 'Hermann Mannheim and Max Grünhut: Criminological Pioneers in London and Oxford', *British Journal of Criminology* 44: 469–95

Hope, Tim (2001) 'Community Crime Prevention in Britain: A Strategic Overview', *Criminal Justice* 1: 421–39.

Horton, John (2002) 'Rawls in Britain' *European Journal of Political Theory* 1: 147–61.

Hudson, Barbara (2006) 'Beyond White Man's Justice: Race, Gender and Justice in Late Modernity', *Theoretical Criminology* 10: 29–47.

Hunter, Caroline and Judy Nixon (2001) 'Taking the Blame and Losing the Home: Women and Anti-Social Behaviour', *Journal of Social Welfare and Family Law* 23: 395–410.

Innes, Martin (2004) 'Signal Crimes and Signal Disorders: Notes on Deviance as Communicative Action', *British Journal of Sociology* 55: 335–55.

Inniss, Leslie and Joe Feagin (1989) 'The Black "Underclass" Ideology in Race Relations Analysis', *Social Justice* 16: 13–34.

Jacobs, Keith; Jim Kemeny and Tony Manzi (2003) 'Power, Discursive Space and Institutional Practices in the Construction of Housing Problems', *Housing Studies* 18: 429–46.

James, David (2000) 'Police Station Diversion Schemes: Role and Efficacy in Central London', *Journal of Forensic Psychiatry* 11: 532–55.

Johnston, David (1997) 'Is the Idea of Social Justice Meaningful?', *Critical Review* 11: 607–14.

Jones, Chris and Tony Novak (1999) *Poverty, Welfare and the Disciplinary State*. London: Routledge.

Jones, Huw and David Short (1993) 'The "Pocketing" of Crime Within the City: Evidence from Dundee Public-Housing Estates', in Huw Jones (ed.) *Crime and the Urban Environment: The Scottish Experience*. Aldershot: Avebury.

Jordan-Zachery, Julia (2001) 'Black Womanhood and Social Welfare Policy: The Influence of Her Image on Policy Making', *Sage Race Relations Abstracts* 26: 5–24.

Juby, Heather and Farrington, David (2001) 'Disentangling the Link Between Disrupted Families and Delinquency', *British Journal of Criminology* 41: 22–40.

Junger, M. and R. Tremblay (1999) 'Self-control, Accidents, and Crime', *Criminal Justice and Behaviour* 26: 485–501.

Junger, Marianne, Robert West and Reinier Timman (2001) 'Crime and Risky Behaviour in Traffic: An Example of Cross-Situational Consistency', *Journal of Research in Crime and Delinquency* 38: 439–59.

Juska, Arunas; Peter Johnstone and Richard Pozzuto (2004) 'The Changing Character of Criminality and Policing in Post-Socialist Lithuania: From Fighting Organised Crime to Policing Marginal Populations', *Crime, Law and Social Change* 41: 161–77.

Keithley, Jane and Fred Robinson (1999) 'Violence and a Public Health Issue', *Policy and Politics* 28: 67–77.

Kelling, George (2001) '"Broken Windows" and the Culture Wars: A Response to Selected Critics', in Roger Matthews and John Pitts (eds) *Crime, Disorder and Community Safety*. London: Routledge.

Kelling, George and William Bratton (1998) 'Declining Crime Rates: Insiders Views of the New York City Story', *Journal of Criminal Law and Criminology* 88: 1217–31.

Kemshall, Hazel (2002) *Risk, Social Policy and Welfare*. Buckingham: Open University Press.

Kemshall, Hazel, Nigel Parton, Mike Walsh and Jan Waterson (1997) 'Concepts of Risk in Relation to Organisational Structure and Functioning Within the Personal Social Services and Probation', *Social Policy and Administration* 31: 213–32.

Kennedy, Catherine and Suzanne Fitzpatrick (2001) 'Begging, Rough Sleeping and Social Exclusion: Implications for Social Policy', *Urban Studies* 38: 2001–16.

Kesteren, John van, Pat Mayhew and Paul Neiuwbeerta (2001) *Criminal Victimisation in Seventeen Industrialised Countries*. The Hague: Ministry of Justice Research.

Kincaid, Jim (1984) 'Richard Titmuss', in Paul Barker (ed.) *Founders of the Welfare State*. London: Heinemann.

King, Michael (1991) 'Child Welfare Within the Law: The Emergence of Hybrid Discourse', *Journal of Law and Society* 18: 303–22.

Knepper, Paul (1996) 'Race, Racism and Crime Statistics', *Southern University Law Review* 24: 71–112.

Knepper, Paul (2001) 'The Historical Prohibition of Multiracial Legal Identity in the United States', in Joan Ferrante and Prince Brown (eds) *The Social Construction of Race and Ethnicity in the United States* (2nd edn). Upper Saddle River, NJ: Prentice Hall.

Knepper, Paul (2007) 'British Jews and the Racialisation of Crime in the Age of Empire', *British Journal of Criminology* 47: 61–79.

Koch, Brigitte (1998) *The Politics of Crime Prevention*. Aldershot: Ashgate.

Kouvonen, Anne and Janne Kivivuori (2001) 'Part-time Jobs, Delinquency and Victimisation among Finnish Adolescents', *Journal of Scandinavian Studies in Criminology and Crime Prevention* 2: 191–212.

Kymlicka, Will (1989) *Liberalism, Community and Culture*. Oxford: Clarendon.

Laakso, Janice and Denise Drevdahl (2006) 'Women, Abuse, and the Welfare Bureaucracy', *Affilia: Journal of Women and Social Work* 21: 89–96.

Lamb, Richard, Linda Weinberger and Bruce Gross (2004) 'Mentally Ill Persons in the Criminal Justice System: Some Perspectives', *Psychiatric Quarterly* 75: 107–26.

Laub, John and Robert Sampson (2003) *Shared Beginnings, Divergent Lives: Delinquent Boys to Age 70*. Cambridge, MA: Harvard University Press.

Lea, John (1987) 'Left Realism: A Defence', *Contemporary Crises* 11: 357–70.

LeBlanc, Marc and Rolf Loeber (1998) 'Developmental Criminology Updated', *Crime and Justice* 23: 115–97.

Lister, Ruth (1990) *The Exclusive Society: Citizenship and the Poor*. London: Child Poverty Action Group.

Lister, Ruth (1996) 'In Search of the "Underclass"' in Ruth Lister (ed.) *Charles Murray and the Underclass*. London: Institute of Economic Affairs.

Loeber, Rolf and Marc LeBlanc (1990) 'Toward a Developmental Criminology', *Crime and Justice* 12: 375–437.

Loveland, Ian (1989) 'Policing Welfare: Local Authority Responses to Claimant Fraud in the Housing Benefit Scheme', *Journal of Law and Society* 16: 187–209.

Lowenkamp, Christopher, Francis Cullen and Travis Pratt (2003) 'Replicating Sampson and Groves's Test of Social Disorganisation Theory: Revisiting a Criminological Classic', *Journal of Research in Crime and Delinquency* 40(4): 351–73.

Luck, Philip, Kirk Elifson and Claire Sterk (2004) 'Female Drug Users and the Welfare System: A Qualitative Exploration', *Drugs: Education, Prevention and Policy* 11: 113–28.

Lynch, James and William Sabol (2001) *Prisoner Reentry in Perspective*. Washington, DC: Urban Institute.

Lynch, Michael and Byron Groves (1989) *A Primer in Radical Criminology*. Albany: Harrow and Heston.

McCarthy, Bill and John Hagan (1991) 'Homelessness: A Criminogenic Situation'? *British Journal of Criminology* 31: 393–410.

MacDonald, Robert and Jane Marsh (2001) 'Disconnected Youth', *Journal of Youth Studies* 4: 373–91.

MacDonald, Robert and Jane Marsh (2005) *Disconnected Youth? Growing Up in Britain's Poor Neighbourhoods*. London: Palgrave Macmillan.

McGahey, Richard (1986) 'Economic Conditions, Neighbourhood Organisation, and Urban Crime', *Crime and Justice* 8: 231–70.

McKeever, Gránne (2004) 'Social Security as a Criminal Sanction', *Journal of Social Welfare and Family Law* 26: 1–16.

Macnicol, John (1999) 'From "Problem Family" to "Underclass", 1945–95', in Helen Fawcett and Rodney Lowe (eds) *Welfare Policy in Britain: The Road from 1945*. London: Macmillan.

McNulty, Thomas and Steven Holloway (2000) 'Race, Crime and Public Housing in Atlanta: Testing a Conditional Effect Hypothesis', *Social Forces* 79: 707–29.

Maher, Lisa and David Dixon (1999) 'Policing and Public Health: Law Enforcement and Harm Minimisation in a Street-Level Drug Market', *British Journal of Criminology* 39: 488–512.

Manucci, Monia (2005) 'Observations on Michael Polanyi's Keynesianism', in Struan Jacobs and R.T. Allen (eds) *Emotion, Reason and Tradition*. Aldershot: Ashgate.

Maplass, Peter and Alan Murie (1999) *Housing Policy and Practice*. Basingstoke: Macmillan.

Marcuse, Herbert (1964) *One-Dimensional Man*. London: Routledge.

Marks, Carole (1991) 'The Urban Underclass', *Annual Review of Sociology* 17: 445–66.

Marquis, Greg (2005) 'From Beverage to Drug: Alcohol and Other Drugs in 1960s and 1970s Canada', *Journal of Canadian Studies* 39: 57–79.

Marshall, T.H. (1950) *Citizenship and Social Class*. Cambridge: Cambridge University Press.

Mateyoke-Scrivner, Allison, Matthew Webster, Matthew Hiller, Michele Staton and Carl Leukefeld (2003) 'Criminal History, Physical and Mental Health, Substance Abuse, and Services Use Among Incarcerated Substance Abusers', *Journal of Contemporary Criminal Justice* 19: 82–97.

Matka, E. (1997) *Public Housing and Crime in Sydney*. Sydney: NSW Bureau of Crime Statistics and Research.

Matthews, Roger (2005) 'The Myth of Punitiveness', *Theoretical Criminology* 9: 175–201.

Meithe, Terance and Robert Meier (1990) 'Criminal Opportunity and Victimisation Rates: A Structural Choice Theory of Criminal Victimisation', *Journal of Research in Crime and Delinquency* 27: 243–66.

Melossi, Dario (2003) 'A New Edition of *Punishment and Social Structure* Thirty-five years Later: A Timely Event', *Social Justice* 30: 248–63.

Mendes, Philip and Badal Moslehuddin (2004) 'Graduating from the Child Welfare System: A Comparison of the UK and Australian Leaving Care Debates', *British Journal of Social Welfare* 13: 332–9.

Mennell, Steven (1977) '"Individual" Action and its "Social" Consequences in the Work of Norbert Elias', in P. Gleichmann (ed.), *Human Figurations: Essays for Norbert Elias*. Amsterdam: Amsterdams Sociologisch Tijdschrift.

Merton, Robert (1938) 'Social Structure and Anomie', *American Sociological Review* 3: 672–82.

Messner, Steven and Richard Rosenfeld (1994) *Crime and the American Dream*. Belmont, CA: Wadsworth.

Messner, Steven and Richard Rosenfeld (2000) 'Market dominance, crime and globalisation', in S. Karstedt and K.D. Bussmann, *Social Dynamics of Crime and Control*. Portland, Oregon: Hart Publishing.

Messner, Steven and Richard Rosenfeld (2006) *Crime and the American Dream* (4th edn). Belmont, CA: Wadsworth.

Michalowski, Raymond and Susan Carlson (1999) 'Unemployment, Imprisonment and Social Structures of Accumulation: Historical Contingency in the Rusche-Kirchheimer Hypothesis', *Criminology* 37: 217–47.

Mika, Harry and Howard Zehr (2003) 'A Restorative Framework for Community Justice Practice', in Kieran McEvoy and Tim Newburn (eds) *Criminology, Conflict Resolution, and Restorative Justice*. Basingstoke: Palgrave.

Miller, David (1978) 'Democracy and Social Justice', *British Journal of Political Science* 8: 1–19.

Miller, David (1999) *Principles of Social Justice*. Cambridge, MA: Harvard University Press.

Miller, Gale (1998) 'Documenting Disputes: Law and Bureaucracy in Organizational Disputing', *Sociology of Crime, Law and Deviance* 1: 203–29.

Minogue, Kenneth (1998) 'Social Justice in Theory and Practice', in David Boucher and Paul Kelly (eds) *Social Justice: From Hume to Walzer*. London: Routledge.

Mishra, Ramesh (1998) 'Beyond the Nation State: Social Policy in an Age of Globalisation', *Social Policy and Administration* 32: 481–500.

Mitchell, Deborah and Mark McCarthy (2001) 'What Happens to Drug Misusers on Release from Prison? An Observational Study at Two London Prisons', *Drugs: Education, Prevention, and Policy* 8: 204–17.

Moore, Mark (1995) 'Public Health and Criminal Justice Approaches to Prevention', *Crime and Justice* 19: 237–62.

Morris, Lydia (1994) *Dangerous Classes: The Underclass and Social Citizenship*. London: Routledge.

Morris, Terence (1958) *The Criminal Area*. London: Routledge and Kegan Paul.

Morrison, Margaret; Grant Macdonald and Terry LeBlanc (2000) 'Identifying Conduct Problems in Young Children: Developmental Pathways and Risk Factors', *International Social Work* 43: 467–80.

Morrow, Marina; Olena Hankivisky and Colleen Varcoe (2004) 'Women and Violence: The Effects of Dismantling the Welfare State', *Critical Social Policy* 24: 358–84.

Murie, Alan (1997) 'Linking Housing Changes to Crime', *Social Policy and Administration* 31: 22–36.

Murray, Charles (1996a) 'The Emerging British Underclass', in Ruth Lister (ed.) *Charles Murray and the Underclass*. London: Institute of Economic Affairs.

Murray, Charles, (1996b) 'Rejoinder', in Ruth Lister (ed.) *Charles Murray and the Underclass*. London: Institute of Economic Affairs.

Mungham, Geoff (1980) 'The Career of Confusion: Radical Criminology in Britain', in *Radical Criminology: The Coming Crisis*. Beverly Hills, CA: Sage.

NACRO (1995) *Crime and Social Policy*. London: National Association for Care and Resettlement of Offenders.

Naffine, Ngaire and Fay Gale (1989) 'Testing the Nexus: Crime, Gender and Unemployment', *British Journal of Criminology* 29: 144–56.

Neal, Sarah (2003) 'The Scarman Report, the Macpherson Report and the Media: How Newspapers Respond to Race-centred Social Policy Interventions', *Journal of Social Policy* 32: 55–74.

Needleman, Herbert, Julie Riess, Michael Tobin, Gretchen Biesecker and Joel Greenhouse (1996) 'Bone Lead Levels and Delinquent Behaviour', *Journal of the American Medical Association* 275: 363–9.

Neild, Jill and Ian Paylor (1996) 'A Case Study Investigating the Criminal Activity Among Residents in an Urban Area', *Environment and Behaviour* 28: 748–63.

Neugebauer, Richard, Hans Hoek, Hans Wijbrand and Ezra Susser (1999) 'Prenatal Exposure to Wartime Famine and Development of Antisocial Personality Disorder in Early Adulthood', *Journal of the American Medical Association* 282: 455–62.

Newman, Oscar (1973) *Defensible Space: Crime Prevention Through Urban Design*. London: Architectural Press.

Nicholson, L (1995) *What Works in Situational Crime Prevention*. Edinburgh: Scottish Office Central Unit.

Nilsson, Anders (2003) 'Living Conditions, Social Exclusion and Recidivism Among Prison Inmates', *Journal of Scandinavian Studies in Criminology and Crime Prevention* 4: 57–83.

Noakes, John and Lesley Noakes (2000) 'Violence in School: Risk, Safety, and Fear of Crime', *Educational Psychology in Practice* 16: 69–73.

O'Beirne, Maria and Jonathan Gabe (2005) 'Reducing Violence Against NHS Staff: Findings from an Evaluation of the Safer Survey Hospitals Initiative', *Crime Prevention and Community Safety: An International Journal* 7: 29–39.

Office of Juvenile Justice and Delinquency Prevention (1993) 'Serious, Violent and Chronic Juvenile Offenders: A Comprehensive Strategy', Fact Sheet. Washington, DC: US Department of Justice.

Orleans, M. (1995) 'The Cochrane Collaboration' *Public Health Reports* 110: 633–4.

Orme, Jackie (1994) *A Study in the Relationship Between Unemployment and Recorded Crime*. London: Research and Statistics Department.

Osler, Audrey and Hugh Starkey (2005) 'Violence in Schools and Representations of Young People: A Critique of Government Policies in France and England', *Oxford Review of Education* 31: 195–215.

Page, D. (2000) *Communities in the Balance: The Reality of Social Exclusion on Housing Estates*. York: Joseph Rowntree Foundation.

Pakes, Francis (2005) 'Penalisation and Retreat: The Changing Face of Dutch Criminal Justice', *Criminal Justice* 5: 145–61.

Pandiani, John (1982) 'The Crime Control Corps: An Invisible New Deal Programme', *British Journal of Sociology* 33: 348–58.

Pantazias, Christina and David Gordon (1997) 'Television Licence Evasion and the Criminalisation of Poverty', *Howard Journal* 36: 170–86.

Parekh, Bhikhu (2000) *Rethinking Multiculturalism*. Basingstoke: Palgrave.

Parton, Nigel (1979) 'The Natural History of Child Abuse: A Study in Social Problem Definition', *British Journal of Social Work* 9: 431–51.

Parton, Nigel (1981) 'Child Abuse, Social Anxiety and Welfare', *British Journal of Social Work* 11: 391–414.

Paternoster, Raymond and Shawn Bushway (2001) 'Theoretical and Empirical Work on the Relationship Between Unemployment and Crime', *Journal of Quantitative Criminology* 17: 391–407.

Paul, Diane (1984) 'Eugenics and the Left' *Journal of the History of Ideas* 45: 567–90.

Peace, Robin (2001) 'Social Exclusion: A Concept in Need of Definition?', *Social Policy Journal of New Zealand* 16: 17–35.

Peffley, Mark (1997) 'Racial Stereotypes and Whites' Political Views of Blacks in the Context of Welfare and Crime', *American Journal of Political Science* 41: 30–60.

Penna, Sue (2005) 'The Children Act 2004: Child Protection and Social Surveillance', *Journal of Social Welfare and Family Law* 27: 143–57.

Petersilia, Joan (2003) *When Prisoners Come Home: Parole and Prisoner Reentry*. Oxford: Oxford University Press.

Pfohl, Stephen (1977) 'The "Discovery" of Child Abuse', *Social Problems* 24: 310–24.

Plant, Raymond (1998) 'Why Social Justice?', in David Boucher and Paul Kelly, (eds) *Social Justice: From Hume to Walzer*. London: Routledge.

Ploeger, Matthew (1997) 'Youth Employment and Delinquency: Reconsidering a Problematic Relationship', *Criminology* 35: 659–75.

Polanyi, Michael (1998) *The Logic of Liberty*. Indianapolis: Liberty Fund.

Postmus, Judy (2004) 'Battered and on Welfare: The Experiences of Women with the Family Violence Option', *Journal of Sociology and Social Welfare* 31: 113–23.

Power, Anne (1989) 'Housing, Community and Crime,' in David Downes (ed.) *Crime and the City*. Basingstoke: Macmillan.

Power, Anne and Tunstall (1997) *Dangerous Disorder: Riots and Violent Disturbances in Thirteen Areas of Britain, 1991–92*. York: Joseph Rowntree Foundation.

Pratt, John and Marie Clark (2005) 'Penal Populism in New Zealand', *Punishment and Society* 7: 303–22.

Pratt, Travis and Timothy Godsey (2002) 'Social Support and Homicide: A Cross-National Test of an Emerging Criminological Theory', *Journal of Criminal Justice* 30: 589–601.

Pritchard, Colin and Malcolm Cox (1998) 'The Criminality of "Former Special Educational Provision". Permanently "Excluded from School" Adolescents as Young Adults (16–23): Costs and Practical Implications', *Journal of Adolescence* 21: 609–620.

Radzinowicz, Leon (1964) *Criminology and the Climate of Social Responsibility*. Cambridge: Heffer.

Radzinowicz, Leon (1988) *The Cambridge Institute of Criminology: Its Background and Scope*. London: HMSO.

Ratcliffe, Peter (1999) 'Housing Inequality and "Race": Some Critical Reflections on the Concept of "Social Exclusion"', *Ethnic and Racial Studies* 22: 1–22.

Reisman, David (1977) *Richard Titmuss: Welfare and Society*. London: Heinemann.

Renzetti, Claire (2002) '"Private" Crime in Public Housing: Violent Victimisation, Fear of Crime and Social Isolation Among Women Public Housing Residents', *Women's Health and Urban Life* 1: 47–65.

Rex, John (1968) 'The Sociology of the Zone in Transition', in R.E. Pahl (ed.) *Readings in Urban Sociology*. Oxford: Pergamon Press.

Roberts, Albert and Patricia Brownell (1999) 'A Century of Forensic Social Work: Bridging the Past to the Present', *Social Work* 44: 359–69.

Robertson, Ann (1998) 'Critical Reflections on the Politics of Need: Implications for Public Health', *Social Science and Medicine* 47: 1419–30.

Robins, Lee (1978) 'Sturdy Childhood Predictors of Adult Antisocial Behaviour: Replications from Longitudinal Studies', *Psychological Medicine* 8: 611–22.

Robinson, Fred and Jane Keithly (2000) 'The Impacts of Crime on Health Services' *Health, Risk, and Society* 2: 253–66.

Roche, Maurice (1987) 'Citizenship, Social Theory, and Social Change', *Theory and Society* 16: 363–99.

Rock, Paul (1988a) 'The Present State of Criminology in Britain', *British Journal of Criminology* 28: 188–99.

Rock, Paul (1988b) 'Crime Reduction Initiatives on Problem Estates', in Tim Hope and Margaret Shaw (eds) *Communities and Crime Reduction*. London: HMSO.

Rodger, John (2006) 'Antisocial Families and Withholding Welfare Support', *Critical Social Policy* 26: 121–43.

Roncek, Dennis, Ralph Bell and Jeffrey Francik (1981) 'Housing Projects and Crime: Testing a Proximity Hypothesis', *Social Problems* 29: 151–66.

Rose, Nikolas (2000) 'The Biology of Culpability: Pathological Identity and Crime Control in a Biological Culture', *Theoretical Criminology* 4: 5–34.

Ruddell, Rick (2005) 'Social Disruption, State Priorities, and Minority Threat: A Cross-National Study of Imprisonment', *Punishment and Society* 7: 7–28.

Rusche, George and Otto Kirchheimer (1939) *Punishment and Social Structure*. New York: Columbia University Press.

Ruttenberg, Hattie (1994) 'The Limited Promise of Public Health Methodologies to Prevent Youth Violence', *Yale Law Journal* 103: 1885–912.

Saarinen, Risto (2003) 'The Surplus of Evil in Welfare Society: Contemporary Scandinavian Crime Fiction', *Dialog: A Journal of Theology* 42: 131–5

Saegert, S., G. Winkel and C. Swartz (2002) 'Social Capital and Crime in New York City's Low-Income Housing', *Housing Policy Debate* 13: 189–226.

Sampson, Robert (1990) 'The Impact of Housing Policies on Community Social Disorganisation and Crime', *Bulletin of the New York Academy of Medicine* 66: 526–33.

Sampson, Robert (1995) 'Community', in James Q Wilson and Joan Petersilia (eds) *Crime*. San Francisco: ICS Press.

Sampson, Robert and W.B. Groves (1989) 'Community Structure and Crime: Testing Social Disorganisation Theory', *American Journal of Sociology* 94: 774–802.

Sampson, Robert and John Laub (1993) *Crime in the Making: Pathways and Turning Points Through Life*. London: Harvard University Press.

Sampson, Robert and John Laub (2005) 'A Life-Course View of the Development of Crime', *Annals of the American Academy of Political and Social Science* 602: 12–45.

Sampson, Robert and Steven Raudenbush (1999) 'Systematic Social Observation of Public Places', *American Journal of Sociology* 105: 603–51.

Sampson, Robert and Stephen Raudenbush (2001) 'Disorder in Urban Neighbourhoods— Does it Lead to Crime?', *Research in Brief*. Washington, DC: National Institute of Justice.

Sampson, Robert and William J. Wilson (1995) 'Toward a Theory of Race, Crime and Urban Inequality', in John Hagan and Ruth Peterson (eds) *Crime and Inequality*. Stanford: Stanford University Press.

Sarls, Jamie and Brendan Bartley (2002) 'Icon and Structural Violence in a Dublin "Underclass" Housing Estate', *Anthropology Today* 18: 14–19.

Savolainen, Jukka (2000) 'Inequality, Welfare State, and Homicide: Further Support for the Institutional Anomie Theory', *Criminology* 38: 1021–39.

Scorcu, Antonello and Roberto Cellini (1998) 'Economic Activity and Crime in the Long Run: An Empirical Investigation on Aggregate Data from Italy, 1951–1994', *International Review of Law and Economics* 18: 279–92.

Scott, Ellen, Andrew London and Nancy Myers (2002) 'Dangerous Dependencies: The Intersection of Welfare Reform and Domestic Violence', *Gender and Society* 16: 878–97.

Scott, Suzie and Hilary Parkey (1998) 'Myths and Reality: Anti-social Behaviour in Scotland', *Housing Studies* 13: 325–45.

Scottish Museums Council (2000) *Museums and Social Justice*. Edinburgh: Scottish Museums Council.

Scourfield, Jonathan and Ian Welsh (2003) 'Risk, Reflexivity and Social Control in Child Protection: New Times or Same Old Story?', *Critical Social Policy* 23: 398–420.

Shaw, Clifford and Henry McKay (1969) *Juvenile Delinquency and Urban Areas*. Chicago: University of Chicago Press.

Shepherd, Jonathan and David Farrington (1993) 'Assault as a Public Health Problem', *Journal of the Royal Society of Medicine* 86: 89–92.

Shepherd, Jonathan, David Farrington and John Potts (2002) 'Relations Between Offending, Injury and Illness', *Journal of the Royal Society of Medicine* 95: 539–44.

Shklar, Judith (1990) *The Faces of Injustice*. New Haven, CT: Yale University Press.

Sidel, Victor and Robert Wesley (1995) 'Violence as a Public Health Problem: Lessons for Action Against Violence by Health Care Professionals from the Work of the International Physicians Movement for the Prevention of Nuclear War', *Social Justice* 22: 154–70.

Simpson, M.K. and J. Hogg (2001) 'Patterns of Offending Among People with Intellectual Disability', *Journal of Intellectual Disability Research* 45: 397–406.

Smith, Dennis (1988) *The Chicago School: A Liberal Critique of Capitalism*. London: Macmillan.

Snodgrass, Jon (1976) 'Clifford R. Shaw and Henry D. McKay: Chicago Criminologists', *British Journal of Criminology* 16: 1–19.

Social Exclusion Unit (1997) *Truancy and School Exclusion*. London: Cabinet Office.

Social Exclusion Unit (2000) *The Social Exclusion Unit Leaflet*. London: Cabinet Office.

Social Exclusion Unit (2002) *Reducing Re-Offending by Ex-Prisoners*. London: HMSO.

Social Exclusion Unit (2004) *Breaking the Cycle: Taking Stock of Progress and Priorities for the Future*. London: Social Exclusion Unit.

Solomos, John (1993) 'Constructions of Black Criminality: Racialisation and Criminalisation in Perspective', in Dee Cook and Barbara Hudson (eds) *Racism and Criminology*. London: Sage.

Sparks, Richard and Tim Newburn (2002) 'How Does Crime Policy Travel?', *Criminal Justice* 2: 107–9.

Spratt, Trevor (2001) 'The Influence of Child Protection Orientation on Child Welfare Practice', *British Journal of Social Work* 31: 933–54.

Sprott, James, Jennifer Jenkins and Anthony Doob (2005) 'The Importance of School: Protecting At-Risk Youth From Early Offending', *Youth Violence and Juvenile Justice* 3: 59–77.

Squires, Peter (2006) 'New Labour and the Politics of Antisocial Behaviour', *Critical Social Policy* 26(1): 144–68.

Stanko, Elizabeth (1990) *Everyday Violence: How Women and Men Experience Sexual and Physical Danger*. London: Pandora.

Starkey, Pat (2000) 'The Feckless Mother: Women, Poverty and Social Workers in Wartime and Post-War England', *Women's History Review* 9: 539–57.

Steinburg, S. (1997) 'The Liberal Retreat from Race During the Post Civil Rights Era' in W. Lubiano (ed.) *The House that Race Built*. New York: Pantheon.

Stevenson, John and Chris Cook (1994) *Britain in the Depression: Society and Politics 1929–39*. London: Macmillan.

Stretesky, Paul and Michael Lynch (2004) 'The Relationship Between Lead and Crime', *Journal of Health and Social Behaviour* 45: 214–29.

Suhling, Stefan (2003) 'Factors Contributing to Rising Imprisonment Figures in Germany', *Howard Journal of Criminal Justice* 42: 55–68.

Sutton, John (2000) 'Imprisonment and Social Classification in Five Common Law Democracies, 1955–1985', *American Journal of Sociology* 2: 350–86.

Sutton, Adam and Adrian Cherny (2002) 'Prevention Without Politics? The Cyclical Progress of Crime Prevention in an Australian State', *Criminal Justice* 2: 325–44.

Svensson, Kerstin (2003) 'Social Work in the Criminal Justice System: An Ambiguous Exercise of Caring Power', *Journal of Scandinavian Studies in Criminology and Crime Prevention* 4: 84–100.

Swanston, Heather, Patrick Parkinson, Brian O'Toole; Angela Plunkett, Sandra Shrimpton and R. Kim Oates (2003) 'Juvenile Crime, Aggression and Delinquency After Sexual Abuse', *British Journal of Criminology* 43: 729–49.

Swift, Roger (1989) 'Crime and the Irish in Nineteenth-Century Britain', in Roger Swift and Sheridan Gilley (eds) *The Irish in Britain 1815–1939*. London: Pinter.

Swift, Roger (1997) 'Heroes or Villains? The Irish, Crime and Disorder in Victorian England', *Albion* 29: 399–421.

Taylor, Claire (2001) 'The Relationship Between Social and Self-Control: Travis Hirschi's Criminological Career', *Theoretical Criminology* 5: 369–88

Taylor, Ian (1997) 'The political economy of crime,' in Mike Maguire, Rod Morgan and Robert Reiner (eds) *The Oxford Handbook of Criminology*. Oxford: Oxford University Press.

Taylor, Ian (1999) 'Crime and Social Criticism', *European Journal of Crime, Criminal Law and Criminal Justice* 7: 180–96.

Taylor, Ian, Paul Walton and Jock Young (1973) *The New Criminology*. London: Routledge and Kegan Paul.

Tham, Henrik (1998) 'Crime and the Welfare State: The Case of the United Kingdom and Sweden', in Vincenzo Ruggerio, Nigel South and Ian Taylor (eds) *The New European Criminology: Crime and Social Order in Europe*. London: Routledge.

Tham, Henrik (2001) 'Law and Order as a Leftist Project? The Case of Sweden', *Punishment and Society* 3: 409–26.

Thornberry, Terence (1987) 'Toward an Interactional Theory of Delinquency', *Criminology* 25: 863–92.

Timms, Noel and A.F. Philp (1957) *The Problem of 'the Problem Family'*. London: Family Service Units.

Timmerman, Stefan and Jonathan Gabe (2002) 'Introduction: Connecting Criminology and Sociology of Health and Illness', *Sociology of Health and Illness* 24: 501–16.

Titmuss, Richard (1954) 'Preface', in John Mays, *Growing Up in the City*. Liverpool: Liverpool University Press.

Tombs, Steve (2005) 'Workplace Injury and Death: Social Harm and the Illusions of Law', in Paddy Hillyard, Christina Pantazias, Steve Tombs, and Dave Gordon (eds) *Beyond Criminology: Taking Harm Seriously*. London: Pluto Press.

Tonry, Michael (2003) 'Evidence, Elections and Ideology in the Making of Criminal Justice Policy', in Michael Tonry (ed.) *Confronting Crime: Crime Control Policy Under New Labour*. Cullompton: Willan Publishing.

Tonry, Michael and David Green (2003) 'Criminology and Public Policy in the USA and UK', in Lucia Zedner and Andrew Ashworth (eds) *The Criminological Foundations of Penal Policy*. Oxford: Oxford University Press.

Tseloni, Andromachi; Karin Wittebrood, Graham Farrell and Ken Pease (2004) 'Burglary Victimisation in England and Wales, the United States and the Netherlands', *British Journal of Criminology* 44: 66–91.

Turner, Jonathan (1988) 'The Mixed Legacy of the Chicago School of Sociology', *Sociological Perspectives* 31(3): 325–38.

Vanderbeck, Robert (2003) 'Youth, Racism and Place in the Tony Martin Affair', *Antipode* 363–84.

Vanttaja, Markku and Tero Järvinen (2006) 'The Young Outsiders: The Later Life Courses of "Drop-Out Youths"', *International Journal of Lifelong Education* 25: 173–84.

Voegeli, Wolfgang (2003) 'Nazi Family Policy: Securing Mass Loyalty', *Journal of Family History* 28: 123–48.

Von Hofer, Hanns (2003) 'Prison Populations as Political Constructs: The Case of Finland, Holland and Sweden', *Journal of Scandinavian Studies in Criminology and Crime Prevention* 4: 21–38.

Von Hofer, Hanns (2004) 'Crime and Reactions to Crime in Scandinavia', *Journal of Scandinavian Studies in Criminology and Crime Prevention* 5: 148–66.

Von Mahs, Jürgen (2005) 'The Sociospatial Exclusion of Single Homeless People in Berlin and Los Angeles', *American Behavioral Scientist* 48: 928–60.

Wacquant, Loïc (1997) 'Three Pernicious Premises in the Study of the American Ghetto', *International Journal of Urban and Regional Research* 20: 341–53.

Wacquant, Loïc (2000) 'The New "Peculiar Institution": On the Prison as Surrogate Ghetto', *Theoretical Criminology* 4: 377–89.

Wacquant, Loïc (2001a) 'Deadly Symbiosis: When Ghetto and Prison Meet and Mesh', *Punishment and Society* 3: 95–134.

Wacquant, Loïc (2001b) 'The Penalisation of Poverty and the Rise of Neo Liberalism', *European Journal on Criminal Policy and Research* 9: 401–12.

Walsh, Anthony and Lee Ellis (1999) 'Political Ideology and American Criminologists' Explanations for Criminal Behaviour', *The Criminologist* (American Society of Criminology) 24: 1, 14–15, 26–27.

Walters, Reece (2001) 'Social Defence and International Reconstruction: Illustrating the Governance of Post-War Criminological Discourse', *Theoretical Criminology* 5: 203–21.

Wardaugh, Julia (1996) '"Homeless in Chinatown": Deviance and Social Control in Cardboard City', *Sociology* 30: 701–16.

Weatherburn, Donald; Bronwyn Lind and Simon Ku (1999) 'Hotbeds of Crime? Crime and Public Housing in Urban Sydney', *Crime and Delinquency* 45: 256–71.

Weil, Simone (1952) *The Need for Roots*. London: Routledge and Kegan Paul.

Weil, Simone (1990) 'On Human Personality', in David McLellan (ed.) *Utopian Pessimist: The Life and Thought of Simone Weil*. New York: Poseidon Press.

Weisburd, David (2002) 'From Criminals to Criminal Contexts: Reorienting Criminal Justice Research and Policy', *Advances in Criminological Theory* 10: 197–216.

Wells, John and Bowers, Len (2002) 'How Prevalent is Violence Towards Nurses Working in General Hospitals in the UK?', *Journal of Advanced Nursing* 39: 230–40.

Welsh, Brandon (2005) 'Public Health and the Prevention of Juvenile Criminal Violence', *Youth Violence and Criminal Justice* 3: 23–40.

Welshman, John (1999) 'The Social History of Social Work: The Issue of the "Problem Family", 1940–70', *British Journal of Social Work* 29: 457–76.

Welshman, John (2004) 'The Unknown Titmuss', *Journal of Social Policy* 33: 225–47.

Welshman, John (2005) 'Ideology, Social Science, and Public Policy: The Debate over Transmitted Deprivation', *Twentieth Century British History* 16: 306–41.

Westergaard, John (1992) 'About and Beyond the "Underclass": Some Notes on Influences of Social Climate on British Sociology Today', *Sociology* 26: 575–87.

Western, Bruce and Katherine Beckett (1999) 'How Unregulated in the US Labour Market? The Penal System as a Labour Market Institution', *American Journal of Sociology* 104: 1030–60.

White, Paul (1997) 'Images of Social Housing Estates in France', *Immigrants and Minorities* 16: 19–35.

Widom, Cathy S. and Michael Maxfield (2001) 'An Update on the "Cycle of Violence", Research In Brief. Washington, DC: National Institute of Justice.

Wiles, Paul (2002) 'Criminology in the 21st Century: Public Good or Private Interest?', *Australian and New Zealand Journal of Criminology* 35: 238–52.

Wiles, Paul and Ken Pease (2001) 'Distributive Justice and Crime' in Roger Matthews and John Pitts (eds) *Crime, Disorder and Community Safety*. London: Routledge.

Williams, Melissa (1995) 'Justice Toward Groups: Political Not Juridical', *Political Theory* 23: 67–91.

Wilson, A.N. (1984) *Hillaire Belloc*. London: Hamish Hamilton.

Wilson, Harriett (1980) 'Parental Supervision: A Neglected Aspect of Delinquency', *British Journal of Criminology* 20: 203–35.

Wilson, James Q. (1974) 'Crime and the Criminologists', *Commentary* 58: 47–53.

Wilson, James Q. and George Kelling (1982) 'Broken Windows: The Police and Neighbourhood Safety', *Atlantic Monthly* 127 (March): 29–38.

Wilson, Sheena (1980) 'Vandalism and "Defensible Space" on London Housing Estates', in R.V.G. Clarke and P. Mayhew (eds) *Designing Out Crime*. London: HMSO.

Wilson, William J. (1980) *The Declining Significance of Race* (2nd edn). Chicago: University of Chicago Press.

Wilson, William J. (1987) *The Truly Disadvantaged: The Inner City, the Underclass, and Public Policy*. Chicago: University of Chicago Press.

Wilson, William J. (1991) 'Studying Inner-City Social Dislocations: The Challenge of Public Agenda Research', *American Sociological Review* 56: 1–14.

Wilson, William J. (1996) *When Work Disappears: The World of the New Urban Poor*. New York: Alfred Knopf.

Wilson, William J. (1996) *When Work Disappears*. Chicago: University of Chicago.

Wilson, William J. (1999) 'When Work Disappears: New Implications for Race and Urban Poverty In the Global Economy', *Ethnic and Racial Studies* 22: 479–99.

Wilson, William J. (2003) 'Race, Class and Urban Poverty: A Rejoinder', *Ethnic and Racial Studies* 26: 1096–114.

Wittebrood, Karin and Paul Nieuwbeerta (2000) 'Criminal Victimisation During One's Life Course: The Effects of Previous Victimisation and Patterns of Routine Activities', *Journal of Research in Crime and Delinquency* 37: 91–122.

Wolfson, Mark and Mary Hourigan (1997) 'Unintended Consequences and Professional Ethics: Criminalisation of Alcohol and Tobacco Use by Youth Among Young Adults', *Addiction* 92: 1159–64.

Young, Jock (1992) 'Ten Points of Realism', in Jock Young and Roger Matthews (eds) *Rethinking Criminology: The Realist Debate*. London: Sage.

Young, Jock (1999) *The Exclusive Society*. London: Sage.

Young, Jock and Roger Matthews (2003) 'Winning the Fight against Crime? New Labour, Populism and Lost Opportunities', in Roger Matthews and Jock Young (eds) *The New Politics of Crime and Punishment*. Cullompton: Willan Publishing.

Young, Malcolm (1991) *An Inside Job: Policing and Police Culture in Britain*. Oxford: Clarendon.

Index

Major, John 108
Mankell, Henning 145
Mannheim, Hermann 5, 8, 102
marginalisation 122
Marcuse, Herbert 158
Marshall, TH 4, 156
Marx, Karl 26, 29, 157–8
mass imprisonment 127–9
Matthews, Roger 13, 128–9
McKay, Henry 20, 54
medicalisation of crime 79–80
media images
  policymaking 16–7
  riots 46
  'scroungers' 43
  welfare recipients 42
mental health
  ASBO 68
  mentally-ill persons125–6
  prisoners 132
  release from care 134–5
  social services 146
Merton, Robert 25, 26–7, 107
Messner, Steven 28
Middlesex Centre for Criminology 13
Mill, John Stuart 156
Mitterand, François 40
Morris, William 159
Murray, Charles 38, 41–2, 44

National Assistance Act (1948)
National Health Service Act (1948) 5
National Health Service (NHS)
  77, 150
National Insurance Act (194)
National Probation Service 149
natural law 158
negative rights 161
neo-liberalism 15, 140, 143
Netherlands
  crime policy 144
  crime victimisation 32–3
  immigration 48
  imprisonment trends 100
  traffic accidents 74
  unemployment and crime 92
  welfare policy 34
new criminology 12
New Deal (USA)
  crime prevention 102–4
  housing 58
New Labour 14, 39, 84, 128–9, 140
Newman, Oscar 59
'New York miracle' 124
New Zealand
  imprisonment trends 100
  mass imprisonment 128

Norway
  child welfare 150
  welfare policy 34

Ohlin, Lloyd 26

Patten, John 90
Polanyi, Michael 168–9
Polanyi, Karl 28
Police and Criminal Evidence Act (1984) 126
policing
  detective fiction 146
  domestic violence 126–7
  drugs 125–6
  families 150
  homelessness 125
  housing estates 62, 65
  left realism 13–4
  mentally-ill 126
  social workers 151–2
  zero tolerance 123–4
policymaking
  experimental criminology 8–10
  causal versus policy 11
  convergence 16
  crime science 10–1
  critical criminology 11–2
  left realism 12–4
  politics of 14
  media viii, 16–7
  unintended consequences 16
policy transfer 16
politicisation of crime 15, 26, 128, 145, 140–2
Poor Laws (1834) 98
populist punitiveness 128
  see also punitive turn
principle of neutrality 168
prisoner reintegration
  employment 129–30
  family issues 133–4
  healthcare 132
  housing 131
  social support 27
'problem families'
  concept of 106–7
  housing estates 56, 63, 64
  unemployment and 103
  recuperative centres 115
  see also families
public health 78, 116–7
public housing (USA) 23, 54–5, 131
punitive turn 142

racialisation of crime 45–7
Radzinowicz, Leon
  definition of criminology 6
  view of social policy 7

traffic accidents 74
truancy 85
Typhoid Mary 75–6

underclass
  'black underclass' 37–8
  'British underclass' 37–9
  labour surplus 99
  truly disadvantaged 24–5
  'Muslim underclass' 47, 49
unemployment
  crime and punishment 97–8
  business cycles 90–1
  embeddedness 96
  housing estates 61, 62
  imprisonment 97–100
  labour markets 94–5
  meaning of 93–4
  murder rates 93
  opportunity effect 91–2
  prisoner reintegration 129–30
  release from care 134–5
  women 94
  worklessness 95–6
unemployment policy
  political problem of 169
  welfare state 5
unintended consequences 41, 54, 62, 160
  see also externalties
unsocial transactions 168
utopianism 12, 59

Wales 87
Walton, Paul 12
war on poverty 15, 26
Weatherburn, Don 63
Weil, Simone 166–7
welfare scroungers 42, 43
welfare dependency 41–2, 101
welfare state
  Beveridge 5
  Bourdieu 143
  crime prevention 27, 41
  culture of control 143
  existential revolution 145
  inclusive, exclusive 143–4
  market forces 29
  Radzinowicz's view 6
  Rawls 162–3
  reform 43, 142
  social justice 156–7
welfare state fallacy 33–4
welfare state solution vii
Wilson, James Q. 11, 123

Wilson, William J. 23–4, 95–6
women
  anti-social behaviour 45
  dangerous dependencies 44
  disciplinary state 149
  fear of crime 83
  health professions 80
  local authority care 135
  poverty 58
  prisoners families 134
  'problem mothers' 106
  public housing 55–6
  victimisation of 77, 80
  victims movement 149
  television license evasion 45
  unemployment 94
  welfare dependency 41–2
workfare 41

Young, Iris 165
Young, Jock 12, 13, 30
youth crime
  alcohol offences 79
  city pattern 20–2, 54
  embeddedness 96–7
  educational deficiency 80–1
  jobs and crime 97
  nutrition 73–4
  policing 65
  resiliency 111
  school exclusions 84–5
  schools 82
  street youth 122–3
  worklessness 96
Youth Justice and Criminal Evidence Act
  (1999) 147
youth policy
  abortions 116
  children's rights 150
  early intervention 114–6
  immigration context 119
  joined-up services 147–8
  parenting orders 116
  risk-focused prevention 116–9
  school exclusions 84–5
  social inclusion 39–40
  'yob culture' 142
  youth offending teams (YOTs) 147

zero tolerance
  benefits fraud 43
  education 86
  medicine 79
  policing 123–4